D1599224

WITHDRAWN

Race Relations in South Africa 1929–1979

Edited by

Ellen Hellmann and Henry Lever

© South African Institute of Race Relations 1979

All rights reserved. No part of this publication
may be reproduced or transmitted, in any form,
or by any means, without permission

First published 1979 (under the title of *Conflict and Progress*) by
MACMILLAN SOUTH AFRICA (PUBLISHERS) (PTY) LTD.
Johannesburg

First published 1980 by
THE MACMILLAN PRESS LTD
London and Basingstoke
Companies and representatives throughout the world

Printed in Hong Kong

British Library Cataloguing in Publication Data

Race relations in South Africa, 1929–1979
  1. South Africa – Race relations
  I. Hellman, Ellen   II. Lever, Henry
  301.45′1′0968   DT763

  ISBN 0–333–29483–1

Contents

Foreword

As the South African Institute of Race Relations approached the completion of its first fifty years of activity in the ever-expanding field of race relations, its Executive Committee decided that it would be fitting to commemorate this anniversary by the publication of analytical surveys of major sectors of South Africa's development during this period by acknowledged authorities in their respective fields. That it could draw largely on members of its own governing councils to write the different sections of this book is one further indication of the Institute's ability, evident from the day of its formation, to enlist the services of men and women of national stature.

To these contributors, many in the midst of numerous other pressing undertakings, I express the deep appreciation of the Institute for this further example of their commitment to the cause of promoting 'peace, goodwill and practical co-operation' in our multi-peopled land – the cause to which the Institute has been dedicated over the past half century. We are most grateful to the writers of the ten sections of this book. We are particularly indebted to the editors, Dr Ellen Hellmann and Professor Henry Lever, for their constant advice and help. Among those who assisted in the preparation of this book, we owe special thanks to Miss E. M. Cadell, Editor for Macmillan South Africa.

The contributions which follow, the products of careful scholarship allied to a keen perception of historical context, cover a wide spectrum of the past fifty years of accelerating economic and population growth, of conflicting social and political changes and of growing racial polarisation. The Institute believes that in facilitating the production of this book, it not only marks its own anniversary but serves South Africa, in that this balanced account of conflict and progress enriches understanding. Such indeed was its purpose – a purpose that reflects the continuing faith of the Institute in the potential of people, all people, to transcend their cultural and environmental limitations.

F. J. van Wyk
DIRECTOR,
South African Institute of
Race Relations

General Note on Race and Nomenclature

During the course of South African history the term used to describe the Bantu-speaking people of South Africa has undergone a number of changes. Before 1951 the term 'native' was official usage. From 1951 the Government began using the term 'Bantu' instead of 'native' in certain of its legislative measures, e.g. the Bantu Authorities Act of 1951. In 1962 the term 'Bantu' was officially substituted throughout for the term 'native'. In 1978, following prolonged criticism of the term 'Bantu', the legislature substituted 'black' for 'Bantu' in all statutes and official documents. The South African Institute of Race Relations has used the term 'African' since its establishment.

While the term 'black' is preferable to 'native' or 'Bantu', and is accepted by the African people of South Africa, it presents certain problems in that the term 'black' has of recent years been used to describe the 'non-white' (in earlier times 'non-European') people of South Africa, that is, the African, Coloured and Asian peoples. This gives rise to ambiguities.

The Department of Native Affairs, which was succeeded by the Department of Bantu Administration and Development, was renamed the Department of Plural Relations and Development in 1978. In the same year the Department of Bantu Education was renamed the Department of Education and Training. On 4 May 1979 it was announced that the name in future would be the Department of Co-operation and Development.

It has not been possible to be consistent in the usage of the above terms in the essays that follow. The terms 'native' and 'Bantu' have been retained in the titles of statues *inter alia* in order to place them in historical perspective. Direct quotations, obviously given as originally written, also reflect the changing terminological usages.

Notes on the Contributors

Dr Ellen Hellmann is a social anthropologist who in the early 1930s pioneered anthropological research in the field of urban Africans in South Africa. She has served in various capacities on a number of organisations concerned with human and inter-group relations. She has been a member of the Executive Council of the South African Institute of Race Relations since 1938 and is a past president of the Institute. She edited the *Handbook on Race Relations in South Africa*, published in 1949 and reprinted in 1975, and is the author of a number of publications, including *Rooiyard: A Sociological Survey of an Urban Native Slum Yard*, 1948, reprinted 1969.

René de Villiers was born and educated in the Orange Free State where he also spent more than half his professional life as a journalist on the staff of *The Friend* newspaper. One of South Africa's best known journalists, he has had over forty years' experience in his chosen field. He has been editor of *The Friend*, the *Daily News*, the *Race Relations News*, the *Star* and the *Forum*. His publications include a chapter on 'Black Politics' in the *Handbook on Race Relations in South Africa* and on Afrikaner nationalism in the *Oxford History of South Africa*.

A former vice-president of the South African Institute of Race Relations, he is currently chairman of its Cape Western region. He is a member of the Executive Committee of the South African Institute of International Affairs and of the English Academy of South Africa. He was a member of the South African delegation to the Commonwealth Press Union conference in Australia and New Zealand in 1955. From 1974 to 1977 he was Member of Parliament for Parktown.

Patrick Laurence obtained his MA from the University of Natal on African Nationalism with a thesis entitled 'Basutoland 1945–60: A Study in Emergent African Nationalism'. Now a senior political journalist on the *Rand Daily Mail*, the author specialises in black politics in South Africa and has written a book on Transkei. He has known many of the founders of the black consciousness movement personally, including Steve Biko, and his role during the unrest of 1976–7 was to co-ordinate the news from the different centres in order to give an overview of events. He is also South African correspondent for the British newspaper, the *Guardian*.

John Dugard is a graduate of the Universities of Stellenbosch (BA in 1956 and LLB in 1958) and Cambridge (LLB and Diploma in International Law). An Advocate of the Supreme Court of South Africa, he is Professor of Law and Director of the Centre for Applied Legal Studies at the University of the Witwatersrand. He has been Visiting Professor at the University of Princeton and Duke University. During the period 1975–7 he was Dean of the Faculty of Law at the University of the Witwatersrand. He was elected President of the South African Institute of Race Relations for 1978 and 1979. His publications include *South West Africa/Namibia Dispute* (1973), *Introduction to Criminal Procedure* (1977) and *Human Rights and the South African Legal Order* (1978).

Dr Sheila T. van der Horst was born in Cape Town, graduated from the University of Cape Town and received her PhD from the London School of Economics, University of London. She lectured in economics at the University of Cape Town and in America and is now a member of the University of Cape Town Council. A past president of the South African Institute of Race Relations, she is now a member of the Executive Committee. She is the author of several books on the South African economy and the labour situation, notably *Native Labour in South Africa* (1971) and *African Workers in Town: A Study of Labour in Cape Town* (1964), and contributed the chapter on 'Labour' in the Institute's *Handbook on Race Relations in South Africa*.

David Welsh, PhD (U.C.T.) and MA (Oxon), was born in South Africa and studied at the Universities of Cape Town and Oxford. He is Associate Professor in Comparative African Government and Law at the University of Cape Town. He is the author of *The Roots of Segregation* (1971), co-editor of and contributor to *Student Perspectives on South Africa* (1972) and *The Future of the University in Southern Africa* (1977), and contributed the chapter on 'The Growth of Towns' to Vol. II of the *Oxford History of South Africa* (1971) and a number of articles to journals and books. He has been a member of the Executive Committee of the South African Institute of Race Relations since 1967. Active in party politics, he concerns himself in particular with constitutional questions.

Dr E. G. Malherbe is a South African educationist who has held a number of posts of national importance during his long and distinguished career. Among these are Chief Investigator, Education Section, Carnegie Poor White Commission, 1929–32, founder and Director of the National Bureau of Educational and Social Research, 1929–39, Director of Military Intelligence and of Army Education Services, 1940–5, Principal and Vice-Chancellor of the University of Natal, 1945–65. He has lectured in education at the Universities of Stellenbosch and Cape Town. His numerous publications on education and related matters include Vols I and II of *Education in South Africa*, a major historical account and analytical survey which has become a standard work on education. Dr Malherbe is a past president of the South African Institute of Race Relations.

Henry Lever studied at the University of the Witwatersrand, Johannesburg, where he obtained five degrees including his Bachelor of Laws (1958) and Doctor of Philosophy (1964). He practised as a lawyer in Johannesburg from 1958 to 1963 before taking up an appointment in the Department of Sociology of the University of the Witwatersrand where he was appointed Professor in 1970. He has studied at the London School of Economics and was visiting Professor of Sociology at Columbia University in 1975. He is the author of *Ethnic Attitudes of Johannesburg Youth* (1968), *The South African Voter* (1972), *South African Society* (1978) and has edited *Readings in South African Society* (1972). He is now Professor in the Department of Behavioral Sciences at Ben Gurion University, Israel.

Born in Idutywa, Transkei, in 1930, **John Barratt** received his higher education at the Universities of the Witwatersrand and Oxford. From 1954 to 1967 he was a South African Foreign Service Officer, and he spent seven of those years with the South African Mission to the United Nations in New York. In 1967 he was appointed Director of the South African Institute of International Affairs, a post he still holds. Author and co-editor of various works on South African external relations, other southern Africa questions and the United Nations, Mr Barratt is a regular commentator in the media on international matters. He is also on the Management Committee of the United States-South Africa Leader Exchange Programme.

Adam Small was born in Wellington in the Boland in 1936. His mother was Muslim and his father a Dutch Reformed schoolmaster. Until the age of nine he lived in Goree, a mission post outside Robertson. The family then moved to the Cape Flats. His primary schooling was Calvinist, but he then attended a Catholic secondary school and went on to the University of Cape Town, where he read Philosophy. As head of the Department of Philosophy at the University of the Western Cape (UWC) for fourteen years, Mr Small introduced concepts of black consciousness to UWC and to the Western Cape and believes that this movement has had constructive results for black communities.

Adam Small is a poet in the medium of Afrikaans and English (*Kitaar My Kruis, Sê Sjibbolet, Black Bronze Beautiful*), a playwright in both languages (*Kanna Hy Kô Hystoe, Joanie Galant, The Orange Earth*), and a commentator on South African affairs.

Married with two sons from a first marriage and a son and a daughter from the second, he is at present Director of the Western Cape Foundation for Community Work, an organisation that concentrates on pre-school care and education.

1 Fifty Years of the South African Institute of Race Relations

ELLEN HELLMANN

The different world of 1929

The South African Institute of Race Relations was born half a century ago in a climate of thought, both national and international, utterly different from that of today. White rule had been firmly imposed over vast areas of the globe during the centuries in which the leading European powers had established their colonial empires. Over these areas colonialism, sustained by the mystique of white superiority, still held sway, despite the growing resentment of the subject peoples against imperialist rule. In Africa, apart from the then Union of South Africa, the only independent states were Egypt, Ethiopia and Liberia. On the map of Africa all the remaining territories were shaded in different colours to indicate which of the colonial powers ruled over their destinies. The race question was not, as it was to become after the Second World War, a dominant issue leading to wars of liberation from colonial bondage and a crucial factor in the conduct of international relations.

In South Africa the problem of race relations has been endemic. Race relations emerged as a problem from the moment the earliest settlers, after landing in the Cape, first encountered Hottentots and Bushmen. Even then, as has been the case ever since, the mirage of total separation lured men with its false promise. The first idea of separation took shape in the proposal to plant an impenetrable thicket of almond trees to enclose the Dutch East India Company's domain. Later, after white settlers advancing north-eastwards met Bantu tribes migrating southwards, followed by a century-long series of wars between them, successive but vain attempts were made to establish final and inviolable boundaries which both parties would respect. There was no finality then, as there is no finality today.

1

In 1929 when the Institute came into being, Union had been in existence for close on two decades. When the two former British colonies and the two Republics (by then all four self-governing colonies) entered into Union, two very different political traditions were brought together. In the Cape a non-racial franchise for men with low electoral qualifications had been in force since 1853. Thereafter there continued to be considerable support, above all for the political aspects of the liberalism of the time expressed in the phrase, 'Equal rights for all civilised men'. The two former Republics permitted no form of racial equality in Church or State, and had a 'whites only' franchise. Union was effected by compromise. It was agreed that each Province would maintain its own franchise system, with existing franchise rights being protected by constitutional safeguards. The Cape, however, made one surrender of principle: it agreed that only whites could be elected to Parliament. It was the hope of Cape liberals, though not the expectation of all of them, that the liberal creed would spread to the north and eventually prevail throughout the country. This was not to be. Under successive governments, and with very little white dissent, the pattern of racial segregation already in existence at the time of Union was extended by a number of discriminatory measures, such as the Mines and Works Act of 1911, which gave statutory force to the conventional colour bar by reserving certain skilled occupations for whites, and the Natives Land Act of 1913, which set aside scheduled Native Reserves for exclusive African ownership and prohibited Africans from purchasing land in rural areas outside the Reserves without the approval of the Governor-General. This Act of 1913 underpinned segregation and laid the foundations for the policies of apartheid and separate development that the future was to bring forth.

Reaction against these measures came from politically conscious Africans, who formed the South African Native National Congress in 1912 and who later, when their opposition to the Land Act failed, sent a fruitless deputation to the Imperial Parliament. Further discriminatory measures followed soon after the end of the 1914–18 war.

African resentment gathered momentum. There was a series of strikes by African workers, in some instances leading to violence and shooting. The Industrial and Commercial Union, an all-embracing organisation of African workers, came into being. It grew to a reputed strength of 100 000 members and extended the range of its activities until, in the late 1920s, fierce internal dissension and rivalries led to its disintegration and finally to its collapse. A confrontation between the white Mineworkers' Union and the Chamber of Mines, when the Chamber announced its intention of opening to Africans a range of semi-skilled operations, together with other white labour disputes, culminated in the Rand Revolt of 1922. This, though suppressed after armed conflict, demonstrated the determination of white workers to retain their privileged position and to safeguard it from encroachment by the growing tide of black workers.

Despite the recurrent turbulence of the period, racial questions were still far from being the predominant concern of the white electorate. White political parties were not primarily divided, as they were to be some twenty years later, on questions of colour policy, although in the 1929 election what was then called Native policy came into more prominence than at any previous election. The question of Dominion autonomy, the Flag Bill, the establishment of state industries, unemployment and the 'Poor White' problem were among the main divisive issues.

In the Cape, the liberal tradition, a long experience of contact between whites and the other racial groups, particularly the Coloured community, as also the need to gain or retain the support of Coloured and African voters, made for a certain degree of interracial mingling in the social and political spheres. Elsewhere, outside the work place, the overwhelming majority of the different racial groups lived in their own watertight compartments. Economic interdependence has always been a fact of life in South Africa, from the early days of slave-owning in the Cape to the complex economic relationships of present-day industrial society. But such co-operation and contact were confined to the place of work, whether farm or factory, mine, business or home. Between individuals of different racial groups there were often, as there are today, relationships of mutual concern and acts of ordinary human kindness. But in the twenties the predominant characteristic of the white group, secure in its hegemony and cushioned in its relative isolation, was its unawareness of the conditions of life under which the other racial groups lived. This unawareness was particularly manifest in the towns where, despite the growing townward flow of Africans, the majority of whites remained largely oblivious of their presence and their needs.

Within this extensive area of unawareness and consequent indifference, there were always certain centres of creative concern coupled with endeavours by whites to ameliorate the conditions under which black people lived. Above all, there was the work of the churches and the missions reaching out not only to bring the Christian faith but to found educational institutions and provide medical services for the people of colour among whom they laboured. John Philip was but the forerunner of a long line of controversial crusaders whose numbers grew with time.

The founding of the South African Institute of Race Relations

The significance of the founding of the Institute in 1929 is that it was the first national multiracial organisation specifically established to promote interracial goodwill and to conduct investigations bearing upon race relations. The two main objects of the constitution it adopted in 1932 read:

(a) To work for peace, goodwill and practical co-operation between the various sections of the populations of South Africa.

(b) To initiate, support, assist and encourage investigations that may lead to greater knowledge and understanding of the racial groups and of the relations that subsist or should subsist between them.[1]

This constitution, not significantly altered since its adoption, provided for co-operation with and assistance to other bodies concerned with such objectives. It also explicitly precluded the Institute from identifying or associating itself with any organised political party. It provided for a governing Council consisting of the ten Foundation Members (later changed to Life Members and increased to fifteen), elected representatives of donor and ordinary members, and two representatives of each affiliated body. This Council, which meets at least once a year, elects an executive committee which meets twice yearly. Members of the executive who live in Johannesburg, where the Institute's headquarters are located, serve on a general purposes committee which meets monthly and is vested with the power to conduct the affairs of the Institute between executive meetings. Both the executive and general purposes committees can set up sub-committees, whose membership is not necessarily restricted to members of the executive. (There were ten such sub-committees in 1978.) Honorary regional representatives were appointed early in the Institute's life. Over the years regional committees were formed in five centres, with their own offices and staff, and a number of branch committees were established. In 1937 the Institute was registered as a non-profit-making company under Section 21 of the 1926 Companies Act.

Prior to the establishment of the Institute various local bodies concerned with race relations had come into existence. In the early years of this century a number of local Native Welfare Societies[2] had been formed which owed much to the initiative of Dr Charles T. Loram, then Chief Inspector of Native Education in Natal and in 1920 appointed to Smuts's first Native Affairs Commission. 'These societies', states Dr Edgar Brookes, a foundation member of the Institute and three times its president, 'consisted of liberal-minded and philanthropic Europeans anxious to help their

4

African fellow-citizens, but there were no African members and few facilities for consultation with African leaders.'

In 1921, in the course of their study tour of education in Africa on behalf of the Phelps-Stokes Fund of the U.S.A., Dr Thomas Jesse Jones and a distinguished African, Dr J. E. K. Aggrey, visited South Africa. They had both had experience of interracial councils in America and were largely instrumental, together with Dr Loram and a close friend of his, Mr J. D. Rheinallt Jones (who came to be known throughout the land as R. J.), in the formation of Joint Councils to promote understanding and goodwill between Europeans and Africans. Rheinallt Jones established the first Joint Council of Europeans and Africans in Johannesburg in 1921. The Joint Council movement gained momentum, largely due to the tireless work of Rheinallt Jones, and gradually replaced the Native Welfare Societies. By 1931 there were close on thirty European-African, three European-Indian Joint Councils and a European-Coloured Joint Council about to commence activities in Cape Town. In all, eighty Joint Councils were established, some playing a prominent role, others having but a brief existence. Eventually, by 1978, there remained only two.

The Joint Councils, like the Institute itself and many other organisations which succeeded them, were attacked by white conservatives, who saw in them a threat to the status quo, and also some blacks and some whites of more militant view, who rejected their conciliatory and reformist approach and taunted them with their powerlessness to right the racial wrongs. The Joint Councils in fact made little impact in their main field of endeavour, which was to combat racial discrimination; nor did they secure the mass following they sought. But many black and white members of Joint Councils learnt there the basic facts of their own society, achieved meaningful contact across the colour line and acquired valuable experience in the conduct of public affairs. A number graduated from the Joint Councils to positions of leadership in political and communal affairs. Above all, the Joint Council movement contributed to the continuing effort to extend the area of awareness.

Dr Jesse Jones paid two further visits to South Africa during the 1920s. Seeing the need to set up a national body to promote interracial activities, to develop the work of Joint Councils and to act as a co-ordinating body for them, he urged Rheinallt Jones to undertake this task. The Phelps-Stokes Fund agreed to provide annual grants of £500 for the first three years and of £200 for the subsequent two years to support this project. Dr Loram succeeded in obtaining annual grants of £750 for five years from the Carnegie Corporation. With this initial financial support it was possible to take the next step. Rheinallt Jones convened an Inter-Racial Conference in Cape Town in January 1929. The response indicated that there would be support for a national organisation.

Accordingly on 9 May 1929 a committee of eight men met in Johannesburg to convert vision into reality. This committee resolved to constitute itself the South African Institute of Race Relations. It elected Dr Loram chairman, Mr Howard Pim treasurer, Mr Rheinallt Jones secretary and appointed Rheinallt Jones as Adviser on Race Relations as from 1 January 1930 – a designation that was changed to Director as from the beginning of 1944.

The Institute's early beginnings and growth

The Institute began its career in two offices, later growing to eight, provided rent-free by the University of the Witwatersrand, which has throughout been most helpful in the provision of much-needed facilities. For a period of ten years after 1946, the Institute operated from a number of premises, until in 1956 it was able to build its own two-storey building, Auden House – named after Dr F. T. Auden, the donor who made its acquisition possible. To start with, Rheinallt Jones's staff consisted of one temporary trained research assistant and one full-time typist. He also had the occasional part-time services of members of the University staff and of the Witwatersrand Council of Education, with both of which Rheinallt Jones was himself closely associated. In addition R. J., through his wide contacts, extensive range of activities and extraordinary initiative, was able to enlist a great deal of voluntary help. Soon thereafter, Rheinallt Jones's wife, Mrs Edith B. Jones, became an officer of the Institute in a voluntary capacity. She served it, until her untimely death in 1944, as Honorary Organiser of the Women's Section (to which were later added Health and Education), with a selfless devotion matched only by the width of her knowledge and her sheer ability.

To commence with and for many years of its existence the Institute was identified with Rheinallt Jones. His own activities shaped the pattern of its development. He held office on a number of other bodies and had close contact with many more: in the first place with Joint Councils, for the inception of many of which he was responsible and the promotion of whose activities continued to be one of his major concerns; and also with missionary bodies, Rotary Clubs, universities, social welfare organisations, Advisory Boards in the then Native Locations and with a host of prominent individuals of all races. As early as 1931 he was directed to add his own

6

report as Adviser in the form of a special appendix to the Institute's annual report in order to define the extent of his own activities. These comprehensive reports, recording the major developments in the field of race relations, are the worthy forerunners of the annual *Survey of Race Relations*, which was first published in 1947.

Rheinallt Jones's extensive activities, which led to the rapid development of the Institute, were made possible because the Institute then, and throughout the fifty years of its existence, was able to draw heavily on the voluntary work of the members of its executive and regional committees and because it has always had on its staff at headquarters and in the regions members who rendered it service of an exceptional quality, service that far exceeded the call of duty.

The records of the Institute testify to the large number of such members, many distinguished in their own field of activitity, who contributed publications and other work of significance or introduced innovations in the Institute's practice and approach. A detailed analysis cannot be given here. But certain people stand out prominently because of the decisive roles they played. Professor R. F. Alfred Hoernlé, a philosopher of international repute, whose Phelps-Stokes' lectures, delivered in 1939 before the University of Cape Town and published as *South African Policy and the Liberal Spirit*, have retained their relevance, moulded early Institute thinking and gave wise and firm leadership as president from 1934 until his unexpected death in 1943. Dr Edgar Brookes was one of the eight who founded the Institute and gave prodigiously both in effort and insight, serving it in many capacities in Natal and elsewhere until his death in 1979. Dr Brookes succeeded Dr Loram, who soon left to take up a professorship at Yale, as president, but relinquished that office in mid-1933 to become Campaign Organiser, in order to build up the Institute's membership and strengthen its finances. A year later the Institute had 546 members, including 24 affiliated bodies, and an annual income of £2 100 from South African sources. Mr Maurice Webb in Durban, Mr Leo Marquard in Bloemfontein and later in the Western Cape, both foundation members, and Mr Donald Molteno, QC in Cape Town from 1938 – all three past presidents – gave inestimable service throughout their lives.

The Institute has had only three directors, all men of exceptional calibre. When the redoubtable R. J. resigned in 1947, he was succeeded by Quintin Whyte, on whose retirement in 1970, Fred van Wyk took over. Deliberately underplaying his own impressive intellectual input, Quintin Whyte organised a departmental system, delegated authority and promoted a sense of collective responsibility to make the Institute a force which transcended the sum-total of the activities of its officers. Fred van Wyk has further developed this structure and in particular has made valuable contributions to enlarging the range of co-operation with other bodies, especially the churches, and to extending the range of contacts in the field of public relations.

Over the years the work of the Institute has expanded, its activities have become more diversified, its staff, income and membership have grown. The graph of the Institute's progress is not a smooth curve without recessions, but on the whole it indicates a steady and substantial growth. When Quintin Whyte became director in 1947 there were 34 members of staff at headquarters and regional offices. By 1977 the number was 77. There were 2 549 members (including 216 donor members) in 1947. They increased to 4 098 (including 439 donor members) by 1977. The Institute has never succeeded in meeting its membership targets, neither in numbers nor in their representative nature. While Afrikaners of distinction – among them J. Reyneke, for fourteen years chairman of the general purposes committee, and past-president Dr E. G. Malherbe – and leading Africans – Professor D. D. T. Jabavu, a vice-president from 1932 until his death in 1959, past presidents Dr W. F. Nkomo and Rev E. E. Mahabane, executive members Dr A. B. Xuma, Dr D. G. S. M'Timkulu, Professor Z. K. Matthews, Mr P. R. Mosaka, to name only some – have been closely associated with the Institute since its inception, its membership has been predominantly white and English-speaking.

Securing the necessary funds to meet the growing costs of actual, let alone desired, expansion has always been and still is a major problem. Deficits have been the rule rather than the exception. At no time has the Institute had an endowment fund of more than trifling proportion. Recurrent financial crises threatened and sometimes compelled cut-backs. Dr Oscar Wollheim, an Institute stalwart who has served on the executive committee since 1940, launched a rescue operation in 1946 when he used his long leave to become Campaign Organiser and conducted a successful membership and fund-raising drive. A number of members devoted much time and effort to raising funds, particularly Dr P. R. B. Lewis, who served as honorary treasurer for fifteen years until 1957 and from whose initiative and guidance the Institute's finances benefited substantially.

Apart from an annual grant of R4 000 for five years from the Department of Education towards the cost of research in literacy work pioneered by Mrs Maida Whyte, the Institute did not apply for nor receive grants from the Government. Membership fees have never met more than part of the Institute's budget. For the rest it relied on donations and contribu-

8

tions, for the last twenty years raised mainly by national five-yearly fund-raising campaigns. In 1972 a Research and Library Trust Fund, exempt from estate duty, was established. Various trusts, chief among them the Bantu Welfare Trust and the Auden Race Relations Trust, have for long made annual grants. In 1953 the Ford Foundation made a grant of $50 000 which enabled the Institute to reach its twenty-fifth anniversary the following year with greatly added impetus to its work. In the years that followed, the Ford Foundation, the Carnegie Corporation, Rocke-feller Brothers Fund and certain other overseas funds, as also a number of Churches in Sweden, Germany and Holland made grants specifically allocated to research and publications, the archives department, youth work, bursaries and the development of D.W.E.P. (Domestic Workers' and Employers' Project). But by far the greater proportion of the Institute funds came from internal South African sources. Bequests, particularly those of Mr E. Lazarus and Dr Bernard Price, although always hopefully intended for the endowment fund, had to be used to meet the costs of the Institute's core administrative structure without which the growing num-ber of service projects could not operate. In the light of the Institute's modest start, the fact that expenditure amounted to R27 430 in 1947 and rose to R507 364 in 1978 speaks for itself.

The evolution of the Institute's approach

The Institute commenced its work with neither a pre-conceived programme nor ready-made policy. It believed in the pursuit of the truth as a value in itself. It believed that the systematic seeking out of facts relating to the conditions which determine the quality of life of the disadvantaged groups in South Africa would increase public awareness and promote inter-racial understanding, an understanding without which there could be no peaceful future for South Africa. It recognised the inherent worth and dignity of every human being and his right to the full development of his innate potential. It affirmed the values of democratic society, with its ac-cepted rights and duties, together with respect for the rule of law and the safeguarding of individual liberty. It pledged itself to pay due regard to opposing views sincerely held.

Within the framework of these beliefs, the Institute gradually came to define its own attitude with increasing clarity. It was a pragmatic process based on the results of research, investigations and fact-finding, analyses of legislative and administrative procedures bearing on race relations and shaped by responses to the issues of the day. The collective thinking of the

Institute crystallised during fifty years, in the deliberations at its annual Council meetings, in conferences on specific subjects which yielded a substantial body of findings, and in the course of the preparation of evidence submitted to numerous government commissions of enquiry.

In the early years it was believed that certain matters appertaining to blacks were 'political' and others not. Only later came the realisation that *all* questions affecting the fate and future of the different racial groups, that labour relations, land and residential rights, sport and social welfare, education and entertainment, the whole area of civil rights – quite apart from the basic matter of political rights – were quintessentially political in the South African context. It was Institute policy for a number of years to refrain from expressing any views on national issues it regarded as 'political'. Consequently, it made no public pronouncement on the Hertzog Native Bills which had been before the country from 1926 and were passed in Parliament in 1936 and 1937. It did provide analyses of these Bills (the 1936 Native Trust and Land Act, the 1937 Representation of Natives Act and the 1937 Native Laws Amendment Act) and other documentation for the Joint Councils and numerous other bodies and individuals. Mrs Rheinallt Jones had compiled two hundred district maps showing in detail the further areas to be released for African occupation, and she assisted in gathering information regarding the extent to which these areas were already in African ownership or occupation. In 1936 Mr A. Lynn Saffery, secretary to the Institute, in his capacity as secretary of the Consultative Committee of Joint Councils of Europeans and Africans, convened a conference of forty organisations to consider the Bills. Significantly, even then, as was repeatedly to occur later, organisations with opposing views did not respond to the invitation to attend the conference. The conference unanimously resolved to oppose the Representation of Natives Bill and appointed a committee to present its view to the public and to Parliament.

From its establishment the Institute concentrated on the investigation of social and economic conditions, with special reference to their effect on race relations. It encouraged and helped other bodies to undertake investigations in their own area of activity and sponsored individual research into relevant matters. As the years passed many research institutions were created by government, university and other bodies and the Institute drew heavily on their material. The Institute made representations to the government and local authorities on many of the matters arising from its investigations, on occasion in co-operation with other bodies. There were deputations to Ministers of different departments of state, in addition to the frequent written submissions.

Rheinallt Jones served in the Senate from 1937 to 1942 as elected representative of the Africans of the Transvaal and the Orange Free State; and he, together with Dr Edgar Brookes in the Senate and Mr Donald Molteno in the House of Assembly, who were both key Institute figures and who were elected for successive five-yearly terms as Native Representatives, established the basis of a valuable and mutually enriching collaboration. In the course of extensive travels in their huge constituencies, they gathered and supplied much vital information to the Institute. At the same time they supplemented their own material with that provided by the Institute and in the speeches they made in Parliament and on other platforms they gave it a wider currency than the Institute on its own could command.

In the forties the Institute presented evidence to a number of important government commissions of enquiry, among them the Native Mine Workers' Commission, the Penal and Prison Reform Commission (of which Mrs A. W. Hoernlé, three times a president of the Institute, was a member) and the 1946 Native Laws Enquiry Commission (the Fagan Commission). This last commission marked a watershed in South African affairs. It reported in 1948, making a number of far-reaching recommendations which, if adopted, would have significantly improved the position and status of urban Africans. It found that Africans constituted a permanent part of the urban population, that their townward movement as a normal economic phenomenon could be regulated and guided but not reversed, and it deprecated the migratory labour system. This report heralded the realisation, destined to grow steadily in importance, that the position of urban Africans constituted the vital nerve centre of South African politics.

It seems passing strange, thirty years later, that the Institute could then recommend a variety of measures designed to stabilise urban Africans, including their right to freehold tenure of land, could commit itself to the recognition of African trade unions and make many other recommendations, all in the conviction that these were not 'political'. The fact that this was indeed the case is a measure of the change that took place when the National Party came into power in 1948, since when all racial matters have become not merely political but party political, in that they constitute the fundamental issues which divide South Africa's political parties.

A further stage in the Institute's development took place in 1952. In the previous year the Institute had presented extensive written evidence to the Commission on 'The Socio-Economic Development of the Native Areas within the Union of South Africa' (the Tomlinson Commission) in which the Institute documented in detail the facts relating to the economic interdependence of all racial groups to support its conviction that with continued economic development, primarily industrial, there would be increasing economic integration. The Commission requested the Institute to appear before it to answer questions relating to the political and social implications of economic integration. This the Institute did. A summary of its evidence was prepared by Quintin Whyte in the booklet *Go Forward in Faith* which, for the first time, stated the broad lines of the Institute's own policy on major racial issues and indicated the course it believed South Africa would have to follow to achieve multiracial harmony, equal opportunity and common citizenship in the interests of all its peoples.

In succeeding years the Institute spoke out clearly and unequivocally against the Government's systematic application of its apartheid policies, which further entrenched white domination and extended the areas of legally institutionalised discrimination. Throughout the 1950s and most of the 1960s the Institute found itself in opposition to the series of government enactments ruthlessly designed to establish a racially segregated society. But the Institute remained, as before, entirely free of alignment with any political party.

In 1972, in view of the many changes that had taken place, the Institute felt that the time had come to give coherent and definitive expression to its statements, findings and resolutions of the preceding twenty years. It therefore published *The Road Ahead*, written by the director, Mr F. J. van Wyk, in consultation with the executive committee. By then, self-governing African homelands had come into being with the likelihood that one or more of them would attain sovereign independence, as did Transkei in 1976 and Bophuthatswana in 1977. The Institute regarded the fragmentation of the Republic as a tragic mistake, but recognised that the extensive development of the homelands had created new political and social realities. It believed then, as it has continued to believe, that a secure and peaceful future can be founded only on the basis of one South African nation composed of different language and racial groups, each group entitled to the right to maintain its own cultural identity, and all united in a common loyalty. It believes that this will be the eventual outcome in that 87 per cent of South Africa's total land area which constitutes what some call 'white' South Africa and others (more realistically, in the opinion of the Institute) the 'common area', even in the unlikely event of all ten African national units opting for independence. The Institute elaborated the grounds for its rejection of the Government's multi-national approach. It reaffirmed its belief that to establish a just society there must be progress towards the goal of a common citizenship for all permanent residents regardless of race. Neither then nor in subsequent years has the Institute attempted to formulate a constitutional blueprint, this clearly being a task for the political parties. But, cognizant of the particular complexities of a plural society and the existing wide differences in the degree of adjustment to a modern industrial society, the Institute, with the help of political scientists and others, has explored this question at meetings of its Council and dealt with it in its publications.

It must not be assumed that the Institute coasted along on a gentle tide of consensus within its governing councils, regional and other committees. It has confronted recurrent crises, both before 1948 and since, when it was riven by internal dissension on issues of policy and action. The continually increasing gravity of the racial situation in South Africa and the sharply mounting black resentment, repeatedly rising to explosive levels, imbued concerned people with an almost intolerable impatience to give real impetus to change. In such circumstances divergence on policy and calls for more militant action were inevitable. At such times the Institute lost some support both to the right and to the left. There were periodic reviews and exhaustive reassessments of its own direction and activities. But while there were changes of emphasis over time, the central fabric of the Institute has endured and it has maintained its basic factual approach. Moreover the Institute was no longer alone, as it had been at the start of its career. Many other organisations, multiracial, black and white, had come into being, in some cases with Institute assistance. They have differed in policy, tactics and the services they offered, but all were positioned on the broad front along which the struggle for racial accommodation is being waged.

Relations with the Government

While the Institute has, in general, been fortunate in the co-operation it has received from senior officials in the public service on such matters as the provision of factual data, its relationship with the Government itself, particularly with Cabinet Ministers in charge of those departments of state relevant to the Institute's work, has varied. During the period of Fusion under General Hertzog and the years of United Party Government under General Smuts from 1939 to 1948, it enjoyed easy access to Cabinet Ministers who, while often not in agreement with the Institute's submissions, were always ready to give them serious consideration. In 1942 General Smuts made a significant speech, in which he declared that 'Segregation has fallen on evil days', from an Institute platform. Jan H. Hofmeyr, soon to be Deputy Prime Minister, delivered the first Hoernlé Memorial Lecture in 1945.

After 1948 the situation gradually changed. The 1950 Council meeting was opened by Dr E. G. Jansen, the Minister of Native Affairs, and Dr W. W. M. Eiselen, the Secretary for Native Affairs, delivered an address on the Native Reserves. Soon thereafter disagreement arose. The Institute, keenly aware of deteriorating race relations, drew up a programme of constructive proposals for immediate African development, deliberately confined to matters on which agreement appeared to be possible, the implementation of which by the Government, the Institute considered, would assist in easing tensions. When it sought an interview early in 1951 to present these proposals to the new Minister of Native Affairs, Dr H. F. Verwoerd, he indicated that he was not prepared to meet a mixed deputation and would prefer to meet the European and Non-European members separately (an approach, it must be noted, which no longer prevails). Consequently the Institute abandoned its plans for this discussion.

The Institute continued to submit written representations on various matters to the appropriate Minister, on occasion accompanied by the request that they be accorded a hearing for further discussion. The reply was often that no useful purpose would be served by such an interview. On a number of occasions written replies were given in response to the Institute's submissions. While the Institute continued to receive helpful co-operation from government officials, its relations with the Government itself became somewhat strained.

Early in 1972 the Government appointed a parliamentary select committee, later converted to a Commission of Enquiry into Certain Organisations (initially the Schlebusch and later the Le Grange Commission) to investigate the objects, activities, financing and related matters of four organisations. The Institute was completely taken aback to find that it was included amongst these four organisations. In the event, when the Report of the Commission appeared the following year, the Institute was vindicated, although the Commission commented unfavourably on the activities of the Institute's youth programme without, however, actually making any substantial allegations of undesirable activities.

The Institute first experienced the effects of the country's security laws in 1966 when its African field officer, now a professor at an American university, was banned. The terms of his banning order, *inter alia*, prohibited his further association in any capacity with the Institute. In the mid-seventies, in the wake of increasing unrest, incidents of urban terrorism and increasingly restrictive and arbitrary security measures, a number of members of the Institute's staff and of its committees were detained without trial, some for recurrent periods, and others were banned. The Institute's reaction was one of mingled incomprehension and acute regret. It repeatedly called on the Government either to charge persons so detained in court or to release them. For the first and only time, an Institute publication, namely a report compiled by the Institute's research staff, *Detention Without Trial in South Africa 1976–1977*, was banned in terms of the Publications Act of 1974 and its possession was prohibited.

Research, investigations and fact-finding

The core of the Institute's work throughout its existence has been the accumulation of factual data relating to the living conditions of the African, Coloured and Asian peoples and to their legal status and civil rights. This included the regular study of the reports of relevant government departments, of commissions and committees of enquiry, the analysis of legislation and ordinances bearing on race relations, and the results of various enquiries the Institute conducted itself. Such enquiries, which varied in depth, ranged from *ad hoc* investigations of specific situations to major research projects. In later years projects were sponsored by the Institute, depending on the Institute's resources in personnel and funds.

The land question, education and particularly the educational facilities available to Africans, farm labour, the employment opportunities and wages of blacks, housing, urban African matters, health and welfare services, juvenile delinquency, the liquor problem, pass laws, migratory labour, the legal disabilities of African men and women, together with the associated high incidence of statutory offences, consequent imprisonment and complaints regarding police treatment, are among the matters to which the Institute, from the start, directed its attention. Education, the provision of health and other social services, the complex of issues relating to urban Africans and the broad area of justice, have been of central concern to the Institute and have been systematically documented. The ongoing study of African wages and the cost of living of African families in the towns commenced early on. From the late 1930s the Institute was able to give considerable assistance to various bodies in the preparation of evidence for submission to the Wage Board. The Institute's early, somewhat generalised, estimates of the cost of living for urban Africans acquired greater precision, particularly in 1943 when the Institute gave evidence to the Bus Services Commission. One of the terms of reference was the ability of Africans to pay the increased bus fares recommended by the Transportation Board; an increase which had, when initially imposed, sparked off widespread bus boycotts on the Witwatersrand, and had then been suspended. In 1944, 1950 and 1954 the Institute drew up and published detailed studies of the costs of basic requirements to support an African family of five in various towns. It assisted in bringing to the attention of commerce and industry the then relatively new concept of the PDL (Poverty Datum Line). In later years, through the work of the Bureau of Market Research, the Institute for Planning Research of the University of Port Elizabeth and other bodies, this concept, with various changes of name, became generally known and gained increasing acceptance as a relevant factor in the determination of wage levels.

As new situations arose, relevant enquiries were undertaken. During the war years, for example, the Institute was active in pressing for better conditions for black recruits, more generous allowances for their dependents, assured and adequate war pensions and a fair share in the 'gifts and comforts' scheme and Y.M.C.A. amenities. It made recommendations aimed at improving demobilisation procedures to facilitate the readjustment of Coloured, Asian and African ex-volunteers to civilian life and, above all, to secure suitable employment for them.

A major impetus was given to the Institute's research and fact-finding work by the establishment of the post of technical assistant in the late forties. Miss Muriel Horrell was appointed to this position in 1949, a post which from 1959 was known as that of research officer. During the twenty-eight years of her dedicated service to the Institute, until her retirement in 1977, Muriel Horrell played a crucial role in extending the Institute's horizons, both in respect of its research work and accumulation of factual data and in respect of its publications. Only during the last six years of her work did Muriel Horrell have the assistance, first of one and later of three research workers who, in their turn, specialised in certain aspects of the complex race relations scene to make their own particular contribution to informed understanding.

Soon after Miss Horrell's appointment, the Institute, using the good offices of Members of Parliament of different political parties, instituted the practice of preparing suitable parliamentary questions in order to elicit factual information on a variety of matters from the Ministers concerned. By 1976 the number of such questions, mostly multiple ones, had reached 161.

The routine work of the research department included the study and summarising of Bills that affected race relations, perusing the Hansard reports of the parliamentary debates on such Bills and on the various

16

Departmental Votes, studying *Government Gazettes*, departmental and homeland reports and other relevant publications and keeping abreast of Government Regulations and changes in administration.

Current developments produced additional matters to which particular attention had to be given. Hence, for instance, after the passage of the Group Areas Act in 1950, Miss Horrell visited a number of towns to assess and map its implications for the Coloured and Asian groups who had borne the brunt of the unhappy consequences of this Act. In 1956 the Institute published *The Group Areas Act – Its Effect on Human Beings*, which was written by Miss Horrell in co-operation with Miss Mary Draper of the Durban office. The gradual implementation of government measures to promote the economic and political development of the homelands demanded the attention of the Institute to a correspondingly increasing extent. One outcome was the publication in 1973 of Muriel Horrell's *The African Homelands of South Africa*, a comprehensive description of the homelands which incorporated available information on their legislative structure and their economic and social development. In the seventies Dudley Horner, the senior research assistant who dealt with employment, labour relations and associated matters, analysed all current wage determinations and agreements, updating them as required, and prepared a memorandum of evidence for a sitting of the Wage Board which proved a useful model for regional committees and others involved in the preparation of such submissions. The business sector made frequent calls on the research department for information on wages, basic costs of living, training opportunities and related questions. Matters arising from the application of the Terrorism and Internal Security Acts claimed increasing attention, particularly after the period of unrest following the disturbances in Soweto on 16 June 1976. Lists of persons who were detained, in so far as their identity was available from Press and other sources, and of persons who died while in police custody, were compiled by the research department. The Institute's research department came to be regarded during that period as the most authoritative source of information on detainees, deaths in detention and political trials.

The Institute's library, an indispensable adjunct to its research and other activities, was started in 1933. In the following years of steady growth, during which a press-cutting system was instituted, it has developed into a comprehensive and specialised library on race relations in Southern Africa. It provides a much-used source for reference. Not only members of the Institute and its staff make use of the library, but members of the public, particularly researchers, turn to the librarian for assistance, ranging from looking up a simple reference to the preparation of a whole bibliography. A number of black students have found the library to be of particular assistance. In 1977 in response to requests the library provided close on 45 000 photocopies of material.

During this long period an impressive store of valuable historical material was collected. It includes complete runs of journals which have long ceased to be published, a large collection of minutes and other documents relating to a number of political, welfare and educational institutions, to black trade unions and multiracial trade union co-ordinating bodies that no longer exist, and valuable collections of private papers, such as those of Dr A. B. Xuma. In addition to a number of records of recent political trials, the Institute has in its possession the complete record, together with the exhibits and judgment, of the lengthy court proceedings of the Treason Trial that ended in 1961. The Institute established a separate archives department in 1973, which has since then been engaged in sorting, classifying and indexing this material. It has also microfilmed a number of important documents, including the minutes of evidence to the 1930–32 Native Economic Commission. The department receives local and overseas orders for microfilm of specific archival holdings.

Making the facts known

The most vital function the Institute has fulfilled during the course of the last thirty years has been the publication of its annual *Survey of Race Relations*. Its development from a slim booklet of one hundred pages to a massive volume of more than six hundred pages has been pre-eminently the achievement of Muriel Horrell. Its compilation is the predominant activity of the research department. Rigorous in its objectivity, the *Survey* presents a comprehensive account of all matters affecting race relations in the Republic during the twelve months under review. It has also included, increasingly over the years with the growing interaction between South Africa and the countries on its borders, accounts of the major developments in these areas, particularly South West Africa/Namibia and Rhodesia/Zimbabwe. It has become an indispensable source book of information for all concerned with South African affairs and is used by individuals and organisations, both inside and outside South Africa, of widely differing outlook and diverse objectives.

From 1933 the Institute produced a quarterly *Race Relations Journal*. Its volumes contain many articles of enduring value contributed by leading economists, educationists, political scientists, sociologists and other experts in their field. Publication was discontinued in 1962 because by then a number of journals, published by research and other bodies, covering in greater detail various aspects of race relations, had come into being. A monthly newsletter to members was started in 1936. After various modifications it became the *Race Relations News*, an eight-page news sheet, primarily distributed to members of the Institute, which contains reports of its activities in the different regions, press releases of the Institute, brief articles and comments on current events, book reviews and other material by members of the Institute and its staff and others. In addition to the *Annual Report*, other regular publications are the annual Presidential Address and the annual Hoernlé Memorial Lecture, many of which have been reported at length in the South African Press and have made a distinct intellectual impact. For many years, as part of its ongoing efforts to promote a better understanding between the English- and Afrikaans-speaking groups, the Institute published *Thought* and *Perspektief* quarterly, summarising respectively Afrikaans- and English-speaking thought on current affairs, particularly as reflected in editorial opinion. Later the Institute introduced and made available to subscribers a daily mimeographed translation of significant editorials from the Afrikaans Press.

The Institute's most ambitious production was the 778-page *Handbook on Race Relations in South Africa* (edited by Ellen Hellmann under the direction of an editorial committee chaired by Rheinallt Jones). It was published by the Oxford University Press in 1949 and reprinted by Octagon Books of New York in 1975. Its thirty-five chapters contributed by different writers, all specialists in their own subject, provided the first comprehensive factual account of the South African racial situation.

Any attempt to describe with the requisite brevity the Institute's output of written material, printed and mimeographed, is from the outset defeated by its magnitude and diversity. It would require pages to catalogue the many writings of Muriel Horrell alone. Among her printed works are: *South African Trade Unionism* (1961); *South Africa's Workers* (1969); *Bantu Education to 1968* and *The Education of the Coloured Community in South Africa 1652–1970*, both prepared as the background for conferences of the Institute on these two subjects; *Action, Re-action and Counter-Action* (1971), an account of the development of black political movements, their response to government legislation, the events leading to the State of Emergency and the Sharpeville tragedy in 1960, the subsequent events and the security measures adopted; *Legislation and Race Relations* (1971) and *South Africa: Basic Facts and Figures* (1973). In 1978 the Institute published *Laws Affecting Race Relations in South Africa 1948–1978*. This book, written by Muriel Horrell after her retirement from the Institute itself, sets a seal on her already distinguished contribution and will undoubtedly prove of enduring value. It includes Parliamentary legislation from 1948 till the end of 1976 affecting race relations, significant Proclamations by the State President in terms of these laws, Ministerial policy statements and administrative action and certain relevant court cases.

The Institute has published summaries of a number of reports of important government commissions of enquiry, among them that of the Fagan Commission by Helen Suzman, of the Tomlinson Commission by Professor D. Hobart Houghton, of the Erika Theron Commission on Matters Relating to the Coloured Population, edited by Sheila T. van der Horst (1976). There are publications dealing with the results of specific research projects, such as those on farm labour; early school-leaving of black pupils; the legal status of African women; sport in the context of race relations; labour relations and many other matters. There have been series of booklets, such as the Topical Talk series, and a great number of occasional publications dealing with a vast variety of subjects, ranging from a factual account of the social pensions applicable to the different racial groups to attitude studies.

The output of roneoed material in the form of fact papers on specific subjects, memoranda of evidence submitted to commissions and committees of enquiry, papers delivered at the Institute's annual Council meetings and its conferences, records of the proceedings of symposia and workshops organised by the Institute and other bodies and matters relating to other subjects too numerous to list, has been prodigious.

From time to time, aware that its publications circulate among a too limited, though influential, section of the public, the Institute attempted to reach the man in the street. It produced a variety of short pamphlets and leaflets to spread the Institute's message of interracial understanding and to convey certain basic facts of the existing situation in a form designed to have popular appeal. A number of leaflets dealing with, for example, workmen's compensation, hire-purchase agreements, certain matters of particular relevance to African women, written in simple direct terms were produced in a number of African languages in the attempt to assist the African at 'grass roots' level. But the Institute would not lay claim to success in the use of the 'popular' medium.

It was of course not only by the written word that the Institute communicated its facts and findings to a wider public. Countless addresses were delivered by the directors during their period of office, by members of senior staff at all centres, by office-bearers and members of the executive committee to audiences large and small over a wide spectrum of the community. Institute personnel participated in numerous conferences organised by other bodies, responded to invitations to be guest speakers at schools and clubs, on the platforms of welfare and other voluntary organisations, to student and other bodies, white and black.

The endeavour to make communication more effective has been a continuing one. There were times of acute discouragement. There were times of relative success. New recruits to the Institute brought new ideas. New methods were introduced. In 1977, on the initiative of Archbishop Hurley, a past president of the Institute, a Human Awareness Programme was started, to operate independently of the Institute, in an effort to reach wider circles of the white power structure and to drive home the urgent need for change, especially in the current attitudes towards power-sharing. The Institute is encouraged in its endeavours by the manifest evidence that many other bodies use its material, have built upon it, have expanded it and have extended the area of communication.

Activities, services and projects

It was self-evident that improvements in the living conditions of the under-privileged sections of South Africa's total society constituted a prerequisite to better inter-group relations. From its earliest days the Institute acted as a pressure group, spotlighting the needs of African, Coloured and Asian communities. Spear-headed by the indefatigable Rheinallt Joneses, the Institute directed its own attention and that of Joint Councils and other bodies on which it was represented to the painfully low level of unskilled wage rates, the gross inadequacy of educational facilities, the housing shortage, the lack of social-welfare benefits and services for blacks, to name only a few major areas of concern. Innumerable representations, factually documented, were made to national, provincial and local authorities.

Sixteen years were to elapse before Africans and Asians became eligible for old-age pensions, which had been introduced for White and Coloured people in 1928. Since 1944, when all population groups became eligible, many bodies, including the Institute, have repeatedly urged the Government to reduce the disparities in the levels of social pensions of the different racial groups. In the early years considerable attention was given to stimulating existing welfare organisations, active almost exclusively in the white community, to extend their services to other sections. Rheinallt Jones in Johannesburg and Maurice Webb in Durban were particularly active in

21

this regard and served as chairmen of many a 'Committee of Europeans and Non-Europeans' dealing with child welfare, the blind and the deaf, formed largely in response to the Institute's representations in the 1930s. From 1960 onwards the position was to be sharply reversed: for at that time the Government decreed that each race group was to conduct and control its own activities. The Institute, as also many interracial national welfare organisations with impressive records of highly developed services to all racial groups, expressed without avail their opposition to this policy, which has gradually been implemented.

In co-operation with church and mission bodies, a great deal of work was carried out in the area of health, the Institute having set up a Standing Committee for Non-European Health Services to continue the work of a conference on Nursing Training and Employment in 1932. For years Mrs Edith Jones persevered and finally succeeded in obtaining full training for black nurses. There were lengthy negotiations regarding the provision of medical training for blacks. In 1940 the Institute was able to report that the University of the Witwatersrand had decided to admit 'a limited number of Non-Europeans to complete medical and dental training'.

An important function of the Institute was to assist other bodies in holding conferences or to convene conferences it was specially requested to hold on matters affecting race relations. Such was the conference held in 1954 to consider the concept of a university and its functions in a multi-racial society. The addresses given on that occasion, together with the Institute's evidence to the Commission on Separate University Education, were subsequently published. On a number of occasions the Institute accepted responsibility for the provision of secretarial services for conti-nuation committees set up by different conferences.

Of particular significance was a series of four conferences of church leaders during the 1950s, organised by Fred van Wyk, then assistant director of the Institute, at the request of various church bodies, including the Dutch Reformed Churches and the Federal Missionary Council of the Dutch Reformed Churches, to discuss the problems Christians face in applying Christian principles to a multiracial country. These were followed by the Cottesloe Conference in 1960, also organised by Fred van Wyk, to discuss the responsibility of the churches in the aftermath of Sharpeville. It was a fully representative interracial conference of Protestant clergy and laity, attended by a number of distinguished representatives of the World Council of Churches. The conference reached a remarkable degree of unanimity. But some months later the two main Dutch Reformed Churches found it necessary to dissociate themselves from the findings of the conference and broke away from the World Council of Churches.

Although not conceived as a social-welfare organisation, the Institute assisted a number of multiracial and black societies engaged in welfare and community activities in their early and formative stages by acting as their secretariat. In later years this aspect of its work increased considerably and included the provision of secretarial, accounting and advisory services to a number of black organisations. From the late sixties, Miss Justine Pike, the secretary of the Institute, conducted a number of courses on administration for the representatives of African voluntary societies and prepared a manual of material on the functions of office-bearers, basic book-keeping and related matters.

At times the Institute itself took the initiative in providing services for which there was a clear need in the anticipation that they would in due course hive off and continue to function under their own auspices. Its first experiment, namely the provision of legal assistance to needy persons charged with criminal offences, was undertaken in 1937. In the following year it established a Legal Aid Bureau in Johannesburg as a department of the Institute, to deal with civil and criminal cases. Assisted by special funding, including grants from the Department of Social Welfare, and the voluntary services of the legal profession, similar bureaux were opened in other centres. In 1942 the Johannesburg Bureau became an independent body, as did the bureaux elsewhere somewhat later. The Institute established the Penal Reform League in 1939, which later likewise became an autonomous organisation.

The origin of the present Bureau of Literacy and Literature goes back to 1946 when the Institute was approached for help in planning a course for the training of African Y.M.C.A. leaders in the technique of teaching African illiterates to read and write English. Assisted by Quintin Whyte, and after consulting those already experienced in teaching adults, Maida Whyte planned and gave this course, using in part the methods of Dr Frank Laubach, an acknowledged international authority on literacy. From then on, for the next ten years of intensive development work, Maida Whyte, as the adult education officer of the Institute, and her assistants designed literacy courses incorporating new techniques, produced primers in English, Afrikaans, Fanakalo and seven African languages, a course in English for Indian women, and an arithmetic course, wrote and commissioned simple follow-up books in the different languages for new literates, taught trainers who in their turn taught other trainers to make countless thousands literate. The work was used in mine compounds and industrial plants, in homes and factories, and it spread to distant mission

23

stations and community centres. Staff and volunteers alike were imbued with Maida Whyte's sense of dedication. In 1956 the stage was reached where the Institute's adult education department could be replaced by the autonomous Bureau of Literacy and Literature, which has charted a further course of development.

In 1971 Mrs Sue Gordon, the secretary of the Southern Transvaal Region, organised a series of meetings in various Johannesburg suburbs at which prominent African speakers addressed groups of white housewives. This was the beginning of D.W.E.P. (Domestic Workers' and Employers' Project). Its main aim was to make employers of domestic workers more aware of the human problems of their workers and of the African people in general. The project spread to other centres and gained the enthusiastic co-operation of women's church and other women's groups which set up Centres of Concern where courses in literacy and in various skills were given. Fifty thousand copies of a five-language leaflet were distributed to workers, and a booklet prepared for employers sold in its thousands, attaining the proportions of a best-seller. D.W.E.P. became a separate department of the Institute under Mrs Gordon early in 1974 and extended its activities nation-wide. In 1977 Mrs Leah Tutu was appointed director of the project, which continued to develop, its Centres of Concern starting a variety of new activities and maintaining contact through a monthly newsletter.

The administration of trust funds and of bursaries has become a major function of the Institute. This activity grew from small beginnings and has expanded at an accelerating rate, particularly during the past ten years. From 1936 onwards the Institute has acted as secretariat to the Bantu Welfare Trust (in 1978 renamed the Donaldson Trust after its founder, Colonel James Donaldson), which has been an agency of creative growth, using its substantial resources to provide schools, bursaries, community facilities, and to meet a variety of other needs of African communities. In the growing realisation of the need to promote the advancement of blacks to higher levels of academic and technical training, other trusts, foundations and a number of local and overseas undertakings allocated varying sums of money to the Institute to administer, mainly for bursaries for black scholars and students. By 1973 the rate of expansion had been such as to require the establishment of a separate department under a trusts officer. When Mrs M. Britten, who had for many years made a vital contribution to this and other aspects of the Institute's work, retired from that position in 1978, twelve trusts, in addition to the Institute's own Race Relations National Education and Research and Library Trusts, had been placed in

24

their entirety under the aegis of the Institute. Their capital at that stage was close to R350 000.

The first impetus to the Institute's bursary work had come in 1954 when the Morris Isaacson Education Trust offered the Institute R4 000 a year for at least three years to start a high school and university bursary scheme for Africans on the Witwatersrand – an offer the Institute accepted eagerly. Soon thereafter the Institute made a public appeal for bursary funds, and repeated this appeal annually. The public response grew. In 1961 a special bursary department was set up. The Isaacson Trust continued and increased its support. Individuals, Rotary Clubs and other voluntary bodies came forward to sponsor one or more bursars. Foundations and trusts and large business concerns made substantial recurrent donations, some for specific objectives, such as teacher training, technical and vocational training, undergraduate courses in science or law, the post-graduate diploma in education, and medical training for African women. Some firms asked the Institute to administer bursary schemes for the children of their African employees; others sought information and guidance. In 1977 the Ford Foundation instituted a bursary scheme to enable members of staff of the five black universities to acquire higher academic qualifications at overseas universities.

The trust and bursary departments have worked in close co-operation in the exacting and ever-proliferating tasks of administration. To bring about more effective national coverage, administration was decentralised, allocations being made to all regions for high-school bursaries, to the Cape Western Region for all university bursaries for Coloured students and to the Natal Region for Asian students. In 1978 the Institute expected to have at its disposal close on R500 000 for bursaries, including R125 000 for the Ford Foundation overseas scheme. The number of bursars has varied depending on the cost of their particular course of study, but in some years it exceeded one thousand. To the amount disbursed by headquarters must be added funds deriving from separate education trusts which the Natal Region and Cape Town had established some years previously. In 1977 the Natal Trust granted bursaries amounting to R28 500, and Cape Town R7 000.

The Education Information Centre, formerly a semi-autonomous body but since 1977 a fully fledged department of the Institute, works closely with the trusts and bursaries departments, supplementing their work and carrying out additional tasks. Among these are an annual Winter School of two weeks' duration, mainly for black matriculation scholars, with attendances of one thousand and more, the publication of an annual

25

Register of Bursaries for the guidance of black students, the production of information sheets on technical and vocational courses and an annual guide to the costs of education for black students. Its services as an education centre are in constant demand.

It requires no special wisdom to understand how important it is for young people to get to know each other across the racial divide, the earlier the better, in informal play and games, in shared activities and in dialogue. Like others, the Institute perceived this need. All regions made attempts to carry out such activities with varying degrees of success.

In 1973, with the aid of funds specifically provided for a youth programme, the youth department of the Institute came into being with a national director of its own. 'Mixed fortunes' has been the keynote of the reports on youth work at the various regions since then. Johannesburg, with the largest staff and budget and its own premises, made progress in providing a variety of activities. Its Open School project, its arts and school tuition programme, its dance, creative writing, electronics and photography workshops, its karate groups attract young people and help them to acquire new skills in congenial company. On the whole, it is mainly African youths who take part in the different activities, with some Coloured and Asian participants, but only occasionally whites. The East London programme, however, with its diverse educational, extra-mural and entertainment activities, succeeds in attracting both voluntary helpers and a substantial number of white participants. In Durban, Cape Town and Port Elizabeth a variety of workshops and other activities make a definite contribution towards meeting the needs of a number of young people. Each regional programme has developed its own character, determined partly by the personality of the organiser and others involved, partly by the nature of the region itself and partly, it should be added, by the degree of supervision security officials consider it necessary to exercise. A number of promising organisers were detained without trial, others were banned. That this has an inhibiting effect needs no stressing.

The temptation to describe at least some of the many successful activities of the different regional offices, each in itself a resource centre meeting a host of public requests, is great: the flourishing African Art Centre which Jo Thorpe, the regional secretary at Durban, developed and its biennial national art exhibition; Pietermaritzburg's growing African Art Centre and non-racial lunch-bar; Cape Town's work at the Athlone Advice Centre and its involvement in the provision of emergency assistance for displaced squatters; Southern Transvaal's 'crash coaching' programme for matric and junior certificate African students, constitute a list which could be, and should be, extended. But space does not permit. The Institute would appear impoverished indeed if, after fifty years of intensive endeavour, to which so many men and women of national eminence in South Africa have contributed, giving freely of their ideas, their time and their writing, it could not point to a considerable number of concrete achievements.

But any general assessment of the worth of its total contribution after fifty years of endeavour cannot be attempted. The essence of the Institute's work, the striving to influence the minds of men, is by its very nature imponderable. Many of us believe that the effort has been meaningful. Some derive a certain wry comfort from the fact that proposals which appeared to be heretical when first expounded on Institute platforms have become the commonplaces of today. One belief we all share: and that is the certainty that, given a different direction in the post-war years, South Africa would have progressed immeasurably further in realising the potential of her rich human and natural resources.

The contributions that follow this introduction examine certain major aspects of South African development over the past half-century. If these analyses prove helpful in charting a wiser course for South Africa as it moves, in a troubled epoch of growing internal tension and international rejection, towards the year 2000, then this book will have been worth the writing.

1. The data on which this introduction is based are taken from the Annual Reports of the Institute 1930 to 1945–6 and 1951–2 to 1976–7, and from the *Survey of Race Relations* 1946–7 to 1950–1, the annual report being incorporated in the *Survey* during this period of five years. I have also drawn on *John David Rheinallt Jones* by the Hon. Edgar Brookes (Johannesburg, 1953). Detailed references are not given since this would be too cumbersome.
2. Names of organisations, of Acts and Bills are given in the terms used. Terminology has changed over the years. 'European' has been replaced by 'white'. The official usage of 'Native' was succeeded by 'Bantu' and has now been changed to 'black'. I follow Institute practice in using the term 'black' to denote African, Coloured and Asian people.

2 South African Politics: The Rising Tide of Colour

RENÉ DE VILLIERS

South Africa was moving into a period of questioning and uncertainty at the time of the founding of the South African Institute of Race Relations. Although party politics was concerned primarily with white people and their domestic problems and differences (colour played an insignificant role in the elections of 1933, 1938 and 1943), thoughtful observers were becoming increasingly worried about the future as they contemplated what in those days would have been called 'the rising tide of colour'.

So we find J. H. Hofmeyr, in the foreword to a book published to commemorate the 21st birthday of the Union of South Africa[1], asking such questions as: 'Is it well with the land and its people? Is the future assured? Are the problems not perhaps insoluble? . . . There is impatience with the slowness of the growth of true national unity. There is a feeling that South Africa is in its economic development falling behind in the race with other peoples. There is fear that after all Anthony Trollope may have been right when he wrote: "South Africa is a country of black men and not of white men – it has been so, it is so and it will be so." Certainly the Union has occupied itself overmuch with controversies between the two great elements of its European population and with unfruitful issues which have arisen therefrom.'

The three principal factors which liberal-minded white South Africans of the early 1930s distinguished as contributing to a sense of national unease were: the delays that had arisen in the attainment of white national unity; the realisation that all was not well with the economic structure of the Union (limited markets for agricultural products, the fallacy of cheap labour, the 'knowledge that the gold of the Witwatersrand is a waning asset'); and finally 'the oppression of the presence of what European South Africa regards as its black cloud – the native with his numerical superiority of three to one'.

Hofmeyr continued: 'A generation ago men gave little thought to the problems of the relations between white man and black. The military power of the Bantu had been broken, he had been forced into subjection, he was giving his labour with docility and submission. . . . But in our day the man in the street and on the farm has become alive to the existence of the native problem; an election has been fought on the issue of "the native menace" and the phrase has come to be part of his thinking. . . his thoughts are of fear, fear not of being overwhelmed physically, but fear lest his position should be undermined in more subtle ways. . . . Fear, apprehension, doubts as to his children's future in this, their only homeland, the anxiety lest some day "little brown children will play among the ruins of the Union Buildings" – from the shadows that these things bring the South African in our day does not find it easy to escape.'

Aware of these fears, the liberals of 1929 urged their fellow-countrymen to see the black man as a helper and a co-worker, not a competitor. They realised that political rights would have to be given people of colour and favoured a qualified franchise on a common roll as a beginning. In the end there would be no differentiation. These men, Hofmeyr, Oliver Schreiner, Edgar Brookes, Herbert Frankel, Rheinallt Jones, among others, set their hopes on 'the nation in action' which would become 'the nation at harmony with itself . . . the nation worthily serving the cause of humanity'.

But to begin with there were the very real problems brought about by the Great Depression of the early 1930s to be tackled. Hertzog and Smuts, who had been fighting one another for nearly three decades, were forced into a coalition in 1933 by the economic blizzard and the devastating drought which accompanied it, but only after the former Nationalist Cabinet Minister turned Appeal Court judge, Tielman Roos, had forced them to take South Africa off the gold standard, thereby paving the way for a period of economic growth and industrialisation which would bring its own human relations and political problems, particularly in the labour field.

But if the South African and National parties could work together in crisis, why not permanently? In both camps there were doubts about the wisdom and the practicality of such co-operation. Hard-line Nationalists muttered aloud about the impossibility of working with 'the jingoes', while on Smuts's side fear and enmity of Afrikaner Nationalists were strong; so strong that in Natal a Devolution group came into being to fight the idea and, if necessary, demand independence for Natal.

But the arguments in favour of co-operation between English- and Afri-kaans-speaking South Africans were overwhelming and a year later the

United Party under Hertzog, with Smuts as Deputy Prime Minister, came into being. The Cape leader of the National Party, Dr D. F. Malan, thought differently however. He not only distrusted Smuts, the 'wily handyman of the Empire': he was determined that the Nationalist Afrikaner should go it alone on his own terms. There could be no watering down of principles: there was to be no 'absorption' of the Afrikaner by the non-Afrikaner: under no circumstances was the Afrikaner to lose his separate identity, his right to decide his own destiny, his *selfbeskikkingsreg*, which a later generation of Nationalists was to claim as their party's greatest gift to people of colour.

Malan's refusal to join Hertzog and Smuts and instead to resuscitate the National Party was to affect the course of South Africa's political life for generations to come. While Hertzog and Smuts stood for a broadly based South Africanism in which Afrikaans- and English-speakers would be equal partners, Malan, with the solid backing, if not primarily at the instigation, of the secret 'service' organisation, the Afrikaner Broederbond, stood for an undiluted Afrikaner nationalism. In essence it was white unity or white sectionalism. And white sectionalism ultimately meant domination by one or other of the two white language groups. In the end it was a question of numbers.

In accusing the Broederbond of trying to wreck national unity and putting the English-speaking community in an underdog position, Hertzog revealed that in a private circular in January 1934, when the Fusion negotiations were in progress, the Bond had said: 'Let us focus our attention on the fact that the primary consideration is whether Afrikanerdom will reach its ultimate destiny of *baasskap* in South Africa. Brothers, our solution for South Africa's ills is that the Afrikaner Broederbond shall rule South Africa.'

There is not the slightest doubt that the Broederbond helped the National Party to win power in 1948. Nor is there reason to doubt that its insistence on separateness in politics, education, youth, welfare, trade and business organisations, to name but a few of the spheres in which it came to be applied, had a decidedly negative effect on relations between the two language groups and militated decisively against the kind of white unity which Hertzog and Smuts envisaged and about which Hofmeyr had written.

A test of Hertzog's sincerity in bringing the two language groups together on equal terms came shortly after the outbreak of the Second World War. Having resigned from the United Party on the war issue, Hertzog agreed to find a basis for an alliance with Malan and his followers. The attempt foundered on the issue of relationships between whites:

Hertzog maintained that the Malanites were not prepared to give the English-speaking South Africans a fair deal politically. That was the end of the public life of the founder of the National Party. He retired and died a year or two later, disillusioned and forsaken by many whose leader he had been.

Twenty years later the National Party of the day, firmly entrenched in power, was again to raise the issue of white unity and to argue that it would be advanced by the establishment of a republic. English-speakers, they said, suffered from a dual loyalty to South Africa. Republicanism would end that. But they did not say that the unity they now talked about would inevitably be a different unity from the one Hertzog and Smuts envisaged, because it would be a unity on Nationalist terms. By 1979, eighteen years after the establishment of a republic, Nationalists claimed that there had been a marked improvement in relationships between the two language groups. Non-Nationalists, on the other hand, believed there had been a distressing polarisation, owing largely to the insistence of Afrikaner Nationalists on trying to remake South Africa in their own ethnic image and in the process tending to treat their English-speaking compatriots as handymen or *agterryers*, unless, of course, they were prepared to accept Nationalist ideology hook, line and sinker.

While the National Party remains overwhelmingly Afrikaner-orientated, English-speaking support for its policies has grown down the years. For this there are two primary reasons: conservative English-speaking South Africans approve of the apartheid approach to colour even though they may not always agree with the techniques of implementation, just as many Afrikaner liberals oppose apartheid and favour an open society. The second is that a proportion of English-speakers, frightened by what has happened in many parts of Africa since independence and *Uhuru* (Zaïre and Uganda are examples, as are South Africa's two neighbours, the former Portuguese colonies of Mozambique and Angola) believe that the Government's handling of security problems is preferable to a more tolerant approach. Finally, there are English-speakers who have identified themselves with the National Party because, they argue, only in that way will the English-speaking section have any influence in determining the country's future.

So, today, forty years after the end of the Hertzog-Smuts experiment in white unity, the problem remains basically unsolved. The Afrikaner, as a result of numbers and technical electoral skills, dominates the political decision-making processes. And, more important: there is total Afrikaner command of the public administration, from ganger to railway general manager, from police constable to commissioner-general, from clerk to departmental secretary, from junior official to chairman of the scores of boards and corporations that control nearly everything from mealies and television to censorship and steel. In the private sector, in mining and finance and big business generally, the English-speaking South African continues to play a dominant role, although Afrikaner entrepreneurs have made spectacular progress in many fields, and are dominant in some, such as liquor and cigarettes.

So it is true to say that white unity will remain a problem as long as Afrikaner Nationalism insists on the strict maintenance of ethnic differences and divisions as embodied, *inter alia*, in Nationalist legislation designed to separate English- and Afrikaans-speaking children in primary schools. While it would not be true today to say that the Broederbond rules South Africa, it is a fact that the Broederbond mentality is a dominant factor in Nationalist and therefore government thinking. The Broederbond, with its *baasskap* mentality, is still a factor behind the scenes, acting both as a sounding-board and as a pressure group when necessary, although the final decisions are taken by the politicians. There is, it is true, a wider acceptance in Nationalist Afrikaner circles today of the need for a more broadly based white South Africanism. But the tribal call to the blood remains compelling and difficult to resist, particularly in times of crisis.

Clearing the decks

When Hertzog and Smuts (the former without the hard-line Nationalist Malanites and the latter without the hard-line anti-Nationalists who were to become the Dominion Party) formed the United National South African Party in December 1934, the decks were cleared for legislation which, in the long run, was to alter the course of South African politics: the Native Bills which Hertzog had first introduced as far back as 1926. The Bills, which had recently emerged from five years in committee, were intended to take the Africans off the common voters' roll in the Cape and substitute a form of communal representation, to deal with the land question and significantly to amend legislation affecting urban Africans. Because the Representation of Natives Bill changed the entrenched franchise provisions of the Act of Union, it had to be passed by a two-thirds majority of both Houses of Parliament, a factor which critics of Hertzog believed was paramount in his desire for Fusion. Years before he had said that the underlying purpose of the legislation was 'clearly to establish the principle that the government of the country must be in white hands, strongly safe-guarded against any encroachment or weakening by non-whites'. The Franchise Bill aroused intense feelings, particularly in the Cape, where Africans had enjoyed common roll voting rights, albeit on a qualified basis, for well over half a century. This opposition, of course, was not confined to whites: black resentment and criticism was bitter, particularly when only eleven out of a total of 180 MPs and Senators voted against the third reading. But the die for political segregation had been cast. For Africans in particular, as Leo Kuper points out,[2] these laws constituted a crisis comparable to those of the Constitution of Union and of the Natives Land Act. 'Their significance for the course of race relations, and for African nationalism, was not that Africans were thereby disillusioned and moved to militant action, but rather that the laws raised formidable barriers to co-operative political action between Africans and whites.' In the words of Selby Msimang, then General Secretary of the All-African Convention, 'Africans had no alternative but to accept the position created by the Native Bills that they were not part of the South African community, that European interests were not bound together with African, and that there was no longer any community of interest between Europeans and Africans.'[3]

Nevertheless, there was prolonged if unavailing opposition at meetings of Africans throughout the country and the movement for political unity between Africans, Indians and Coloured people was given new, albeit short-lived, life. The All-African National Convention, which Professor D. D. T. Jabavu had convened specially to fight the legislation, sent a strong deputation to the Government, but it achieved nothing.

Since the Hertzog Bills were to be the foundation on which the edifice of apartheid was to be erected by Malan and his successors in the years to come, it may well be asked why Smuts and his more enlightened followers supported legislation which was so short-sighted and retrogressive. Smuts clearly did not find the decision an easy one. Although he did not like communal representation, he did not see it as inherently wrong. More importantly, he feared that public feeling about the Cape franchise was such that Africans might sooner or later be deprived of it and he wanted to avoid that and salvage something from the wreckage; so he agreed to Hertzog's plan as a compromise. Thirdly, there was the vital issue of white unity. At the National Convention in 1909–10 he had said 'Let us have unity first and settle the native problem afterwards'. There was a good deal of that sentiment left in him a quarter of a century later, when, in addition, the Second World War was casting its shadow over South Africa.

So it was left to Hofmeyr and ten others to vote against the third reading of the Representation Bill. Hofmeyr did so because he objected to the Africans being given an inferior, a qualified citizenship 'which has the marks of inferiority in clause after clause. . . . By this Bill', he warned, 'we are sowing the seeds of a far greater political conflict than is being done by anything in existence today.'

How right Hofmeyr was is obvious today. But much was to happen before then. With the 111 seats it won at the general election of 1938 (the Nationalists' total was twenty-seven, Mr J. G. Strydom, the future Prime Minister, being the Transvaal's sole representative), the United Party ruled as it wished. But a great deal of trouble was in store and on the issue of whether South Africa should go to war on the side of the Allies against Germany, the Party was to break in two. This not only ended the Fusion experiment of white unity, but ushered in an era when Nationalism's primary aim was Afrikaner unity, the goal which would give it political power. Before Malan was able to 'bring together all who, out of inner conviction, belong together' and so win power, he had to fight off a challenge from inside his own camp. The para-military Ossewabrandwag not only attempted to sabotage South Africa's war effort, but threatened to usurp the National Party's position as the mouthpiece of Nationalist Afrikanerdom. Hitler's defeat made Malan's task easier and when he resolved his domestic differences with N. C. Havenga, Hertzog's erstwhile lieutenant, the scene was set for the vital 1948 or apartheid election, the outcome of which was in time to change the course of South Africa's history and launch Afrikaner Nationalism on an unprecedented period of office which has already lasted thirty-one years.

The Nationalists won the 1948 election not because the word 'apartheid' was emotionally irresistible (that was to come later) but primarily because they were able to frighten the white electorate with the word 'integration', a concept which they imbued with all the horrors of *verbastering* and of being swamped in a black tide. Onto J. H. Hofmeyr, Smuts's second-in-command and the focus of liberal hopes, they managed to pin the label 'integrationist', a philosophy which they maintained would lead to the end of the white man in South Africa. They also exploited the Communist threat to the utmost. And when, over and above this highly emotional double-barrelled indictment, the Nationalists were able to offer the vague philosophy of apartheid with its enticing promise of 'safety' and privilege for the white man, the battle was all but won. It needed only those who blamed the Smuts Government for the food and housing shortages and the unemployment and disillusionment which followed the long years of war to join the floating vote and the disgruntled who thought it was time for a change, to ensure victory for Dr Malan – a victory, incidentally, of which not more than a handful of Nationalists ever dreamt. Dr Malan himself, it has been said, did not realise even on the day after polling, that he would be called upon to form a government.

The corollary of this surprise, of course, was something akin to stunned incredulity on the part of Smuts and his followers. A search for scapegoats began. For some there was an obvious one at hand: Hofmeyr, the liberal. It was all his fault. He must not be allowed to succeed Smuts. However, before the movement to 'purge' Hofmeyr could get under way, he died and a 'great light went out in the land, making men more conscious of its darkness'.[4]

The Nationalists came to power in a South Africa that was different from that which they ruled when they last held office, namely, 1931–32. The Great Depression of the early thirties had seen the beginning of a process that was to last until the closing years of the Second World War and to change the face and the economy of South Africa drastically: the trek to the towns, first by whites driven off the land by economic necessity; and secondly, and in larger numbers, by Africans, drawn to urban areas by economic opportunities attendant on industrialisation, which, in turn, had been given tremendous momentum by the war and the growth of manufacturing industries. Large-scale urbanisation not only had a profound effect on the economy itself, but also on the lives and thinking of both white and black. The unaccustomed juxtaposition of the races in shops and offices and factories produced, among other things, a new economic interdependence, particularly in the labour field; and in time it would introduce a new dimension into politics: the urgent demand of the aspiring black worker for political rights and a realisation of his bargaining power as a worker.

The decade from 1943 saw black politics assume a far more militant character which was destined, henceforth, to impress itself more and more on white consciousness and white politics. Strikes, boycotts and civil disobedience were among the weapons of the recently formed Youth League under men like Nelson Mandela, Walter Sisulu and William Nkomo. The Natives' Representative Council, set up under the 1936 legislation, had become increasingly frustrated by the ineffectualness of the consultative procedures and was increasing its demands for a share of power. It was not surprising, therefore, that the Nationalists' accession to power in 1948 was the signal for renewed and intense activity in black politics. This culminated, four years later, in the Defiance Campaign, during which 8 000 people at least were arrested and countless leaders charged under the Suppression of Communism Act.

The Malan Government saw these activities as a direct threat to apartheid, the policy aimed at the maintenance and protection of the white population 'as a pure white race', the maintenance and protection of the indigenous race groups 'as separate national communities', with possibilities of developing in their own areas to 'self-protecting national unities and the development of national pride, self-respect and mutual respect *vis-à-vis* the different races of the country'.

The Government therefore embarked upon a legislative programme which was almost wholly negative, restrictive and even punitive: the withdrawal of the communal franchise given to the Indians of Natal and the Transvaal; the abolition of the Natives' Representative Council; the Group Areas Act; race classification; the Suppression of Communism Act with its far-reaching powers to restrict individuals and organisations and more; and the first stages of the statute designed to deprive the Coloured people of the Cape of the common roll franchise which they had had for a century.

The United Party Opposition in Parliament failed to satisfy many white voters and for a time at least, the most effective criticism of Nationalist policy came from two extra-parliamentary bodies, the War Veterans Torch Commando (which at one stage had an effective membership of about 250 000 men and women) and the Women's Defence of the Constitution League, from which the Black Sash developed, a movement of conscience and protest against the violation of the spirit of the constitution.

In spite of all this (some will say because of all this), the National Party won the 1953 election with a considerably increased majority of 33 (94 seats to the U.P.'s 57 and Labour's 4). Not only was the Government emboldened by its success to carry on with its restrictive legislation and its policy of *kragdadigheid vis-à-vis* its opponents, but what was as bad was that its white opponents became increasingly dispirited and disillusioned and therefore less effective. The Torch Commando, already weakened by dissension over goals and tactics in the run-up to the election, withered and died; and in doing so it revealed the almost fatal dichotomy and indecision which were to beset white opposition politics for the next generation and more: how far to go in opposing the excesses of Nationalism's restrictive and/or repressive legislation; to what extent to identify with the political strivings of people of colour; how far to go in pleading for political and economic rights for black people; and finally, how to determine the nature of such rights.

When, in due course, security became the crucial issue of the day, the Opposition ranks were in even greater difficulty. They now had to decide just what the requirements of security were and how to counter Nationalist taunts of a lack of patriotism. This dichotomy and indecision led, ultimately, to the death of the United Party in 1977. However, the process had begun in 1954, when six right-wing MPs, led by Mr Bailey Bekker, were expelled from the party because they regarded its policy as 'too radical', and formed the Conservative Party. The break-up of the party continued with the resignation of Dr Bernard Friedman, MP for Hillbrow, over the Coloured vote issue (the U.P. was too indecisive, he argued). This was followed in 1959 by the break-away of eleven liberal-minded MPs on the issue of land for Africans and the consequent formation of the Progressive Party.

The Progressive Party adopted an unequivocal multiracial stance from the start. It declared that there was only one nation in South Africa embracing various groups, each entitled to participation in government. Therefore, it decided on a two-tier non-racial franchise in a Federal bicameral system and a Bill of Rights in a rigid constitution, involving a large measure of decentralisation of power.

White politics was never to be quite the same again. For the previous twenty-three years a group of seven representatives of the Africans led by Mrs Margaret Ballinger, a remarkably effective parliamentarian, had pleaded the cause of black people persistently and eloquently. There was, as Professor W. K. Hancock wrote in his biography of Smuts, 'an immense disproportion between their number and the impact they made on Parliamentary discussion'.[5] That task was taken over by the Progressive Party in 1960, the year in which, by coincidence, even this minimal form of African representation by whites in Parliament was terminated.

Despite the fact that the Progressive Party had but a single representative in the House of Assembly from 1961 to 1974, it did its job magnificently, thanks almost entirely to the efforts of another exceptionally gifted woman MP, Helen Suzman. For fourteen years Helen Suzman *was* the Progressive Party, not only resisting the oft-times unbridled onslaughts in Parliament, but articulating Progressive practice and philosphy with a clarity and incisiveness which were to influence the outlook and thinking of countless South Africans of all colours.

It was by the Progressive Party that the real choice before South Africa was put clearly in the early 1960s: Was the white man to share power fairly with blacks in an undivided South Africa? Or was he to try to govern by himself that 87 per cent of the land surface that he claimed as his own, giving the eight different African ethnic groups independence to rule themselves in their own homelands? The place of the Coloured and Asian peoples in this set-up had not been clarified at that stage. Nearly two decades later the government of the day was to announce a plan to create separate 'parliaments' for the Coloured and Asian peoples to operate alongside a white parliament, the white man retaining ultimate authority in matters of dispute. The issue boiled down to whether there was in fact one sovereign nation in an undivided South Africa or whether there were a number of separate nations each to become sovereign in its own sphere, with limited local jurisdiction for the Coloured and Asian peope 'in their own affairs'.

But much was to happen before the battle lines were drawn as clearly as that. Between 1953 and 1958 the South African Labour Party faded out after a long and at times honourable history which began in 1910. It died because it could not decide whether it should serve white interests primarily or whether it should take its stand on a basis of equality between white and black workers. It lurched from near-left to right in the political spectrum and failed to stay at one end or the other. From nine MPs in 1943, it slid to nought in 1958 and then disappeared from the scene. Its decision to fight the 1953 election on the basis of an agreement with the United Party and the Torch Commando angered both liberals and conservatives in its ranks and contributed to its demise – another party that could not make up its mind about the place and role of people of colour in 'white' politics.

Even the short-lived Liberal Party, formed in 1953 (after the death of the Torch Commando) with the object of working for a common South African citizenship irrespective of race, had some difficulties in deciding on the precise nature of a non-racial franchise (qualified or not) as well as on the extent to which the party should identify itself with the black resistance movements of the 1950s and early 1960s. It settled, in the end, for the principle of adult suffrage. By doing so, incidentally, it was able to retain the support of moderate African opinion.

Although it was never officially represented in Parliament, the Liberal Party's case was persuasively put by MPs such as Margaret Ballinger and Donald Molteno and the Senators Edgar Brookes and Rheinallt Jones. Outside Parliament it had distinguished spokesmen such as Alan Paton and Leo Marquard. After the passage of the Prevention of Political Interference Bill in 1968, which made it mandatory for parties to be uniracial, the Liberals disbanded rather than continue under conditions which made nonsense of their philosophy.

The years of crisis

When Dr H. F. Verwoerd succeeded Mr J. G. Strydom as Prime Minister in 1958, he was to usher in a new era in Nationalist politics by giving to apartheid the connotation of separate freedoms. He thereby invested the apartheid philosophy with a moral dimension and content it had formerly lacked. His theory of independence for the homelands was new; but it came nine years after a seasoned observer (Mrs A. W. Hoernlé, president of the Institute of Race Relations) had experienced 'a growing sense of bitterness on one side and on the other a reorientation to a purely sectional outlook among Africans'. Whereas formerly the black person had no other aspiration than to be a South African, 'today he is more and more imbued with the idea of African nationalism and freedom from control of the white man'.[6] So in a sense Verwoerd anticipated and helped to provoke the philosophy of African nationalists of a later period who in their turn would reject a common society and opt to go it alone.

Dr Verwoerd also gave South Africa a republican constitution (after having narrowly won the 1961 referendum on the issue) and followed this up by taking the Republic out of the Commonwealth, the start of a new and increasingly uncomfortable period of isolation. Not even those who were unhappiest about South Africa's departure from the Commonwealth could have foreseen a time when, through a combination of circumstances and the close interplay of national and international policies, the Republic would become more isolated than ever before. This was almost wholly due to the abhorrence which the rest of the world developed for the policy and practice of apartheid, a factor which Nationalism's opponents at home tried to exploit for electoral purposes but without great success.

The process of isolating South Africa began in the early days of the United Nations, when Third World countries in particular started looking at South Africa's race policies very critically, and in particular at the treatment of her Indian peoples. As more and more independent African and Asian states became members of the U.N., an increasingly censorious interest was taken in the Republic's colour policies and above all in the question of political rights. When the future of the mandated territory of South West Africa/Namibia became a live issue at the U.N., South Africa's isolation deepened as world pressures grew to force a solution.

The Nationalist Government's retort to charges that it was responsible for South Africa's growing isolation was to blame it on various factors: a world-wide communist conspiracy to isolate the Republic and hand it over to black rule; the Western world's unconcern for the white man in Africa and its preference for the black; the free world's failure to recognise

39

the value of the Cape sea route in the East-West confrontation. At the same time the Nationalists accused the West of being soft on communism, of failing to realise the communist threat, and of allowing the rest of mankind to interfere in South Africa's domestic affairs at the U.N. Nationalism's domestic opponents, in turn, blamed the Government and its colour policies for the country's isolation. They pointed out that the real menace in southern Africa was the Nationalist-dominated white minority government and that if Marxism was to be repulsed, this situation must first be rectified. As Western nations pointed out, South Africa, with a small and privileged ruling class surrounded by a poverty-stricken proletariat lacking any effective political power, represented a classical Marxist situation.

Events were to show that neither a republic nor homelands freedom would smooth Verwoerd's path noticeably, and the 1960s were to be more traumatic and turbulent than any other comparable period. The decade was ushered in by Harold Macmillan's 'wind of change' speech (3 February 1960) and Verwoerd's subsequent retort: 'we will see to it that we remain in power in this white South Africa'. Sharpeville (21 March 1960), with its 69 men and women shot dead by the police, was to take South Africa to the brink of disaster. It echoed round the world and led, among many things, to the declaration of a national state of emergency, to a march on the Houses of Parliament in Cape Town by 30 000 Africans, and to the detention of approximately 11 000 Africans throughout South Africa.

Drastic government action followed. The African National Congress and its breakaway offshoot, the Pan-Africanist Congress, under the leadership of Robert Sobukwe, were outlawed, and such black leaders as had not managed to go underground or who had not been previously banned, such as Chief Albert Luthuli, the Nobel Peace prize-winner, were imprisoned or restricted. A state of near-open warfare developed between the police and the more militant African leaders. John Vorster became Minister of Justice in 1963 and almost immediately, at the request of the police,[7] took powers to detain without trial, to begin with for twelve days, then for ninety (1963), then for 180 (1965) and finally for an unlimited period if authorised by a judge (such authorisation was done away with ten years later).

The courts were increasingly by-passed as individuals were held incommunicado and organisations declared unlawful by administrative edict. *Habeas corpus* ceased to exist. By 1961 the black leadership had abandoned all ideas of peaceful change and had openly resorted to violence to achieve their ends with bodies such as Umkhonto we Sizwe (Spear of the Nation) and Poqo (We go it alone) indulging in sabotage wherever and whenever possible. Public buildings, railway lines and power installations were their main targets.

Fifteen years after the event the police claimed to have smashed the P.A.C. and saved South Africa from a bloodbath when they thwarted a detailed plan to blow up the centre of Johannesburg on 9 April 1963.[8] Be that as it may, the arrest of nearly the entire A.N.C. leadership at Rivonia, outside Johannesburg, in July 1963, and the subsequent life imprisonment of Nelson Mandela, Walter Sisulu and Ahmed Kathrada (and in 1965 of Abraham Fischer, the leader of the long-outlawed Communist Party) marked the end of an era of violent resistance which had reached its zenith shortly after Sharpeville and at times attained an intensity not known in South Africa's history.

The end of an era, but not by any means the end of the striving by people of colour for what they thought was their due – a share in the decision-making processes of government. However unapparent this striving was on the surface, the Institute of Race Relations found at the end of the turbulent sixties 'much frustration and bitterness among Africans, particularly those in urban areas'. Through fear of informers and of police action, however, 'few of these people are willing to give open expression to their feelings'.[9]

While the banned A.N.C. and P.A.C. set up headquarters outside South Africa and tried to carry on the struggle from such centres as Dar-es-Salaam, London, Cairo, Algiers and New York, all the while lobbying where they could at the United Nations and the World Council of Churches, the South African Government directed more and more attention and activities to the homelands. It accelerated the development of African towns and resettlement villages[10] with the object of getting as many Africans as possible out of the white urban areas and so reducing the black-white population ratio outside the homelands. Unintentionally, by offering the homelands self-government and later independence, the Government was instrumental in shifting the focus of African political attention and action from the urban to the homeland areas.

In time, therefore, men such as Kaiser Matanzima (Transkei) and Gatsha Buthelezi (KwaZulu) were the ones who articulated the political aspirations of the African people. While Matanzima worked inside the separate development framework, getting what he could out of the system, Buthelezi steadfastly refused to accept homeland independence, expressing vigorous opposition to the fragmentation of South Africa on a variety of platforms both inside the homeland and outside. Whether or not the

Government anticipated it, the Verwoerd policy of independent home-lands came to provide African leadership with a far more effective plat-form than had existed previously. Not only did the homeland leaders have status, but their positions virtually safeguarded them against intimidation and arrest or banishment.

So it came about that by 1979 it was Buthelezi who was claiming to be able to speak for all African people and work for a black political alliance with which he hoped some day to compel the Republican Government to negotiate. And it was Matanzima, at one time thought to be a puppet of the Nationalists, who was breaking off diplomatic relations with Pretoria and agitating in the most strident terms for more land for Transkei.

Meanwhile what was the effect on white political thinking of the crisis events of the early sixties? Even the National Party's cohesion was strained by Sharpeville,[11] particularly in the context of the findings of an inter-church conference held at Cottesloe in Johannesburg, in which a number of Dutch Reformed Church ministers had participated and at which apartheid was vigorously attacked and repudiated. After the hated pass laws, which had been the direct lead-up to Sharpeville, had been very briefly suspended in an attempt to get the country on an even keel again, Paul Sauer, the most senior member of the Cabinet after the Prime Minister, had said: 'We cannot simply go on as in the past. The time has come for adaptation to the new thinking which is taking place in our country'.[12]

But from his hospital bed (whither he had gone after a near-successful attempt on his life in Johannesburg a week or two earlier) Verwoerd cracked the whip, the 'new thinking' was put in cold storage and party unity was restored. Even within the Dutch Reformed Church criticism of the regime and its policy became muted if not stilled altogether. Afrikaner unity had again been put first.

It was different with the United Party, which, in the face of growing in-ternal tension and increasing threats from beyond the country's borders, showed signs of buckling. It voted against the Sabotage Act in 1962, but when the General Law Amendment Bill, with its unlawful organisations clause, came up in the following year, the U.P. supported the second read-ing, albeit 'with great regret', in the words of its leader, Sir de Villiers Graaff. The party acted similarly over the Terrorism Act in 1967: while opposing certain provisions at the committee stage, it agreed to the princi-ple of the Bill. Elements in the party seemed incapable of standing up to Nationalist taunts that the party was 'soft' on communism and on security and that the quality of its patriotism was questionable.

42

So it was not altogether surprising that in 1972 it finally agreed to take part in the Schlebusch Commission of Inquiry into the activities of the University Christian Movement, the National Union of S.A. Students, the Christian Institute of Southern Africa and the Institute of Race Relations. When after what many of its critics described as a McCarthy-type witch-hunt, the Government banned eight NUSAS leaders for five years although no action had been recommended against the student body itself, and the United Party supported the Government's action, criticism of the party mounted and unhappiness in party ranks escalated. The result was the loss of six seats to the Progressive Party in the 1974 general election. But this was by no means the end of the United Party's troubles. The breakaway of the so-called Young Turks (four MPs) in 1975 and of the Basson group in 1977 (six MPs) was further proof that the party had still failed to find inner cohesion on the essential issue of colour. The dissolution of the party in 1977 was almost inevitable against the background of questing and indecision, indecision which spilled over into such issues as group areas and trade union rights for Africans.

It remains to be seen whether its lineal successor, the New Republic Party, under new leadership (Sir de Villiers Graaff stepped down from the post of Leader of the Opposition after twenty-one years) will be able to find the unity and direction of purpose – in a word, a colour policy – which evaded the party that Hertzog and Smuts had founded over forty years before.

The dispossessed

The Coloured and Indian peoples have this in common today: neither has direct or indirect representation in the central legislature, and both demand it; each has a primarily elected council looking after its own affairs; both groups have been promised their own parliament under the Nationalist Government's new constitutional proposals and both have rejected the idea. Finally, both communities, over the years, have been divided on whether they should seek their political salvation in co-operation with other dispossessed groups, whether they should seek an alliance with the whites, or whether they should go it alone within the system as they find it and in that way get what they can out of it.

When the Coloured people of the Cape were on the common electoral roll with whites (there were nearly 24 000 by 1929, and it was estimated that in ten of the 58 Cape constituencies they could exercise a decisive influence on the outcome of an election even though from 1930 onwards they did not have the vote on the same basis as whites – women being excluded, for one thing) the question of co-operation with Africans and/or Indians was not a live issue. Yet so strong were feelings on the Hertzog Bills in the mid-thirties that Dr Abdurahman, president of the African (that is, Coloured) People's Organisation, took the lead in convening a series of Non-European Conferences to fight the measures. Subsequently, in the All-Africa National Convention established for the same purpose, Coloured people worked harmoniously with Africans and Indians. To that extent white politics even in those days drove people of colour together to make common cause with each other.

During the days of the Coloured Advisory Council (set up in 1943 to advise and assist the Government in the field of Coloured affairs) the minds of community leaders were focused on how to achieve full citizenship rights for all Coloured people throughout the country. The extension of the Coloured franchise to the northern provinces was their objective. The National Party, on the other hand, wanted precisely the opposite; and since 1922 it had been agitating for the removal of all Coloured voters from the common roll. Significantly, Hertzog had strenuously opposed the removal of the Coloured people from the common roll when he led the United Party in the mid-thirties. He condemned Malanite proposals to do so as 'making insincerity, disloyalty, dishonesty and faithlessness the hallmark of the white man in his dealings with the non-White'.

Hence, while it was not really a surprise to the Coloured leadership to hear in 1951 that the Nationalists proposed to deprive them of their century-old right, the publication of the Separate Representation of Voters Bill in that year nevertheless came as a real shock. True, they had been warned in the Sauer report on apartheid that they should be given communal representation in Parliament and the Cape Provincial Council; but nevertheless they had hoped against hope that it would not come to pass.

Thus began five years of bitter struggle in which Coloured leaders and the white opposition inside and outside Parliament had a common objective. Together they fought against the monstrosity of the High Court of Parliament and opposed the packing of the Senate to give the Government the two-thirds majority it needed.

In 1955 the South African Coloured People's Organisation made a last despairing plea and reiterated the community's determination to fight not only for the right to remain on the common voters' roll, but also for the extension of the full franchise, without qualification, 'to all non-white South Africans'. And six Coloured leaders issued a statement showing how their people felt. Because of previous assaults on their rights, 'with con-

44

tinuous humiliation', the leaders said, there was 'a feeling of hopelessness and despair' in the Coloured community which could be wrongly interpreted as a lack of interest. The vast majority of Coloured people, they stressed, did not want to be removed from the common roll. There was some division among them, but this was not on the removal issue, rather on how to oppose it.

All was in vain and in February 1956 the Cape Coloured voters were finally removed from the common roll 'and South Africa took another stride away from the Western conception of shared government and government by consent'.[13] Humiliation had already been heaped on the Coloured people by the Population Registration Act of 1950 (in many ways the cornerstone of race separation), which classified every individual according to race, and which caused untold misery to countless individuals and families. The forced removals of hundreds of thousands of Coloured people under the Group Areas Act caused bitter resentment, as did job reservation, the reservation of amenities to whites, the exclusion of Coloureds from the open universities, differential salary scales for workers similarly qualified, deprivation of the municipal franchise and absurdities such as the one and only Coloured orchid-grower being told to form his own and separate orchid society. All this and more caused estrangement between Coloured and white and drove Coloureds further into the folds of the other dispossessed groups.

At the same time the Coloured community continued to be plagued by division. The first elections for the Coloured People's Representative Council took place in 1969, and two parties emerged. The Labour Party stood for direct parliamentary representation for all South Africans and accepted the Representative Council as an interim measure only and a stepping stone to full democratic rights. The Federal Party, on the other hand, came out in favour of parallel development and expressed a willingness to co-operate with the Government in promoting the advancement of the Coloured people. In the event the Labour Party won twenty-six of the thirty-seven contested seats. But because the Government was empowered to nominate twenty councillors, the Labour Party was relegated to the opposition benches. And when the Government included in its quota no fewer than thirteen of the defeated Federal candidates, the action, labelled 'an insult to democracy', contributed to mounting cynicism about the sincerity of the white man and the honesty of his intentions.

When, subsequently, the Labour Party boycotted the opening of the C.P.R.C. and refused to appropriate money for the implementation of the budget, the Government revoked the appointment of Mr Sonny Leon, the Labour leader, as chairman of the Executive Committee and replaced him by Mrs Alathea Jansen, a Government-nominated Independent member. Division again revealed itself when, after the urban violence of 1976–7, the leader of the Federal Party, Dr W. J. Bergins, turned down a plea by the Labour Party leadership for a multiracial convention to 'formulate a non-racial democratic constitution' for the country. He believed that through negotiation and dialogue with the Government, the Coloured people could best further their interests. Similarly, when the Prime Minister announced that he was to form an Inter-Cabinet Council as part of his process of consultation with Coloured and Indian people, the meeting was not attended by Labour Party representatives. In the event the Inter-Cabinet Council went out of existence in 1977 when the Government produced its three-parliament constitutional plan. On these proposals, too, the Labour Party has taken a stand of non-collaboration, while minority elements in the Coloured community favour participation.

Labour spokesmen took much the same line as in former disputes: the Coloured people will not be content with crumbs from the white man's table. They want full citizenship rights and direct representation in Parliament. Moreover, they stressed that they saw no sense in any constitutional arrangements which excluded over 70 per cent of the population, that is, the Africans. As the party had pointed out after the black urban rioting of 1976–7, when young Coloured people in the Western Cape and elsewhere had taken part in some of the demonstrations and marches, it was the Government's erosion of the democratic processes and its policy of separate institutions which were the cause and breeding-ground of dissension and unrest among people of colour.

Indian aspirations

There was a time in the 1940s when the politics of the Indian community was dominated by determined men of radical views, some of them on the far left. They came to the fore during the campaign against the so-called Pegging Act which froze Indian land transactions in parts of Natal and the Transvaal. It was the first of two measures (the other was the Asiatic Land Tenure and Indian Representation Act) which the Smuts Government enacted at the instigation of Natal (whose anti-Indian sentiments, particularly at that time, were notorious). These measures caused bitter resentment in South Africa and elsewhere, particularly in India. It was the Land Tenure Act that led directly to United Nations' demands for an inquiry into South Africa's race policies and which resulted in due course in the Indian Government's decision to break off diplomatic and trade relations with South Africa.

After the passing of the Pegging Act the Natal Indian Congress (founded as far back as 1894 by Mahatma Gandhi) and the Transvaal Indian Congress, always a more radical organisation than its counterparts elsewhere, persuaded the South African Indian Congress to change its attitude to the issue of political co-operation with other people of colour. For a while the emphasis in Indian politics was on the need for black unity to achieve political rights for the coloured races of South Africa. The introduction in 1946 of the Asiatic Land Tenure and Indian Representation Bill (which extended the Pegging Act provisions to the whole of Natal and the Transvaal and brought the acquisition of all land within its scope while introducing a measure of communal political rights) was the signal for the Indian community to resist to the utmost. The Natal Indian Congress, under the leadership of Dr G. M. Naicker, decided on a campaign of passive resistance, in the course of which nearly 2 000 were jailed. Significantly, India sent messages of encouragement to the local community, thereby introducing a new element into the discussion of South Africa's race problem: 'interference' by a foreign power. At the U.N., General Smuts, to his surprise and dismay, was called upon to justify his Government's illiberal stand.

In the course of the political struggle of the Indian people against segregation and its concomitants, however, there developed a polarisation of political attitudes between moderates and radicals. In 1945 the Anti-Segregation Council, which favoured a united front with Africans and Coloureds, took over the leadership of the Natal Indian Congress. In the Transvaal, too, the radicals under Dr Yusuf Dadoo were in control and the feeling for a united front with Africans was very strong. But in Natal there emerged a body of moderates, representing mainly the interests of merchants, who broke away from the main body and formed the Natal Indian Organisation, oriented towards and seeking an accommodation with whites while rejecting compulsory segregation and subordinate status.

Official National Party policy in 1948 was unequivocal: Indians were regarded as 'a strange and foreign element which is not assimilable . . . they must be treated as an immigrant community'. They were to be given no part in the law-making processes and would be settled in separate areas. This latter objective was to be realised through the Group Areas Act, a measure which further angered and embittered the Indian community at home and abroad and which encouraged South Africa's critics at the U.N.

to redouble their attacks on South Africa's official policy of separation and discrimination.

Indian resistance to discriminatory legislation reached its peak in Natal with the Defiance Campaign of 1952 in which segregation and restraints on travel between the provinces were specific targets. But the repressive powers of the State proved too strong and most of the Indian leadership was proscribed under the provisions of the far-reaching Public Safety and Criminal Law Amendment Acts. By the end of the year the campaign had been called off.

Although the South African Indian Congress helped to sponsor the 1955 Congress of the People at which the Freedom Charter was adopted, a good deal of the spark had gone out of the Indian will to resist by the end of the 1950s. No other community had suffered so much from being deprived of its active leadership; perhaps no other community had had, proportionately speaking, so many of its rank and file jailed. At its Council meeting in 1960, the South African Institute of Race Relations observed the 100th anniversary of the arrival of the Indians in South Africa, and found, *inter alia*, that 'while the Indian community enters upon its second century in South Africa with a sense of gloom and frustration it has not failed to detect the small ray of hope cast by the recent spontaneous actions of its white compatriots in open defence of Indian rights and freedom. If this is a symptom of awakening white conscience, the hope is not entirely lost that the Indian South Africans might yet attain their legitimate heritage to grow in peace to the full stature of their manhood like all their fellow-citizens . . . no more and no less.'[14]

Whatever awakening of white conscience there might have been, it had little effect on government policy. In 1961 the Verwoerd Government announced the establishment of a Department of Indian Affairs and a council to deal with the interests of Indians, very similar to the set-up for the Coloured people. The Indians would be given full control over their residential areas 'so that they can have their own local government on parallel lines'. What was significant about this decision was the admission, by the Government, that repatriation, on which Nationalists had set their hopes, had failed as a 'solution', and that there was no choice but to regard Indians as permanent inhabitants of South Africa. It was cold comfort, but it was *some* comfort, as was shown by the fact that the Indian National Congress offered to co-operate with the new department, albeit on a very limited basis. When a nominated twenty-one-member Indian Council was set up in 1964, some Indians regarded it as serving a limited purpose, others not. However, it did discuss local problems and irritations and constantly drew attention to the hardships caused by the Group Areas Act. As late as 1971 there were leaders of the community who believed that the position of Indians was the most precarious in South Africa: because of the stifling of Indian opinion, it was pointed out, there was no real expression of Indian political aspirations for the first time in eighty years.

However, Indian politics in Natal gradually came to life again. In 1972 the Natal Congress, recently revived, discussed a motion to change its name to People's Congress and to include members of all communities as a contribution to black solidarity for effective opposition to 'racist domination'. The motion was narrowly defeated but showed that some Indian thinking had advanced since the early 1960s because there was no opposition to co-operating with 'other oppressed peoples'.

On the question of whether the Indian community should take part in the Prime Minister's Inter-Cabinet Council (1976) there was again a difference of opinion. Some were in favour of boycotting it, others for giving it a trial. As far as the Government's new three-parliament constitutional plan was concerned, however, there was greater unanimity than previously. The Indian Council, partly nominated and partly elected, decided unanimously not to support the proposals. By doing so, South Africa's Indians, like the vast majority of their Coloured compatriots, showed once again that they would not be satisfied with second-best and that they would continue to strive for full citizenship rights.

The race against time

We have seen that the story of the last fifty years is primarily the story of how the Afrikaners have taken political control of South Africa and of what the Afrikaner Nationalists have done to secure their future. In the process they have created a state which has many of the attributes of a Western-style democracy but also many of the defects of a dictatorship.

So we find that just over four million whites have sole and absolute control over 87 per cent of the land surface of the country; that 18,5 million African people have to be content with sovereignty over the remaining 13 per cent although over 40 per cent of them live permanently in the 87 per cent of the 'white' or common area, where they are officially regarded as *gastarbeiter;* that the 2,5 million Coloured people and the 750 thousand Asians possess no homeland over which they can be sovereign and consequently fall under white control without a say in the decision-making processes at the highest level.

All opposition, whether it has come from whites or blacks, from inside the country or outside, has been interpreted as a threat to the continued existence first of the Afrikaner (ordained by God to a christianising role in the southern tip of Africa, they believe), and then of the white man. Hence the attempts to justify a battery of repressive laws and regulations; exclude the jurisdiction of the courts, thereby making a mockery of *Habeas corpus* and the rule of law; inhibit the freedom of the Press and, in one instance, close down a daily newspaper and detain its editor for five months; detain people without trial and gag individuals, including ministers of religion; withhold passports; outlaw (as it did at a stroke of the pen in October 1977) a whole range of organisations set up by Africans; apply political and other censorship through the Publications Control Board; demarcate separate racial group areas and move scores of thousands of people without their consent; regulate labour, withhold trade union rights from Africans and reserve categories of work for specific race groups; encourage the extension of migrant labour and justify the resultant break-up of family life as an unfortunate necessity; and every year jail hundreds of thousands of African men and women for technical offences such as contravention of the pass laws.

All this and more, like the suspension of normal democratic procedures, was done and justified as being essential for the continued existence of the white man and for the maintenance of law and order. Mr Vorster's Security Chief, General H. J. van den Bergh, said in 1978: 'For me the choice [in the 1960s] was between revolution, violence and a bloodbath and the so-called rule of law, about which there was all the noise. I looked at my children and those of others and said: "To the devil with the rule of law".' He added later: 'I am very thankful that I could always count on John Vorster's support.'[15]

The pure theory of separate development contains a streak of idealism, but it is not always possible to distinguish between realism, cynicism and idealism. The whole idea of separate freedoms which emerged when Dr Verwoerd developed the idea of independent homelands (a vision that was not in the minds of those who first outlined the apartheid blueprint) has attractions, provided it is practically attainable. But that is the crux. What kind of freedom, opponents of Nationalism ask, can nations enjoy when they have no prospect of ever becoming economically viable and when their political dependence on 'Big Brother', that is, South Africa, is total? QuaQua, for instance, has a de facto population of 190 000; of its de jure population, 98,2 per cent live beyond its borders; a gross domestic product of R2 million and a population density of 415 per square km compared with South Africa's 13. A quasi-official research organisation

50

has written that QuaQua is little more than 'a haven for the wives of migrant workers, unemployed men and children and the aged'.[16] This is admittedly the most extreme example; but the situation of some of the other ethnic states is not very much better. Under such circumstances independence is a farce.

Afrikaner Nationalism still has to disprove the contention that by placing all the emphasis on group freedom, on the right of separate nations to determine their own destinies, sight is being lost of the individual and of individual rights. The danger is that the end-result might be a negation of personal liberty, of the individual in fact.

And there is another danger in Nationalist policy which the leadership has refused to face. Taken to its logical conclusion, the policy of separate freedoms will produce a situation where, in today's South Africa, there will be seven or eight independent nations (assuming, of course, that those opposed to the independence concept can be talked or cajoled into it) and that in the 'white' part of South Africa there will be more 'foreigners' than citizens. All Africans will, according to present thinking, be foreigners; none will be South Africans in a country which belongs to them as much as to the whites. The fact that many of them may never have seen or visited their 'own country', that they may in fact be four or five generations removed from their 'homeland', and that they reject the tribal citizenship being forced on them in place of the South African citizenship of which they are being deprived, has not disturbed the ideologues. In the eyes of many of its critics, however, the Government's idea is not only amoral but so fanciful as to border on the grotesque. A nation whose mines and industries and factories and farms and shops and offices are all dependent, to a greater or lesser degree, on foreign labour will certainly be a constitutional rarity in the modern world. But then, *Ex semper Africa aliquid novi.*

The gravamen of the charge of Nationalism's rational critics is that in the field of human relations it has done far too little that is positive, far too much that is negative and destructive, and a deal that is downright dangerous. There are those who claim that apartheid or separate development has come to be the end of the road and has no answer to the political and economic problems of the day. They point in particular to the National Party's failure to find an acceptable formula for non-homeland Africans to participate in the government of 'white' South Africa and to the rejection, by the Coloured and Asian peoples, of the three-parliament constitutional plan – itself, they argue, an admission of failure of a thirty-year-old separatist policy, at least as far as effective consultation is concerned.

Above all, such critics point to the sometimes frightening hatred and bitterness which Nationalism's race ideology and practices have produced, particularly among the more sophisticated and the young black people – a hatred which manifested itself starkly in the violence of 1976–7 and which, it is believed, is often a response to what many blacks look upon as the white institutionalised violence of the apartheid regime. This polarisation, which has spawned black consciousness and power, has made many younger people of colour reject the open shared society of white liberals and opt (perhaps largely for tactical reasons, who knows?) for a go-it-alone approach. Just as Afrikaner Nationalists have rejected the concept of shared power, so many young black people are setting their sights on an eventual take-over of power on their terms alone. South Africa, in fact, may be said to be nearing the situation foreshadowed by one of Alan Paton's characters in *Cry, the Beloved Country*: 'The danger is when they have come to loving us we shall have come to hating them'.

There are still black leaders who believe in an open shared society such as liberal thinking down the years has envisaged. The present Coloured and Indian leadership favour it, as do a number of African homeland leaders whose ideal, in the words of Chief Buthelezi, is to find 'a non-racial basis for political participation in a just South African society'. Again the danger is that by the time a majority of the white electorate has come to see shared power in a non-racial society as the answer to South Africa's problems, the black people will have rejected this idea and be determined to try to take over complete power and total control.

In a very real sense, therefore, South Africa has embarked on a race against time: a race between those who choose consultation and co-operation and those who choose separation with its inbuilt high-risk factor of violent confrontation and conflict. The answer lies largely with those who wield power, the Afrikaner Nationalists. They, too, seek change, but insist that it must be change within the framework of the separate devlopment philosophy. Recent events in South West Africa/Namibia and even in the Republic suggest that it would be wrong to underestimate Nationalist capacity for pragmatic change and adaptation even within the Party's ideological framework. There has, for instance, been a good deal of change in the last ten years, much of it admittedly cosmetic, but some of it very real change, particularly in the economic sector, where, for instance, the living standards of the urban Africans have risen significantly. And some progress has been made in the attempt to do away with discrimination based on colour. Interracial games were anathema even five years ago; mixed entertainment and worship were similarly frowned upon and prohibited. Parks and libraries and a few beaches in the big cities have been opened to people of colour and some bus services have become integrated. Black traffic police operate freely in some cities. Job reservation, although still on the statute book, applies minimally, and in some sections of the pro-government press the demand for swifter and more fundamental change in all spheres is insistent. The rise and increasing independence of Nationalist newspapers is itself a hopeful sign that there will be more *ontplooiing* of Nationalist policy, however much it is resisted inside the party and in the Herstigte Nasionale Party, a party which has failed signally to establish a base in Parliament, but whose fundamental philosophy is shared by a considerable proportion of grass-roots Nationalists of the traditionalist school.

What South Africans of all races were asking themselves as the 1970s drew to a close was whether the change that was coming would be basic enough to satisfy those needs which so badly needed satisfying if racial accord was to be achieved in South Africa and whether it would come soon enough. Time alone would tell whether there was an acceptable and satisfying alternative to the kind of open multiracial society many of the founders of the South African Institute of Race Relations envisaged fifty years ago, and for which many liberal-minded people of all races are working today. Were South Africans going to be compelled to choose between go-it-alone white Nationalists and go-it-alone black Nationalists? Or would they be given an opportunity to choose between conflict and consensus?

1. Edgar Brookes *et al.*, *Coming of Age* (Maskew Miller).
2. *Oxford History of South Africa*, ed. Monica Wilson and Leonard Thompson (Oxford University Press).
3. *Ibid.*
4. Alan Paton, *Hofmeyr* (Oxford University Press, 1971).
5. W. K. Hancock, *Smuts: The Fields of Force* (Cambridge University Press).
6. *Survey of Race Relations* (S.A. Institute of Race Relations), 1958.
7. *Die Burger*, 13 July 1978, interview with General H. J. van den Bergh, ex-head of State Security.
8. *Ibid.*
9. *Survey of Race Relations* (S.A. Institute of Race Relations), 1970.
10. T. R. H. Davenport, *South Africa: A Modern History* (Macmillan, 1977).
11. Dirk en Johanna de Villiers, *Paul Sauer* (Tafelberg).
12. *Ibid.*

13. *Oxford History of South Africa, op. cit.*
14. *Survey of Race Relations* (S.A. Institute of Race Relations), 1960.
15. *Die Burger*, 12 July 1978, interview with General H. J. van den Bergh.
16. *QuaQua, Economic Review* by Buro vir Ekonomiese Navorsing i.s. Bantoe-ontwikkeling (Benbo) 1977.

3 Black Politics in Transition
PATRICK LAURENCE

Introduction

The history of African nationalism and its resistance to South Africa's race policies has been thoroughly charted up to the Rivonia trial of 1963–4, which marked the virtual end of the underground campaign following the Sharpeville shootings and the banning of the African National Congress (A.N.C.) and the Pan-Africanist Congress (P.A.C.) in 1960. Black politics since then has been explored less fully. After the imprisonment or flight of many of the leaders of the 1950s and early 1960s there was a three- to four-year period of quiescence. Then came a resurgence of African political activity.

In his book on African nationalism in South Africa, Walshe looks briefly at the Black People's Convention (B.P.C.) and remarks that 'one gets a sense of *déjà vu*, of having seen it all before'.[1] That was in 1973, shortly after the founding of the B.P.C. and four years before it was banned. Walshe was right. There were threads reaching back thirty years to the founding of the A.N.C. Youth League. Comparing the B.P.C. and the Youth League, one is struck by the same impatience with white liberals, the same disregard for the caution of more conservative Africans and the same search for a formula to galvanise the masses into action against race discrimination.

But of course there were crucial differences. The B.P.C. emerged after the critical years of the early 1960s, which saw the prohibition of the A.N.C. and P.A.C. and the crushing of their underground offshoots, Umkhonto we Sizwe and Poqo. The B.P.C. did not have the option of re-vitalising existing organisations. It had to start afresh without borrowing too heavily or too obviously from older and outlawed movements. That may account in part for B.P.C.'s initial emphasis on 'psychological libera-tion' through promotion of black self-sufficiency and black self-help. As the B.P.C. *ad hoc* committee declared of black people: 'Their future destiny and ultimate happiness [are] in their hands.' The belief that blacks had to organise their own lives and shape their own political destiny had its corollary in the injunction: 'No co-operation with government institutions.'[2] The assumption was that institutions created *for* the black man were ultimately designed to ensnare rather than free him.

At about the same time a different set of black men were striving to fill the vacuum which had overtaken black politics since Sharpeville and the subsequent state of emergency. These were men who accepted the government-created framework of separate institutions for Africans, of which the ethnically based homeland legislative assemblies were prime examples. By 1973 the African homeland leaders had made their mark. They were outspokenly critical of official race policies. They were taken seriously by the media rather than dismissed contemptuously as stooges. Looking back, one might have noted similarities between these men and African leaders before them who had served in government institutions: the outspokenness of the homeland leaders had its parallel in the forthright speeches made by some members of the old Native Representatives' Council (N.R.C.) of 1936–46.

But there were differences, too. The new homeland policy earmarked the homelands for independence as mini-ethnic-states. Its *sine qua non* was the 'fragmentation' of South Africa and the division of the African majority into ethnic units. This added a dimension that was lacking in the decade of the N.R.C.'s existence. It accounted for much of the bitterness which radical blacks felt toward the homeland leaders, a bitterness which appears to have exceeded even that of the old Non-European Unity Movement toward 'collaborators' serving in government-approved institutions.

Within a year of B.P.C.'s inaugural conference at Hammanskraal, near Pretoria, in December 1972, homeland leaders met at Umtata, capital of Transkei. The primary purpose of the 'Umtata Summit' was for the homeland leaders to seek a formula for collective action in their dealings with Pretoria and thereby counter the danger of becoming victims of a divide-and-rule strategy. Among the resolutions taken at Umtata was one in favour of federation, which was at the least an implicit commitment against fragmentation of South Africa into minuscule black states. An associated but unpublished agreement was not to conclude separate deals with Pretoria until their collective demand for more land than the roughly 14 per cent allocated under the 1936 Land Act was granted.[3] Another formal demand was for the repeal of the pass laws. In championing African demands for more land and abolition of the pass laws, the homeland leaders had taken up two popular issues. Their stand held out the hope of some *modus vivendi* with the new black consciousness movement as personified by B.P.C. and its fraternal organisations. But it was not to be.

Enmity between the homeland leaders and the black consciousness movement was to grow. Fuelled by the later decision of Paramount Chief Kaiser Matanzima of Transkei, Chief Lucas Mangope of Bophuthatswana and Chief Patrick Mphephu of Venda to opt for Pretoria's offer of independence, it was to become one of the features of black politics in the 1970s. There had been similar quarrels in the past over participation in government institutions, but they lacked the acrimony of the 1970s. Overlapping areas of agreement made not an iota's difference to the central dispute. Until the outburst of unrest triggered by a student march in Soweto on 16 June 1976, it was to be the predominant debate in black politics.

Black consciousness

Early in 1970 Anthony Sampson, British author and former editor of *Drum*, remarked on the withdrawal of many blacks from white-controlled institutions into a world of their own.[4] Sampson, an astute observer of events, had put his finger on an important development in the black community at that time. It was the beginnings of black resurgence after the crushing of the older nationalist movements and the subsequent lull: the withdrawal was the prelude to renewed self-assertion. The process started with the withdrawal of black students from the multiracial National Union of South African Students (NUSAS) and the founding of their own student union. The new student union was the harbinger of a series of interrelated black organisations united by common allegiance to the philosophy of black consciousness.

As Professor Kotzé notes,[5] black consciousness finds its closest ideological relative in the Africanist tradition of Anton Lembede, pre-eminent theoretician of the A.N.C. Youth League, and Robert Sobukwe, founding president of the P.A.C. Steve Biko, founder of black consciousness, explicitly linked the two in an essay presented at a seminar in January 1971. Referring to Africanist criticism of the A.N.C. leadership for adopting the Kliptown Charter of 1955 in conjunction with non-black organisations, he wrote: '. . . these were the first real signs that blacks in South Africa were beginning to realise the need to go it alone and to evolve a philosophy based on and directed by blacks'. Then, significantly, he added: 'In other words, black consciousness was slowly manifesting itself.'[6]

Black consciousness shares many traits with Africanism, although, of course, it articulates them with different emphases and in a different context. At the core of both philosophies is the belief that blacks must determine their own destiny. It is expressed succinctly in the black consciousness slogan: 'Black man, You are on your own'. The stress on black self-reliance has two corollaries: (1) insistence that ultimately all whites, even those who profess radicalism, are beneficiaries of the white-controlled status quo and therefore defenders of it; (2) consequently their only role in predominantly black movements is to de-radicalise them by pacifying the black masses and restraining the black leaders. Both philosophies attach importance to the elimination of black dependency and feelings of inferiority. They therefore have psychological as well as political dimensions. Both implicitly accept a Hegelian dialectic, in the sense that they presume the way forward lies in the polarisation of society into mutually hostile camps and believe the desired non-racial society will emerge as a synthesis between the opposing forces. Both are labelled as racist by their opponents and are taxed with the question of how a non-racial society can be the product of racial polarisation.

But if black consciousness and Africanism share a common conviction that whites must be excluded from black political movements, black consciousness is less exclusivist in a broad sense than Africanism. Its definitition of blacks is broad and includes all South Africans who are not white: Africans, Indians and Coloureds. Africanism, as manifested in the short life of the P.A.C., excludes Indians. Although the P.A.C. defined as an African any person who owes his loyalty to Africa and who accepts the democratic right of the African majority to rule, closer scrutiny of the concept shows that it related to the future non-racial society and *not* to the struggle toward that society.[7] Study of Sobukwe's speech at the inaugural conference of the P.A.C. is instructive. It contrasts 'indigenous African people' with 'foreign European and Indian minorities'. It insists on the right of Africans to organise under the banner of African nationalism and to decide on the methods of struggle for themselves without the interference of minorities 'who arrogantly appropriate to themselves the right to think and plan for the African'.[8]

It is interesting to note that one of the charges levelled against the Natal Indian Congress by the black consciousness movement was that by restricting its membership to Indians it was 'guilty of exclusivism'.[9] It is idle but fascinating to contemplate what attitude black consciousness might have adopted toward the P.A.C. for its exclusion of Indians. It would be unlikely to have been impressed with the view that the Indians were under the domination of the 'merchant class'[10] and therefore unready to identify with the oppressed Africans. Black consciousness considered that the white establishment 'stratifies the black world' by giving preferential treatment to certain blacks. Its response was to counter that by uniting all blacks, Africans, Indians and Coloureds, under the banner of black solidarity.

Another difference between black consciousness and Africanism lies in the formal structures to which the two philosophies gave birth. Where black consciousness inspired the formation of several different organisations (no less than seventeen black consciousness organisations were banned in the October 1977 crackdown by the South African Government), Africanism led to the emergence of the P.A.C. Black consciousness was both more inclusive ideologically and more diffused organisationally. In retrospect black consciousness seems to have adopted a strategy of forming different organisations to concentrate on different segments of the black community.

The South African Students' Organisation (SASO) was the first of the black consciousness organisations to emerge. Its ideological roots reach back into the Africanist tradition, but its immediate antecedents lie in the University Christian Movement (U.C.M.). As a relatively radical movement, U.C.M. attracted black students to its conferences.[11] Within U.C.M. a black caucus emerged as the nucleus of a blacks-only student movement. With University of Natal medical students playing a leading role, the black caucus initiated the conference at Mariannhill in December 1968 at which SASO was formed. The inaugural conference was held at the University of the North, near Pietersburg, in July 1969, amid accusations that the decision to launch an exclusively black student movement was fundamentally apartheid-inspired. SASO's refusal to acknowledge either ethnic differences between Africans or race differences between blacks was an implicit repudiation of the accusation.

At its 1970 conference SASO formally severed ties with NUSAS, declaring that the emancipation of blacks depended on themselves and denying that NUSAS was capable of representing black aspirations.[12] SASO, however, held out the hope of an eventual re-merging of black and white after blacks had consolidated their strength and were able to negotiate on equal terms with whites.[13] But it was patently clear that the theoretical unification lay in the remote future and that for the moment the two streams would have to go their own way.

Within two years of its formation SASO had established branches at all black university campuses and had made its mark on the student scene.

Student unrest at most black universities in mid-1972 helped to spread knowledge of SASO. The unrest started at the University of the North after a student, Onkgopotse Abraham Tiro, made an 'impudent' speech at a graduation ceremony. Tiro was expelled and attempts by the students to secure his re-instatement merely resulted in their mass expulsion. Solidarity demonstrations, in which SASO played a key role, then took place at the remaining black universities: the Universities of the Western Cape, Durban-Westville, Fort Hare and Zululand. At this time SASO issued a statement, the Alice Declaration, calling for a national boycott of 'racist' universities.[14]

SASO did not succeed in forcing closure of the 'apartheid universities'. But the campus unrest of 1972 was important for at least three reasons. First, there were subsequent moves to meet SASO demands (though this was never admitted) through the appointment of black rectors at the University of the Western Cape and, later, at the Universities of the North and Zululand. Secondly, the solidarity shown by students across the barriers of ethnicity and race proved that the message of black consciousness was getting through. Finally, the way in which unrest spread from one campus to another was a warning that the black community was not nearly as segmented as whites were wont to believe. The full accumulative significance of the university unrest of 1972 was manifest only after black high-school students launched their own campaign for educational reform in 1976.

The 1972 SASO annual conference was particularly important because it highlighted the degree of hostility within the black consciousness movement to black leaders operating from officially approved separate development platforms. It was demonstrated by the deposition of the then SASO president, Temba Sono, and his expulsion from the conference, because he advocated some form of accommodation with selected leaders operating from within the separate development system.

Appealing to the conference not to stagnate in 'servitude of ideology' Sono said: 'We agree among ourselves, but we have to seek out those who differ from us and try to sway them to our way of thinking.' SASO had to learn to talk even to its enemies. Apparently anticipating objections that it would result in contradictions between theory and practice, he added: 'We have to accommodate even contradictions in our struggle.'[15] To those who might object to the compromise implied in talking to people operating from within the hated system, he pointed out that black students had already made their own compromises by carrying reference books and attending segregated 'tribal' universities.[16]

60

The reaction was quick and decisive. Sono's speech was dubbed 'very dangerous' by the founder president of SASO, Steve Biko. Sono was slated for not consulting his executive about the speech, which was purportedly calculated to embarrass SASO and confuse rank and file blacks.[17] He was deposed and summarily expelled. In retrospect it is significant that Chief Gatsha Buthelezi, then Chief Executive Councillor of KwaZulu, figured prominently in the controversy. He was one of the men Sono had in mind when he pleaded some sort of agreement with selected leaders within the 'system'. Rejecting that specifically, Biko described Chief Buthelezi as the 'one man who had led the entire world to believe in the bantustan philosophy'.[18] Before his departure for the United States, Sono reiterated his point by describing Chief Buthelezi as a 'force you cannot ignore'.[19]

From 1973 to its banning in October 1977 SASO went through one crisis after another as it battled to survive in the face of counter-action by the Government. The opening shots in the counter-action came in March 1973 with the banning of eight black consciousness leaders. Among them were four executive office holders of SASO, Jerry Modisane, the president, Strinivasa Moodley, editor of the SASO newsletter, Barney Pityana, the secretary general, and Harry Nengwekhulu, the permanent organiser. It was indicative of the spread of black consciousness that members of newer organisations were also restricted in March of that year.

The March crackdown was but the prelude to further action against SASO. After the election of new office-bearers at the annual conference in July 1973, it became evident that the Government's strategy was to systematically deprive SASO of its leaders. Within days of his election as SASO president, Henry Isaacs was served with a five-year banning order. It both restricted his movements and prevented him from holding public office. The theology student who took over as acting president, Hamilton Qambela, suffered a similar fate. Several SASO office-holders who filled key positions were banned at about the same time. Though hard hit, SASO recouped and held a special conference in January 1974. Muntu Myeza, later sentenced to six years' imprisonment, was elected president. At the annual conference in July 1974 Myeza stepped down from the presidency to take up a full-time position on SASO's executive as secretary general. A University of the North student, Pandelani Nefolovhodwe, was elected president.

By mid-1974 SASO began to take up a defiant and even provocative stance toward the authorities, in spite of the battering it had taken the previous year. Several factors contributed to the more aggressive mood. The bannings were clearly resented and helped to produce a reckless, almost desperado anger. That was reinforced by the murder of Tiro in February of 1974. One of the moving spirits behind the idea of extending black solidarity beyond South Africa's borders to campuses in Botswana, Lesotho and Swaziland, he had fled from South Africa to Botswana in 1973. In February of the following year he received a parcel bomb which blew him to pieces. Only a few weeks before he had said in a letter to SASO: 'No struggle can come to an end without casualties.'[20] Of possibly greater import to the black consciousness movement, however, was the collapse of the Portuguese in Africa and the triumph in Mozambique and Angola of anti-colonialist guerrillas. To many blacks in South Africa, Frelimo became the symbol of the irresistible force of black nationalism.

These events were to lead to a serious trial of strength between the black consciousness movement and the authorities in September of 1974. By that time SASO was merely one of several movements subscribing to black consciousness. Instead of being the leading actor, SASO was one of a series of actors whose roles were largely interchangeable since they talked the same language and shared common goals. But SASO's role in the emergence of black consciousness as a viable force was crucial. SASO took black consciousness into the university campuses. From that psycho-political 'beachhead' black consciousness spread upwards and downwards chronologically: upwards into the adult community and downwards into the high schools and even primary schools. The organisational vehicles through which black consciousness was spread ran to a total of a score or more. Pre-eminent among them were B.P.C. and Black Community Programmes as the 'conscientisers' of the adult community, the South African Students' Movement (SASM) and provincially based youth movements under the aegis of the National Youth Organisation as the politicisers of the youth.[21]

Having recovered to some extent from the bannings of 1973–4, the black consciousness movement sought to celebrate the triumph of Frelimo in Mozambique. The B.P.C.-SASO axis was the driving force behind rallies to commemorate the handing over of power to a transitional Frelimo government. It planned rallies in four main centres, including Durban.[22] A similar rally was later planned at the University of the North under the authority of the Students' Representative Council, but SASO was later found to have been involved as well.

On the evening before the rallies the Minister of Justice, Mr J. T. Kruger, announced that all rallies organised by SASO and B.P.C. were prohibited under the Riotous Assemblies Act until 20 October of that year. In spite of the proclamation, however, rallies took place at Curries Fountain in Durban and at the University of the North. At both there were clashes between blacks and baton-wielding police backed by dogs. These events led to the arrest of scores of blacks and, later, to the trial under the Terrorism Act initially of thirteen and finally of nine leading members of the black consciousness movement.

The trial of the nine was critical for the future of black consciousness. It deprived the SASO-B.P.C. alliance of much of its already depleted leadership. But it did more than that. It put black consciousness itself on trial, in the sense that many of the original charges under the Terrorism Act related to SASO and B.P.C. speeches and manifestos which articulated much of the underlying philosophy of black consciousness. Although the accused were charged with fostering racial hostility through the propagation of anti-white views, the central charge was that they had conspired to 'transform the state' by violent and unconstitutional means.[23]

Judgment was given on 15 December 1976, more than twenty-two months after their first appearance in court and twenty-six months after they were first detained. The nine were found guilty, with six of the accused sentenced to six years' imprisonment and three to five years. They were, however, acquitted of the main charge of being party to a revolutionary conspiracy. Their sentences were for conspiring to commit acts capable of endangering the maintenance of law and order and for the organisation of the pro-Frelimo rallies of September 1974. Black consciousness *per se* was not declared illegal. Neither were the movements committed to it, provided, of course, that they did not emulate the activities of the nine accused.

However, by the time of the judgment the focus of political attention had swung away from the universities and the young men and women at the head of SASO and B.P.C. The high-school students in Soweto had upstaged them. From the fatal clash in Soweto on 16 June 1976 between protesting high-school students and police, black school students dominated the political arena. Only the death in detention of Steve Biko in September 1977 and the crackdown on black consciousness organisations in October of that year shifted attention away from them.

The exact role of black consciousness in the unrest or, as some would prefer to label it, 'resistance' of 1976, is a matter best left to detailed scholarship. But, without anticipating the findings of the Cillié Commission of Inquiry into the causes of the unrest and mindful of charges of sedition brought against student leaders in connection with the unrest, one broad conclusion seems legitimate: black consciousness helped to create the climate of black self assertiveness which saw black youngsters take to the streets to protest against compulsory instruction in Afrikaans.

Several people have attempted to coin labels for the new generation of high-school students who defied the authorities in Soweto and elsewhere for months on end. Bishop Desmond Tutu, general secretary of the South African Council of Churches, refers to them as youngsters with 'iron in their souls'. Professor David Welsh, of the University of Cape Town, describes them as youth who are not afraid of death. The combination of circumstances which produced that state of mind is obviously complex and deeply-rooted in the South African situation. But one of the vital components was black consciousness and its exhortation to blacks to 'Go-it-alone'.

Within the secondary schools of Soweto, SASM was a key vehicle for transmitting the message. Founded in 1972 by Soweto high-school students, SASM had as its main aim co-ordination of high-school activities, dissemination of programmes 'concerning injustices in society'[24] and propagation of black consciousness. It was affiliated to the Transvaal Youth Organisation, which fell under the National Youth Organisation. The Transvaal Youth Organisation stood for 'liberation of the black community from psychological and physical oppression'.[25]

It is not coincidental that the first two presidents of the Soweto Students' Representative Council, Tsietsi Mashinini and Khotso Seathlolo, were leading members of SASM in Soweto. Nor is it surprising that they played a leading role in organising protest against compulsory instruction through the medium of Afrikaans. These statements should not be interpreted as an endorsement of the view that the unrest was the work of a clique of conspirators. But they do seek to highlight the underlying importance of black consciousness without minimising the insensitivity and myopia of the authorities in refusing to acknowledge that its education policies had aroused deep resentments in Soweto, as evidenced by the series of strikes and attacks on police which preceded 16 June.

The hallmarks of black consciousness are apparent in the S.R.C.'s campaign against Bantu Education. SASM has been described as the youth wing of SASO.[26] Its agitation against Bantu Education paralleled that of SASO against the 'tribal' universities. Another black consciousness aim which the S.R.C. propagated was the rejection of government-created institutions. It was most clearly manifested in its campaign against the Soweto Urban Bantu Council (U.B.C.).

The anti-U.B.C. campaign opened in April 1977 as a fresh S.R.C. initiative when it looked as though its planned boycott of schools was beginning to peter out. By June of that year, twenty-three U.B.C. members, including the chairman, David Thebehali, had resigned. Not even the reprieve won by the U.B.C. against proposed higher house rents could save it.

Another measure of the antipathy toward government institutions was the way in which the wave of arson spilled over from Soweto into the homelands. In general arson in the homelands, like the burnings in Soweto, was not aimless. It focused on targets associated with Pretoria's policy of creating special institutions for the African peoples. The burning down of the Bophuthatswana Legislative Assembly early in August 1976 was unequivocal evidence of political direction behind the arson. These observations do not prejudge the question of whether the S.R.C. deliberately planned and/or encouraged attacks on government institutions. But it is contended that by attacking these institutions verbally the S.R.C., and indeed the black consciousness movement as a whole, helped to categorise them as the instruments of 'oppressors and collaborators' and thereby heightened the likelihood of their being attacked in outbursts of violence.

In a psycho-political sense black consciousness is subversive of apartheid and its ideological derivatives in the homelands. To a considerable degree Pretoria's policies depend on co-operation from 'moderate' blacks. By dubbing the 'moderates' as 'collaborators', black consciousness strikes at one of the pillars of the present order. In that context the drastic blow struck against black consciousness on 19 October 1977 was hardly surprising. On that day, a little over a month after the death of Steve Biko in detention, seventeen black consciousness organisations were banned. That the bannings came before the inquest into Biko's death is not surprising either. It required no great perspicacity to note that his death had brought about a re-dedication to the cause by black consciousness cadres. Similarly it needed little foresight to anticipate that the inquest, with its brutal details, would incite black anger.

Black consciousness *per se* was not banned in terms of the restrictive measures taken by the Government in October. Anyone propagating it, however, ran the risk of being charged with furthering the aims of an unlawful organisation. But for many blacks that was a risk rather than a deterrent. As Kotzé observes of black consciousness: 'It is not something which can be countered merely by suppressing specified organisations. It is a movement with psychological and spiritual dimensions . . . which transcend organisational forms.'[27] Black consciousness was no more eliminated by the October crackdown than Africanism was by the banning of the P.A.C. in 1960. Like Africanism, black consciousness is an idea that lies at the heart of the tradition of black resistance to white hegemony. It will survive as long as white rule survives. Already there are signs of a resurgence of black consciousness after the October bannings. New organisations have been formed which have their roots in black consciousness. The Soweto Students' League, the Azanian People's Organisation and the Writers' Association of South Africa come to mind.

Black consciousness had added another chapter to the history of black resistance in South Africa. The full balance sheet must await historians of the future. But some kind of interim assessment can be made. It helped fill the vacuum created by the outlawing of the A.N.C. and P.A.C. by providing an independent outlet for the political energies of blacks who viewed the government-created institutions with suspicion. These organisations, which were independent of government approval and immune to white liberal advice, helped create the psychological pre-conditions for the protests which swept through South Africa in 1976–7. If Africanism had its Sharpeville, black consciousness had its Soweto. Both added to the martyrs and heroes who had inspired protest in the past.

Black consciousness found itself fighting on two fronts. Its outlook made reaction from the authorities inevitable. But it opened a second front by attacking homeland leaders. While it had to ward off attacks from two directions, Chief Buthelezi and his Inkatha movement, shielded to a high degree from official repression by their position 'within the system', were steadily building up strength. After the October bannings Chief Buthelezi and Inkatha were seen by many as the main obstacle to Pretoria's policy of denationalising Africans by making them citizens of independent homelands instead of South Africa. But that did not make Chief Buthelezi any more acceptable to black consciousness radicals.

The antipathy of black consciousness militants towards Chief Buthelezi came to a head at the funeral of Robert Sobukwe in Graaff-Reinet in March 1978. Taught to regard Chief Buthelezi as a 'collaborator' because he served as KwaZulu Chief Minister and operated from a legislative assembly set up under the Bantu Homelands Constitution Act, the young militants turned on him at Graaff-Reinet. Having worked themselves into a frenzy, they abused him verbally, threatened him physically and demanded that he leave the sports ground where the service was held. At the request of Bishop Tutu, Chief Buthelezi left. Stones were thrown as he walked a gauntlet of jeering youths and his bodyguard fired two shots into the ground. Chief Buthelezi escaped with his life. But in the acrimonious exchanges which followed, the little that was left of black unity was destroyed.

Homeland leaders

In June 1970 Chief Gatsha Buthelezi was elected Chief Executive Councillor of KwaZulu. His election and the establishment of a Zulu Territorial Authority were significant for several reasons. Chief Buthelezi, a former member of the A.N.C. Youth League, was the logical successor as the dominant political figure in Zululand after the death of Chief Albert Luthuli, president of the A.N.C., in 1967. His acceptance of a position within the legislative framework of the Bantu Authorities Act gave a new kind of legitimacy to the idea of working within the system. As Alan Paton, author and former president of the Liberal Party, remarked at the time: 'Chief Gatsha will be no stooge. . . . If the government acts honourably, it will not regard him as its servant but as a servant of the Zulu people.'[28]

In a remarkably short time the English-language press underwent a complete change in attitude toward homeland leaders. Until Chief Buthelezi's election, it tended to regard homeland leaders and homeland politics as irrelevant, a subject for disdain rather than analysis. Chief Buthelezi changed that. He popularised the idea of using an 'apartheid platform' to attack Pretoria's race policies. His lead was soon followed by his fellow homeland leaders, who began to take up the cudgels against the distribution of land between white and black, the pass laws, the industrial colour bar, the bannings and detentions, the inequalities in education and income and so on.

The press was not alone in its changed view of the homeland leaders. The South African Institute of Race Relations reflected the new perspective when it made the future of the homelands the theme of its annual congress in 1974. Significantly, Chief Buthelezi was singled out for the special honour of delivering the Alfred and Winifred Hoernlé Memorial Lecture. Diplomats took the homeland leaders seriously as genuine opponents of both grand and petty apartheid, of independent bantustans and separate amenities.

But the black consciousness movement retained its sceptical attitude. It did not believe that it was possible to fight apartheid from within. The separate development platforms had been designed to thwart black aspirations by encouraging ethnicity as a political antidote to black unity. To expect positive results from 'the system' was illogical, black consciousness averred. There could be no solution to the problem from the people who caused the problem in the first place, black consciousness militants insisted. Black consciousness scepticism was personified by the columnist in the SASO newsletter, who said of the concept of challenging Pretoria from one of its own platforms: 'If you want to fight your enemy, you don't accept the unloaded of his two guns and then challenge him to a duel.'[29]

The high water mark for the homeland leaders came with the Umtata Summit of November 1973. The summit, brainchild of Chief Mangope, came after a ringing series of statements by Chief Buthelezi and the Matanzima brothers of Transkei, Chiefs Kaiser and George, in favour of a federation of black states.

Until then the Matanzima brothers had been looked on askance by most South Africans who were not members of the ruling National Party. The declaration in favour of solidarity helped change that. The *Weekend World* praised Chief Kaiser Matanzima for moving 'into line with the real thinking of the black man'.[30] The summit was predicated upon the assumption that it would consolidate the avowals of unity.

In a formal statement issued after the summit the six leaders who attended committed themselves in principle to propagation of the idea of federation. More important was the informal agreement to act in concert in pursuit of their objective of more land for Africans. Fulfilment of their aim was indispensable to the aim of creating a viable federation of homelands. A corollary to their informal agreement was the undertaking not to conclude separate deals with Pretoria until the 1936 Land Act had been revised.[31]

But within five months Chief Matanzima was to break the agreement and formally announce his decision to negotiate independence unilaterally. Later, when he was questioned on his about-face, he replied cynically: 'We never had solidarity with the rest of the black Africans. We had our own United Territories General Council. We started a self-governing state in 1963 long before the others thought of doing it. We've never aligned ourselves with them as far as our progressive political situation is concerned.'[32]

At another summit meeting of homeland leaders in November 1974 an attempt was made to paper over the cracks in their 'solidarity' which had appeared since Chief Matanzima's decision. Chief Buthelezi had expressed regret that his 'Transkei brothers' should have broken the unity forged at Umtata. Collins Ramusi, then Minister of Interior in the Lebowa government, had accused Chief Matanzima of 'treachery' at about the same time. The statement issued after the 1974 summit reaffirmed black solidarity and unity and declared that none of the men present questioned the right of Transkei to opt for independence.[33] But it was whistling in the dark. Their united front was broken. Within a year it was to disintegrate when Chief Mangope announced that he, too, intended opening unilateral negotiations for independence. His surprise decision drew a rebuke from Chief Buthelezi, who said: 'It is a matter of courtesy that we consult with each other.'[34]

By opting for Pretoria-style independence, Chief Matanzima and Chief

Mangope, and later Chief Patrick Mphephu of Venda, virtually destroyed the credibility of those who asserted they were opposing separate development, alias apartheid, from within. Whatever the vehemence of the three chiefs in their protests about racism, however loud their proclamations of unity, they were party to the partition of South Africa and the creation of mini-ethnic-states. Since that was the *raison d'être* of grand apartheid, they could convince few people that they were authentic opponents of Pretoria's race policies. The scepticism which they drew rubbed off on the homeland leaders who still declared their opposition to independence. Many blacks shared Prime Minister Vorster's conviction that it was merely a matter of time before all the homeland leaders exercised their option to independence.

At their respective independence ceremonies at Umtata in October 1976 and Mmabatho in December 1977 both Chief Matanzima and Chief Mangope tried to dissociate their infant states from Pretoria's race policies. Chief Matanzima said: 'It has been alleged in certain quarters that our independence is an essential element of South Africa's policy of apartheid. . . . I must reject it with the contempt it deserves.' Chief Mangope expressed the hope that Bophuthatswana's independence would 'go down in history as marking the beginning of the end of racial discrimination in South Africa'. But they were speaking into a void. The people who needed persuading on these points were boycotting the birth of the new states.

The fragmentation of South Africa into mini-states apart, there was another aspect of Pretoria-style independence which helped bring the three chiefs into disrepute and which added to the suspicion surrounding all homeland leaders. It was the price that they paid for their independence: loss of South African citizenship for all Africans with ethnic ties with Transkei and Bophuthatswana, irrespective of whether they were permanently in white-designated South Africa or not. Initial protestations by Chiefs Matanzima and Mangope that they would not be party to compulsorily depriving Africans in South Africa of South African citizenship only served to harden feelings against them.

Chief Matanzima repeatedly insisted that people of Transkei descent living permanently within South Africa were Pretoria's 'indaba'.[35] Chief Mangope was even more emphatic. In a letter to the South African Cabinet he threatened to withdraw from the independence deal unless people of Tswana descent were given the option of renouncing Bophuthatswana citizenship and automatically regaining South African citizenship. 'We are not to accept independence at all costs', he said.[36]

In the end, however, both were signatories to laws, the Status of Transkei and Status of Bophuthatswana Acts, which stripped millions of Africans (and their descendants) of South African citizenship even though they were born and bred in white-designated South Africa. That, in turn, made it difficult for their fellow homeland leaders to justify the contention that they were opposing apartheid from within. It is significant that the period of Transkei and Bophuthatswana independence coincided with the phase during which the label 'homeland leaders' took on its most derisive connotations. Seemingly sensing that all participants to the Umtata summit would be smeared as 'collaborators' because of Transkei and Bophuthatswana independence, those leaders who were still opposed to independence began to distance themselves from the 'homeland leader' tag.

Even before Chiefs Matanzima and Mangope had made their final moves toward independence, Chief Buthelezi had taken a step of his own which was of equal, if not greater, import to South Africa's politics. It was his decision to revive the Zulu cultural movement, Inkatha ka Zulu, founded by his uncle, King Solomon ka DiniZulu. The revived Inkatha, however, was wider in outlook. Chief Buthelezi renamed it first *Inkatha YaKwaZulu* and then *Inkatha YeNkululeko YeSizwe*, both of which reflected the revived movement's wider vision. Inkatha YaKwaZulu means 'in or of KwaZulu', leaving open the option of founding different Inkathas in other parts of South Africa and of their being linked federally to Inkatha YaKwaZulu, all serving under a central Inkatha. But that idea, which Chief Buthelezi seemed to favour initially,[37] later gave way to the concept of making the existing Inkatha the Inkatha for all South Africa by opening its ranks to all Africans. That change is reflected in the term YeNkululeko YeSizwe or 'national liberation movement'.

Described by Welsh as the 'prototype of a mass mobilisation-type political party'[38] shortly after it first began to attract wide attention, Inkatha quickly forged ahead as one of the potentially decisive political forces in South Africa. Committed to rejection of colonialism, neo-colonialism, racism and discrimination,[39] Inkatha's immediate political aim was to thwart fragmentation of South Africa by blocking Pretoria's design to create independent bantustans for Africans.[40] Chief Buthelezi's first major speech in Soweto as president of Inkatha reflected a change in emphasis and a more radical tone.

Whereas in the Hoernlé Memorial address in January 1974 Chief Buthelezi was advocating adaptation of homeland policy toward some form of federation[41] (and, incidentally, using the term 'homeland leaders' quite happily), in his address at Soweto's Jabulani Amphitheatre in March 1976 he called openly for majority rule. In 1974 the 'emergence of independent homelands' did not necessarily contradict the association of black and white states on matters of general concern. In 1976 the whole world had to be told that separate development was despised by Africans as disguised *baasskap*. In 1974 there was association with Chief Matanzima as a co-advocate of a South African 'federal commonwealth'. In 1976 there was an implicit challenge to Chief Matanzima and unequivocal rejection of his independence decision. 'I challenge anyone to prove to me that the majority of blacks do in fact want the so-called independence which is offered to our reserves, now called homelands', he said. 'No single black leader will dare to go to his people to decide the independence issue on the basis of a referendum.'

By 26 October 1976, the date on which Transkei became independent, the differences between Chief Buthelezi and Chief Matanzima were apparently irreconcilable. Chief Buthelezi made his feelings about Transkei independence clear by his refusal to attend Transkei's independence celebrations. Chief Matanzima had earlier hit back against Chief Buthelezi for his Soweto speech, describing him as a 'well-fed, well-dressed and well-paid' person who held a position in the 'hated establishment' but who incited the black masses by 'not so subtly' suggesting that the revolutionary changes which overtook Angola and Mozambique were imminent in South Africa.[42]

Events in Soweto in 1976 were to justify Chief Buthelezi's right to be accorded a special status among African leaders working within the officially sanctioned framework. Where observers were wont to write the homeland leaders off as 'irrelevant' after 16 June 1976, that was a label that simply could not be hung around Chief Buthelezi's neck. The unrest which swept through African townships throughout South Africa after 16 June helped further to emphasise the differences between the anti-independence camp of Chief Buthelezi and the pro-independence corral of Chief Matanzima.

On 24 August 1976 the unrest in Soweto took a new turn when hostel dwellers, drawn mainly from Mzimhlophe hostel, attacked Soweto residents. Zulu migrant workers were blamed for the attacks. Chief Buthelezi flew to Soweto from KwaZulu. He was the first and only homeland leader to enter Soweto during the unrest, a time when feelings were running strongly against 'collaborators'. Chief Buthelezi addressed workers at Mzimhlophe hostel, deploring the manner in which Zulus had been singled out for blame and pointing out that the men in the hostels were drawn from all ethnic groups. Appealing for a cessation of intra-African violence, he said: 'We must heal the wounds that we have inflicted on each other in the past few days. We dare not play the game of turning against each other, as this diverts our attention from facing up to our oppressors.'

At a press conference the next day, Chief Buthelezi minced no words in apportioning a major share of the blame on the police for the violence. 'They emerged as not only the instigators of the hostel dwellers but also as having aided and abetted them when the rampaging took place.' In retrospect the significance of Chief Buthelezi's visit is that he was probably the only leader working within the government framework who would have been able to address a gathering in Soweto in safety.

Shortly before Chief Buthelezi's visit to Soweto, representatives of seven homelands met at a hotel near Jan Smuts Airport to assess the situation and to attempt to move in from the political periphery to which they had been confined since 16 June. Convened by Professor Hudson Ntsanwisi of Gazankulu, the day-long meeting culminated in the release of a joint communiqué. Perhaps the key point in the communiqué was their plea for a meeting with the Prime Minister, Mr Vorster, to discuss the unrest. A ten-point list of African grievances in the communiqué formed a proposed agenda. Two items in the five-page statement are worth emphasising. (1) realisation by the signatories that they were in danger of being swept aside by events; (2) reiteration, with the exception of Bophuthatswana's representatives, of their opposition to abdicating the African birthright to South African citizenship by accepting independence. Their statement on government institutions, including their own legislative assemblies illustrates the first point. It read: 'Failure to implement the genuine aspirations of blacks, as presented by black leaders, has done great harm to government-recognised statutory bodies and has given a lot of credibility to the accusations that these institutions are foisted on our people and are of no value.'

Since the homeland leaders are constantly accused by black consciousness militants of collaborating with Pretoria in repression of the 'real' leaders, it is worth noting that their communiqué included a demand that all detained blacks should be charged or released and that detained leaders should be included at a proposed new national convention. In the ten days before their summit meeting about 140 black consciousness leaders had been detained in country-wide police swoops.[43] Chief Buthelezi's confidential memorandum to the meeting is important on the same issue. He pressed for representatives from areas that had been affected by the unrest to be included in the proposed talks with the Prime Minister. In an implicit but clear reference to black consciousness leaders, Chief Buthelezi pressed the homeland leaders to agree to a dialogue with 'representatives of black organisations whose political views may differ from ours'. He added: 'I

72

we do not ensure a common purpose we may find ourselves engulfed in a civil war which [will] further delay the day of our liberation.'

The meeting between the homeland leaders and Mr Vorster took place on 8 October, but it yielded very little in terms of the hopes set out in the joint communiqué after the homeland leader summit of 21 August. Mr Vorster refused to discuss the unrest as it was under investigation by a judicial commission of inquiry. He similarly stalled demands for the release of detained leaders with the response that he would not 'interfere with the law', which provided for regular review of detentions. The plea for a national convention brought the riposte that it was an idea without any merit.[44] Mr Vorster was apparently unmoved by a special 'viewpoint' presented to the meeting at the start of the talks by Chief Buthelezi. Chief Buthelezi's viewpoint described the Africans present as 'leaders who are serving our people within the framework of your policy'. It warned that they would face a 'politically impossible task' if they returned empty handed from that day's meeting.

The impasse which the homeland leaders believed they had come to after their meeting with Mr Vorster led to the formation of the Black Unity Front (B.U.F.). A stearing committee for B.U.F. was elected that night, within hours of the meeting with Mr Vorster. Its chairman was Dr S. M. Nyembesi, a top Inkatha man from Soweto. Its mandate was to bring together a wide cross-section of the African community with a view to taking concerted action to solve the problems they faced. B.U.F., which had the backing of at least three homeland leaders, Chief Buthelezi, Professor Ntsanwisi and Dr Cedric Phatudi, declared its objectives more specifically at a press conference about six weeks later. It rejected separate development unequivocally as *baasskap* and advocated majority rule within a non-racial society. Homeland legislative assemblies were acceptable only as potential provincial councils, not as surrogates for African participation in Parliament.

B.U.F., however, never really got off the ground. Within a year or so it was moribund and about to be replaced by another alliance, the South African Black Alliance (SABA). But Inkatha continued to thrive and by mid-1978 Chief Buthelezi could boast with some justification: 'It is a grass-roots movement. It has by far the best organised and largest constituency South Africa has ever seen.' Within a short three years Inkatha's paid-up membership had burgeoned to 150 000 as against the peak of 100 000 achieved by the A.N.C. in the wake of the Defiance Campaign of 1952.

Chief Buthelezi's stature had grown with Inkatha. He emerged as the 'leading personality' in a survey of African political leadership preferences carried out in urban areas by the German-based Arnold-Bergstrasse Institute. With a preferential rating of nearly 44 per cent, Chief Buthelezi drew twice as much backing as his nearest rival, the imprisoned A.N.C. leader, Nelson Mandela (18 per cent). On the basis of the survey, Professor Theodor Hanf and his co-authors state: 'The outstanding political phenomenon in urban black politics is without doubt Chief Gatsha Buthelezi. . . . He is *the* political figure of black South Africa in general.'[45]

But in spite of Chief Buthelezi's popularity and Inkatha's rapid growth, both the chief and his movement remained targets of criticism from black consciousness cadres. Where Chief Buthelezi was rejected because of his role within the government-sanctioned system, Inkatha was repudiated because it was seen as a Zulu tribal organisation. One of the first statements by the Soweto Black Parents' Association condemned 'bantustan leaders' and all related politicians operating from government platforms for misrepresenting the people. The association, which was formed in the immediate aftermath of 16 June, made no exception to accommodate Chief Buthelezi. The most important reason for rejecting Inkatha was the belief that it was inimical to black solidarity because of its 'tribal' orientation.

The Inkatha constitution does little to counter these accusations. Membership of the all-powerful, policy-making central committee is limited to KwaZulu citizens who are both conversant with the languages of KwaZulu and registered voters for the KwaZulu Legislative Assembly.[46] Moreover, no person may stand as a candidate for president of the movement unless he is a citizen of KwaZulu who qualifies for election as KwaZulu Chief Minister, which effectively limits candidates to Zulu chiefs.[47] In a speech to the Association of Third World Affairs in Washington, U.S.A., Chief Buthelezi appeared to emphasise Inkatha's link with KwaZulu. Referring to the 'partnership between Inkatha and the KwaZulu Legislative Assembly', he said: 'Every member of the [KwaZulu] cabinet . . . is an important central committee member and every member of the assembly . . . is a candidate nominated by Inkatha. Inkatha and the Legislative Assembly are now ineradicably tied together. The destruction of one is the destruction of the other.'

One outcome of the close relationship is that there is no chance of Chief Buthelezi being removed and replaced by a pro-independence chief minister, as the whole of Inkatha is firmly committed against independence. That is what Chief Buthelezi may have had in mind when he defended the controversial citizenship clauses in Inkatha's constitution as necessary tactical manoeuvres.[48] But that outcome has a price: Inkatha is overwhelmingly Zulu and is reportedly polarising urban Africans on a near

74

one-to-one basis, with adherents of the black consciousness movement and the Africanist tradition among its most vocal opponents.[49]

It is perhaps not coincidental that the confrontation between Chief Buthelezi and young militants in the black consciousness movement should have taken place at Sobukwe's funeral. Sobukwe was bound to attract some of Chief Buthelezi's bitterest enemies to his funeral. In the heady atmosphere of ideology and death, Sobukwe's personal friendship toward Chief Buthelezi counted for nothing. The aftermath of the clash left the African community deeply divided, as Chief Buthelezi hit back against the B.P.C.-SASO axis and their real or suspected sympathisers. At a meeting in Soweto after the Graaff-Reinet funeral, Chief Buthelezi expressed amazement that he, who had stood firmly against independence, should be lumped with Chiefs Matanzima and Mangope, who had 'sold' the South African birthright of their people. But, as the 1970s drew to a close, that was an accurate pointer to the confused acrimony and bitter division in black politics.

Chief Buthelezi had in the meantime forged links with the Coloured Labour Party and the Indian Reform Party to form the Black Alliance, of which he was elected chairman. One of the alliance's major aims was the holding of a national convention to work out a new dispensation for South Africa. Another was to act in concert to give black solidarity a dimension in reality as well as rhetoric. But the testing question which lay ahead was whether it would hold together in the face of consistent attempts by the ruling National Party to woo Coloureds and Indians as junior partners of its proposed tripartite alliance of non-African minorities.

Conclusion

Looking back, with the advantage of hindsight, a broad pattern is detectable. The triumph of white reaction against the revolutionary force of African nationalism created a political void in the African community. The new black consciousness movement, working from a base in the black universities, and a renewed African self-assertiveness, emanating from the relatively safe platform of homeland legislative assemblies, started to fill the vacuum at roughly the same time. They became locked in a struggle for supremacy and a tussle over who were to be the legitimate heirs to the long tradition of black resistance in South Africa.

Pleas by people like Temba Sono for a *modus vivendi* seemed only to stiffen the resolve of the black consciousness movement to wage relentless political war on the 'imposters' who spoke in the name of black solidarity but who accepted positions within a government system which stressed ethnic and race differences within the black community. Chief Buthelezi's view that there was room for a variety of forces on the frontline of resistance to Pretoria's race policies made no impact. The attack on him at Graaff-Reinet aggravated the situation immensely. It constituted a decisive setback to the hopes of black unity. Chief Buthelezi underlined this fact in his policy speech to the KwaZulu Legislative Assembly. He declared: 'We have in the past bent backwards to have our relations with them patched up for the sake of black unity. . . . We are no longer prepared to do so.'

The events of 16 June and the reaction they sparked throughout South Africa opened the way for the re-entry of the banned A.N.C. and, to a lesser extent, of the P.A.C. into the arena as a 'third force'. They returned as clandestine organisations committed to armed struggle. But they came back. The Commissioner of Police acknowledged the new situation in his annual report for the year ending June 1977, when he said: 'The wave of widespread rioting and unrest to a certain extent gave rise to new hopes among members of the banned P.A.C. and A.N.C.' In contrast to his report for the previous year, the Commissioner reported that there had been 'no large-scale political unrest'.[50]

There are other yardsticks with which to measure the situation. The rising number of security trials, reaching a total of 186 in the two years after June 1976, would be one. The flight of youngsters from African townships and their recruitment in neighbouring countries by the A.N.C. and P.A.C. for military training would be another. Some idea of the scale of these developments can be gleaned from official statistics. According to the United Nations Deputy High Commissioner for Refugees, a total of about 3 000 South African refugees were living in neighbouring states.[51] In 1978 about 4 000 South Africans were estimated to be undergoing training in A.N.C. and P.A.C. camps. In the two years immediately after 16 June some 2 500 people were charged with activities relating to insurgency, including undergoing military training, recruiting people for military training and transporting arms.[52]

Just as important as numbers are considerations of a different nature. Although the South African authorities had faced and defeated saboteurs in the early 1960s, the re-emergence of A.N.C. and P.A.C. insurgents in the 1970s took place in a different context. In the 1960s South Africa was surrounded by a *cordon sanitaire* of white-ruled states: Rhodesia, the Portuguese colonies of Mozambique and Angola, and Namibia. By the late 1970s the *cordon sanitaire* had disintegrated. That, plus the immense pressure exerted against South Africa as the only white-ruled state left in southern Africa, constituted an obvious shift in the geo-political balance of power. Added to that was the psycho-political significance of the youth who fled as students to return as insurgents. It provided a link across a generation between the old-style African nationalists and the new generation of angry young men. The link came at a time when the old nationalist movements were in danger of atrophying in exile. Nothing symbolised the new situation so much as the killing of two whites in broad daylight by the Goch Street killers on 13 June 1977.

As the 1970s drew to a close the independent homelands seemed destined to play an important role in helping South Africa to contain the insurgents. With their leaders compromised as 'sell outs' in African nationalist eyes, their survival depends increasingly on the survival of the white-ruled South African core. In that sense the pressures on the new states, particularly those on the Botswana-Zimbabwe borders, to commit their infant armies and meagre resources to checking insurgents seem very strong. The interception of two guerrillas in Bophuthatswana in August 1978 and the handing over of them to South Africa seemed to point to the pattern of events for the future.[53] In spite of Transkei's severing of diplomatic relations with South Africa over Griqualand East (which did not prevent it from accepting R113 million from Pretoria), the independent homelands seemed more likely to end up as captive South African buffer states than Trojan horses within the South African fortress.

1. P. Walshe, *Black Nationalism in South Africa* (Johannesburg, 1973), p. 39.
2. *Black Review*, 1972, p. 11.
3. P. Laurence, *Transkei: South Africa's Politics of Partition* (Johannesburg, 1976), p. 101.
4. *The Star*, 28 March 1970.
5. *Politikon*, June 1974, p. 54.
6. S. Biko, 'White Racism and Black Consciousness' in H. W. van der Merwe and D. Welsh, *Student Perspectives on South Africa* (Cape Town, 1972), p. 186.
7. T. Karis and G. Carter, *From Protest to Challenge* (Stanford, 1977), vol. 3, p. 317.
8. *Ibid.*, p. 515.
9. *Black Review*, 1972, p. 6.
10. Karis and Carter, *op. cit.*, p. 515.
11. *Black Review*, 1972, p. 19.
12. *Ibid.*, p. 20.

13. Saso Information Pamphlet, 1972.
14. *Black Review*, 1972, p. 22.
15. *Ibid.*, p. 23.
16. Muriel Horrell *et al.*, *A Survey of Race Relations in South Africa*, 1972, p. 30.
17. *Black Review*, 1972, p. 25.
18. *The Star*, 3 July 1972.
19. Horrell *et al.*, *op. cit.*, p. 30.
20. *Black Review*, 1974–75, p. 108.
21. *Black Review*, 1973, p. 64.
22. *Black Review*, 1974–75, p. 77.
23. *Ibid.*, p. 82.
24. *Black Review*, 1972, p. 182.
25. *Black Review*, 1973, p. 183.
26. Horrell *et al.*, *op. cit.*, p. 22.
27. *Politikon*, *op. cit.*, p. 62.
28. Quoted in B. Temkin, *Gatsha Buthelezi, Zulu Statesman* (Johannesburg, 1976), p. 125.
29. *Black Review*, 1972, p. 77.
30. Laurence, *op. cit.*, p. 100.
31. *Ibid.*, p. 101.
32. *Ibid.*, p. 103.
33. *Ibid.*, p. 101.
34. *Ibid.*, p. 102.
35. *Ibid.*, p. 114.
36. *Hansard*, vol. 77, 1977, cols. 8684 and 8685.
37. Personal interview, mid-1975.
38. *Reality*, March 1976.
39. Preamble to Inkatha constitution.
40. Inkatha Bulletin, September 1976.
41. G. Buthelezi, *White and Black Nationalism, Ethnicity and the Future of the Homelands* (Johannesburg, 1974).
42. Laurence, *op. cit.*, p. 102.
43. South African Institute of Race Relations, *South Africa in Travail* (Johannesburg, 1978), p. 20.
44. *Rand Daily Mail*, 9 October 1976.
45. Summarised version of Arnold-Bergstrasse Institute findings released by Chief Buthelezi on his return from Europe, 24 June 1978.
46. Inkatha constitution, Section 9 (1).
47. *Ibid.*, Section 8 (4).
48. *Rand Daily Mail*, 26 April 1978.
49. From Buthelezi's summarised version, see n. 45.
50. Quoted in *Financial Mail*, 11 August 1978.
51. Loraine Gordon *et al.*, *A Survey of Race Relations in South Africa*, 1977, p. 130.
52. *Rand Daily Mail*, 15 June 1978.
53. *Beeld*, 12 August 1978.

4 Racial Legislation and Civil Rights

JOHN DUGARD

The life of the South African Institute of Race Relations spans a crucial period in South African history. For the first nineteen years of the Institute's life South Africa was governed by a succession of administrations under the premiership of J. M. B. Hertzog and later J. C. Smuts which, although responsible for the introduction of racially discriminatory legislation and responsive to the demands of race politics in an overwhelmingly white political order, were nevertheless not founded primarily on a race-policy platform or ideology. Since 1948, however, South Africa has been ruled by the National Party, which came to power on the platform of apartheid and still persists in placing this racial ideology in the forefront of its legislative programme and its political appeal. Consequently there is a marked tendency, both at home and abroad, to divide South African history into two phases: pre-1948 and post-1948. This approach to history accounts for the popular belief that the present evils of South African society are of post-1948 origin. The correctness of this assertion in general will not be examined in this essay. However, racial legislation and the laws affecting civil liberties will be studied with a view to answering the question whether, and if so to what extent, the modern apartheid legal order predates 1948.

Race laws and civil liberties before 1948

The seeds of modern South African race laws are clearly to be found in earlier legislative enactments. A wide range of laws attempted in a somewhat unsystematic manner to divide the community into different racial groups;[1] and, while no law prohibited marriages between persons belonging to different race groups, it was a punishable offence for a 'European' to have illicit carnal intercourse with a 'native' of the opposite sex.[2]

79

Severe restrictions were placed on the freedom of movement of Africans by the pass laws, which can be traced back to 1809,[3] and which were once described by a National Party spokesman as being 'as old as civilisation in our country'.[4] A pass, in the sense of a document required for lawful movement into, out of, or within a specified area which must be produced on demand by a policeman, was essential for the movement of African males in most parts of the country, but certain categories of Africans, attaching mainly to middle-class occupations, were exempted from these laws.[5]

Economic separation was maintained by a number of laws which reserved certain jobs for whites[6] and by the prohibition placed on Africans from joining recognised trades unions.[7] The territorial division of South Africa into areas for African occupation and areas for occupation by other population groups was prescribed by the Bantu Land Act of 1913[8] and the Bantu Trust and Land Act of 1936.[9] Residential zoning laws designed to prevent Indians from owning land or occupying premises outside 'bazaars' set aside for their exclusive use date back to 1885. Separate schools for different races were already the rule well before Union and in one of its earliest pronouncements on race, in *Moller* v. *Keimoes School Committee*,[10] the Appellate Division gave its approval to this practice. While there were no legislative restrictions on the admission of blacks[11] to universities, in fact only the University of Cape Town and the University of the Witwatersrand admitted students on academic merit, with no regard to race.[12]

The South African courts, with no power of judicial review over Acts of Parliament, displayed a fluctuating attitude towards racial legislation but generally could be said to have been sensitive to the expectations of the white community. In 1911, in *Moller* v. *Keimoes School Committee*, the Appellate Division gave its approval to legislation aimed at school segregation and, speaking through the Chief Justice, Lord De Villiers, declared:

As a matter of public history we know that the first civilized legislators in South Africa came from Holland and regarded the aboriginal natives of the country as belonging to an inferior race, whom the Dutch, as Europeans, were entitled to rule over, and whom they refused to admit to social or political equality. . . . Believing, as these whites did, that intimacy with black or yellow races would lower the whites without raising the supposed inferior races in the scale of civilization, they condemned intermarriage or illicit intercourse between persons of the two races. Unfortunately the practice of many white men has often been inconsistent with that belief, but the vast majority of Europeans have always condemned such unions, and have regarded the offspring of such unions as being in the same racial condition as their black parents. These prepossessions, or, as many might term them, these prejudices have never died out, and are not less deeply rooted at the present day among the Europeans in South Africa, whether of Dutch or English or French descent. We may not from a philosophical or humanitarian point of view be able to approve this prevalent sentiment, but we cannot, as judges, who are called upon to construe an Act of Parliament, ignore the reasons which must have induced the legislature to adopt the policy of separate education for European and non-European children.[13]

While the Supreme Court of the United States gave its imprimatur to the 'separate but equal' doctrine as early as 1896 in *Plessy* v. *Ferguson*,[14] the South African courts hesitated in this regard and, in some decisions, inclined to the view that separate facilities could never be reasonable.[15] It was only in 1934 that the Appellate Division, in *Minister of Posts and Telegraphs* v. *Rasool*,[16] upheld the validity of regulations establishing separate facilities for white and black on the ground that separation coupled with equality was not unreasonable.[17]

Laws designed to maintain white domination and secure racial separation resulted in serious inroads being made on the freedoms of person, movement, speech and assembly. Wide powers to detain without trial were vested in the Governor-General as the supreme chief of all Africans in Natal, the Transvaal and the Orange Free State.[18] The Executive was empowered to confine political dissidents to particular areas without judicial authorisation by the Riotous Assemblies Act and the Native Administration Act. The former statute gave the Minister of Justice the power to prohibit any person from being in any area when he was satisfied that such person was 'promoting feelings of hostility' between whites and blacks,[19] while in terms of the latter the Governor-General might banish any African to a particular part of South Africa in much the same way as successive Russian regimes have banished political opponents to Siberia.[20] Freedom of speech was curbed by laws which made it a criminal offence to utter any words or publish material calculated to engender hostility between whites and blacks[21]: laws which were generally enforced in such a way as to restrict criticism of white supremacy.[22] Freedom of assembly was seriously undermined by a proclamation issued in 1928 prohibiting the holding in any reserve of 'gatherings or assemblies of natives in excess of ten in number', except in the case of religious or other exempted meetings, and by the Riotous Assemblies Act which provided for the banning of meetings where hostile feelings between Europeans and Africans might be engendered.

The pre-Second World War situation was summed up in the following manner by W. P. M. Kennedy and H. J. Schlosberg in the standard work on South African constitutional law:

> Nowhere in the world, we venture to suggest, does there exist a system of executive despotism similar to the executive administration of native affairs in South Africa. In other portions of Africa we may see an absolute control of the native population; but this control is by an external power; there is no pretence to parliamentary government. In the Union, however, we see all the trappings of parliamentary government side by side with the absolute and autocratic power of despotism.[23]

Procedural safeguards are an important component of liberty. In South Africa, which follows the English law of criminal procedure and evidence, few attempts were made to tamper with due-process-of-law rights before 1948. Trial by jury was, however, abolished in 1914 in respect of political trials[24] and, during the Second World War, the accused was denied the right to bail and to a preparatory examination when charged with certain political crimes.[25]

New approaches to the role of the Law

The South African legal order was not free from discriminatory and repressive features in the period 1929 to 1948. But, compared with the contemporary response to laws of this kind, there was little reaction to such laws. This can be explained on both historical and jurisprudential grounds. While Africa was under colonial rule the legal orders of most colonies were not substantially different from that of South Africa. Moreover, in the United States many southern states had laws on the statute book which were remarkably similar to South Africa's racial laws. There was little concern over the use of the legal process to achieve a discriminatory order as, in the pre-Second World War era, law was seen essentially as a mechanism of control by lawyers and politicians reared on the positivist legal tradition, which denies the importance of legal values.

The post-Second World War period brought about fundamental changes to this way of thinking. The advancement of human rights and the elimination of racial discrimination now became primary goals of the international community. The Charter of the United Nations set the scene by declaring its commitment to work for 'universal respect for, and observance of, human rights and fundamental freedoms for all without distinction as to race, sex, language, or religion'. This was followed by the Universal Declaration of Human Rights (1948), which contains a detailed code of freedoms to which states are expected to aspire, and by multilateral treaties such as the European Convention on Human Rights and Fundamental Freedoms (1950), the International Convention on the Elimination of All Forms of Racial Discrimination (1965) and the International Covenant on Civil and Political Rights (1966). This international human rights programme, together with the decolonisation movement, has been one of the major forces in international politics in the post-war era and has contributed substantially to a new approach to the legal process.

The revolution in thinking about the role of law is undoubtedly the result of the Nazi experience. The debasement of the German legal system by Hitler made lawyers and politicians alike cognisant of the need for law to adopt a more purposive function in the promotion of equality and respect for fundamental freedoms.[26] This was reflected not only in the new approach of international law but also in the adoption of national constitutions with Bills of Rights. In the United States the Supreme Court initiated change to the edifice of American law with its decision in *Brown* v. *Board of Education*,[27] in which the 'separate but equal' doctrine was held to violate the requirement of equal protection of the law contained in the Fourteenth Amendment. This was followed by a host of decisions of the Warren Court designed not only to achieve racial equality but also to promote freedoms of speech and association and to protect the procedural rights of an accused person in a criminal trial.

While nations and the international community increasingly invoked the legal process to further equality and individual rights, the South African legislature, firmly controlled by the National Party, continued to use the law as an instrument of discrimination and repression. Herein lies the root cause of South Africa's present situation. In 1929 the South African legal system was not seen as being particularly out of step with international expectations or as being fundamentally different from other legal systems. But after 1945 the new idealism brought about heightened international expectations which prompted many states, particularly in the Western world, to introduce domestic reforms. South Africa not only remained impervious to this jurisprudential wind of change: it rejected it.

Racial legislation since 1948

In 1948 the National Party came to power on the platform of apartheid.

For the first decade of National Party rule apartheid was generally perceived as a policy of racial domination and there was little talk of self-determination as a component of this policy. This was reflected in the laws enacted during this period, which set out to institutionalise and consolidate racial discrimination. After 1959, and the passing of the Promotion of Bantu Self-Government Act[28] which set the legislative scene for a commonwealth of nations in South Africa, new emphasis was placed on separate development and self-determination for ethnic groups. But by then the harm had been done: racial domination had been entrenched.

The first ten years of National Party rule witnessed the systematisation and consolidation of racial legislation. Whereas pre-1948 racial legislation relied partially on social convention to ensure racial separation, as for instance in the case of marriage, every effort was now made to divide South African society by legislative means.

Race classification was given new form by the Population Registration Act of 1950[29] that provides for the compilation by the Secretary of the Interior of a register of the entire South African population, which is to reflect the classification of each individual 'as a white person, a coloured person or a Bantu'.[30] The Act contains elaborate definitions of each racial group, based on the criteria of appearance, social acceptance and descent, which have been amended frequently in order to obstruct attempts to cross the colour line. In order to maintain the 'purity' of race classification the Prohibition of Mixed Marriages Act of 1949[31] was introduced to forbid marriages between black and white and the Immorality Act was extended in 1950,[32] to prohibit extra-marital sexual relations between whites and all blacks; that is, including Coloureds and Asians.

The 'separate but equal' approach to public amenities, approved in *Minister of Posts and Telegraphs* v. *Rasool*,[33] was vigorously enforced by the Appellate Division in a number of cases where public bodies had provided substantially unequal facilities for different races.[34] The invocation of the separate but equal doctrine in the face of apartheid legislation, which made no pretence at equal treatment, incensed the Government and in response it introduced the Reservation of Separate Amenities Act of 1953,[35] which allows any person in control of public premises to reserve separate but unequal facilities for different races and ousts the power of the courts to declare such unequal reservations invalid. This resulted in separate and substantially unequal amenities for different races in all spheres of life: buses, trains, restaurants, libraries and parks, and others.

The limits of movement were laid down by two enactments of 1952. The Bantu (Urban Areas) Consolidation Act[36] was amended to make it an offence for an African to remain for longer than seventy-two hours in an urban area unless he is able to show that (a) he has resided in such area continuously since birth; or (b) he has worked continuously in such area for the same employer for ten years; or (c) he has lawfully resided continuously in such area for at least fifteen years; or (d) the African is the wife, unmarried daughter, or minor son of a male falling under (a), (b) or (c); or (e) permission has been granted him to remain by a labour bureau. The pass laws, a necessary concomitant to this influx control measure, were consolidated and extended by the Bantu (Abolition o Passes and Co-ordination of Documents) Act.[37] This law did not – despite its title – repeal the pass laws, but instead co-ordinated them by providing for the carrying of 'reference books' instead of 'passes' and extended them by requiring women to carry reference books as well. In terms of this Act every African over the age of sixteen must be fingerprinted and furnished with a reference book that contains his identity card and information about his employment. A policeman may at any time call upon an African to produce his reference book and failure to produce it on demand constitutes a criminal offence. The impermanent nature of the African's right to be in urban areas was further emphasised by laws empowering the authorities to banish Africans from the cities and by the Bantu (Prohibition of Interdicts) Act of 1956[38] which prevents an African from obtaining a court interdict to suspend the operation of any banishment order pending an attack on the validity of such an order.

In 1950 the piecemeal, regional attempts to secure residential and occupational segregation were replaced by a uniform scheme contained in the Group Areas Act,[39] which provides for the creation of separate group areas in towns and cities for whites, Africans and Coloureds. (The 'Coloured' group has, however, been further subdivided into Indian, Chinese, Malay and 'other Coloured' groups.) This has resulted in large-scale population removals. By the end of 1975, 58 834 Coloured families, 30 646 Indian families and 1 594 white families had been moved from their homes and resettled in group areas. These figures testify to the discriminatory manner in which the Act is implemented, but the Appellate Division has indicated that such discrimination is inherent in so colossal a social experiment.[40]

Job reservation was endorsed by new statutes[41] which expanded the number of jobs withheld from Africans while the ban on the recognition of African trade unions continued.[42] Moreover, Africans were totally prohibited from striking in terms of the Bantu Labour (Settlement of Disputes) Act of 1953.[43]

Segregation in the field of education was intensified at both school and university level. The Bantu Education Act of 1953[44] removed African Education from provincial control and brought it under a national policy directed by the Department of Bantu Education. University segregation was later introduced by the Extension of University Education Act[45] which prohibited black students from attending any 'white' university without governmental permits. The same Act provided for the establishment of separate universities 'for Bantu persons' and for 'non-white persons other than Bantu persons' from which white students were excluded.

By 1959 the legal foundation of racial domination had been laid and it was now left to the administrative apartheid machine to implement these laws. This process continued unabated until the early 1970s when the National Party Government started to adopt a new policy towards discrimination. This departure from previous policy was given historic utterance in 1974 when, in the course of the debate on South Africa's continued membership in the United Nations, Mr R. F. Botha, then South Africa's Ambassador to the United Nations, declared:

> Our policy is not based on any concepts of superiority or inferiority, but on the historical fact that different peoples differ in their loyalties, cultures, outlooks and modes of life and that they wish to retain them . . . we do have discriminatory practices and we do have discriminatory laws. . . . Those laws and practices are a part of the historical evolution of our country. . . . But I want to state here very clearly and categorically: my Government does not condone discrimination purely on the grounds of race or colour.[46]

Since 1974 government rhetoric has changed dramatically and public support for racial superiority has been relegated to the outlands of the National Party and to congresses of the Herstigte Nasionale Party. To date, however, the commitment to 'move away' from discrimination – as it is generally termed – has been translated into administrative but not legislative action. The rigours of the Group Areas Act have been softened by the granting of exemption permits, which have resulted in the opening of some hotels, restaurants and theatres to blacks and in the occupation of some premises reserved for whites by blacks. Moreover, in 1973–4 several city councils desegregated facilities such as libraries and parks which were under their control, and later the desegregation of post-office counters was commenced on the instructions of the Postmaster General. Job reservation has been significantly relaxed by administrative fiat and Africans have been given a limited right to strike.[47] Black students are increasingly being allowed to study at white universities by means of special permits issued by the Executive and major efforts are under way to improve the quality of African education.

Undoubtedly these administrative acts provide evidence of the Government's commitment to 'move away' from discrimination. But unfortunately administrative relaxation of the laws has not been accompanied by legislative repeal. To date, only the masters and servants laws, which made it a criminal offence for an employee to breach his contract of employment, have been repealed,[48] and this action was prompted more by the threatened invocation of the United States Tariff Act of 1930, which prohibits the importation of goods produced by indentured labour under the threat of penal sanction, than by the determination to move away from discrimination. Until the laws which comprise the edifice of apartheid have been abolished it will be impossible to speak of the dismantling of apartheid. Although administrative departure from the full rigours of the law is to be welcomed, this cannot be viewed as final evidence of a determination to 'move away' from discrimination as it affects only 'the few' and is in any event susceptible to a reversal in policy. The apartheid order is in essence a legal order. Only the abolition of the laws that comprise this order will convince a sceptical public, both at home and abroad, of the Government's commitment to abandon racial discrimination.

Civil liberties since 1948

Inevitably the intensification of discrimination promoted increased black resistance which, in turn, led to new legislative curbs on individual liberty. During the 1950s legislative restrictions sought mainly to outlaw communism and to limit the activities of the African National Congress. Since then, however, following the failure of temporary emergency measures in 1960, the Government has embarked upon a legislative programme which has virtually resulted in a permanent state of emergency.

In 1950, at the height of the Cold War, Parliament enacted the Suppression of Communism Act.[49] Like its American counterparts, the Smith Act[50] and the McCarran Act,[51] this statute was directed mainly at the Communist Party. But in addition to banning the Communist Party, it placed serious restraints on black political activity by including within the definition of communism – which the Act sought to suppress – any doctrine which aims at bringing about any political, industrial, social or economic change . . . by the promotion of disturbance or disorder, by unlawful acts

87

or omissions' or which 'aims at the encouragement of feelings of hostility between the European and non-European races of the Union of South Africa' where the consequences are calculated to further the achievement of political, industrial, social or economic change by the promotion of disorder by unlawful acts. Consequently, members of the African National Congress (A.N.C.) were as much, if not more, exposed to prosecution[52] and administrative harassment under the Act as were members of the Communist Party. One form of administrative harassment which was increasingly used was the 'banning order'. The Suppression of Communism Act empowers the Minister of Justice to impose severe restrictions by means of a banning order on the freedoms of movement, speech and association of any person whose activities he deems to be furthering the achievement of the objects of communism. There is no appeal to the courts against such an order, with the result that the Executive has been able to silence many of its political opponents by executive decree.[53]

Despite the restraints imposed by the Suppression of Communism Act, the A.N.C. organised a massive passive resistance campaign in the early 1950s in the course of which some 8 000 volunteers deliberately violated laws, such as the pass laws, and went to jail by way of protest against the legislative structure of apartheid. Parliament's response was to enact the Criminal Law Amendment Act,[54] which makes it an offence punishable by imprisonment for three years and/or a whipping for any person to violate any law 'by way of protest against a law', and the Public Safety Act,[55] which allows the Government to declare a state of emergency and rule by emergency regulations when it considers public safety to be threatened.

In 1960, following the shooting of Africans demonstrating against the carrying of passes at Sharpeville, the Government declared a state of emergency and issued regulations which prohibited meetings and permitted detention without trial. Shortly thereafter the A.N.C. and the P.A.C. were proscribed under the newly enacted Unlawful Organisations Act.[56] During the 1960 emergency 11 503 persons were detained[57] and there is little doubt that the drastic action taken under the emergency measures succeeded in restoring order. On the other hand, judged from an economic point of view, the emergency proved to be disastrous as foreign investors lost faith in the country's political stability. Consequently the Government set about devising measures which would enable it to deal effectively with its political opponents without the necessity of declaring a state of emergency.

Detention without trial now became a regular feature of South African law. In 1963 the ninety-day detention law[58] was passed, which empowered a senior police officer to arrest without warrant and detain any person whom he suspected on reasonable grounds of having committed, or having information about the commission of, the crime of sabotage or offences under the Suppression of Communism Act and the Unlawful Organisations Act. A detainee might be held for the purpose of interrogation until he had, in the opinion of the Commissioner of South African Police, replied satisfactorily to all questions or for 'ninety days on any particular occasion'. A ninety-day detainee was denied the right to be visited by anyone other than an official of the State and the courts were expressly prohibited from ordering the release of a detainee. This measure was, however, a temporary one in the sense that it required annual renewal by the State President.

In 1965, after 1 095 persons had been held under the ninety-day detention law, it was repealed and replaced by the 180-day detention law. This took the form of an amendment to the Criminal Procedure Act,[59] which authorised an attorney-general to order the arrest and detention of 'any person likely to give material evidence for the State in any criminal proceedings' in respect of certain political and common-law offences, whenever he was of the opinion that such a person might be intimidated or abscond or whenever he deemed 'it to be in the interest of such person or of the administration of justice'. A detainee might be held for six months and no person, other than a state official, was permitted to have access to him. As in the case of the ninety-day detention law, the power of the courts to order the release of a detainee was excluded. This provision became a permanent part of the South African system of criminal procedure and required no annual renewal. Formally, this law differed from its predecessor in that it did not expressly authorise police interrogation of a detainee and was intended simply to detain witnesses. In practice, however, these formal differences proved of little relevance, since detainees were vigorously questioned by the police and often appeared in court as accused persons rather than as state witnesses.

By 1967 the white electorate had become accustomed to detention without trial. There was thus little outcry when the Terrorism Act[60] was introduced. Section 6 of this statute permits a senior police officer to detain a person indefinitely for the purpose of interrogation in solitary confinement when he has reason to believe that such person is a terrorist or has information relating to terrorism. As before, the jurisdiction of the courts to order the release of a detainee is excluded and no person other than an official of the State may visit a detainee. 'Terrorism' is widely defined in the Act, with the result that any person who engages in extra-constitutional political activity is exposed to arrest and detention under this law. In any event the decision whether to detain a person rests with the police and this may not be questioned by the courts.

Incommunicado pre-trial detention for the purpose of interrogation has become a regular feature of investigations into political offences and most accused and state witnesses who have appeared in recent political trials have undergone lengthy periods of detention under section 6 of the Terrorism Act before being brought to trial. The period of pre-trial detention varies considerably from case to case but it is not unusual for a detainee to be held for over six months. As detainees are completely isolated there is no way of ascertaining how they are treated. Since 1963 over forty detainees have died in circumstances that warrant an in-depth judicial investigation, but the Government has consistently refused to appoint a judicial commission of enquiry. Suspicions that detainees are maltreated under interrogation have not been removed by inquest proceedings before magistrates as inquest magistrates have consistently declined to examine the methods of interrogation employed and have not hesitated to attribute death in the most suspicious circumstances to natural causes, suicide or prison accidents – as illustrated by the Biko inquest. Although designed to combat terrorism, the Terrorism Act has itself become an instrument of terror and a symbol of repression. It, more than any other law, has contributed to the poor image of the law among black South Africans and in the international community.

The tentacles of the Suppression of Communism Act – renamed the Internal Security Act in 1976 – have also tightened their grip on the South African body politic. The Act may now be invoked to proscribe organisations, silence newspapers, detain and ban individuals without access to the courts where the Executive considers that such organisations, newspapers or individuals are engaged in 'activities which endanger the security of the State or the maintenance of public order'. The full horror of this law was revealed on 19 October 1977 when the Executive declared eighteen organisations unlawful, silenced three publications (including *The World*), detained forty-seven black leaders and banned seven prominent whites (including Dr C. F. Beyers Naudé and Mr Donald Woods).

The freedom of assembly and the right of political protest are seriously undermined by a number of statutes, and in particular by the Riotous Assemblies Act as amended in 1974.[61] In its new form this Act permits the Minister of Justice to prohibit any gathering in order to maintain peace or prevent the engendering of racial hostility – with no limitation on the duration of the prohibition. In 1976, after demonstrations and disturbances in Soweto had sparked off nation-wide protests, the Minister of Justice banned 'any gathering' in South Africa except sports meetings, meetings held inside buildings and specially authorised meetings. The ban was originally imposed for twelve days but it was repeated regularly and, at the time of writing, is still in force.

Although the Government claims to respect the freedom of the press, the truth is that this freedom is seriously curtailed by the general restrictions on freedom of speech, by the use of arbitrary detention and banning laws against journalists and editors, and by legislation such as the Internal Security Act which empowers the Executive to silence newspapers without appeal to a court of law. Happily the press is excluded from the wide scope of the Publications Act of 1974[62] but, in order to secure this relief, it has been compelled to subject itself to a disciplinary code enforced by a Press Council appointed by the Newspaper Press Union. This code lays down standards which, *inter alia*, require newspapers to exercise due care and responsibility as to 'subjects that may cause enmity or give offence in racial, ethnic, religious or cultural matters in the Republic . . . [and] matters that may detrimentally affect the peace and good order, the safety and defence of the Republic and its people, the economy and the country's international position'. A newspaper which violates these standards may be ordered to pay a fine of up to R10 000 by the Press Council.

Censorship has been intensified by the Publications Act of 1974 which excludes the jurisdiction of the courts and vests the screening of publications (other than newspapers) and films in government-appointed committees, and, ultimately, in an administrative tribunal, the Publications Appeal Board. The decisive standard under the Act is 'undesirability' and any publication, object, film or public entertainment is deemed to be undesirable if it:

(a) is indecent or obscene or is offensive or harmful to public morals;
(b) is blasphemous or is offensive to the religious convictions or feelings of any section of the inhabitants of the Republic;
(c) brings any section of the inhabitants of the Republic into ridicule or contempt;
(d) is harmful to the relations between any sections of the inhabitants of the Republic;
(e) is prejudicial to the safety of the State, the general welfare or the peace and good order.[63]

These standards have been widely interpreted by the committees and Publications Appeal Board charged with their implementation with the result that a considerable number of literary and political works are with-held from the South African public.

The above-described laws, which permit persons to be detained without trial and 'banned', allow organisations to be proscribed, newspapers to be silenced, meetings to be prohibited and publications to be outlawed, have in effect introduced a permanent state of emergency. This explains why, despite periods of unrest and a general deterioration in the security situation, the Government has not declared a state of emergency under the Public Safety Act since 1960.

A common feature of the above laws is the exclusion of the jurisdiction of the courts. *Habeas corpus* has been excluded expressly by all the detention-without-trial laws and there is no appeal to the courts against the silencing of organisations, individuals, newspapers or other publications. Consequently the courts no longer stand as a shield between Executive and individual where political dissent is concerned. The common-law crime of treason has been replaced by statutory forms of treason such as sabotage[64] and terrorism[65] and trials under these laws have become a regular feature of the South African scene. But the basic rules of criminal procedure have been heavily weighted in favour of the prosecution and it is no longer possible to see in these rules a safeguard of individual liberty.[66]

While the Government is on record as being opposed to discrimination on the ground of race, there is no such commitment in respect of repression. On the contrary, South Africa's formidable array of repressive security laws is added to regularly and there seems little awareness on the part of the Government of the extent of the resentment to these laws and their implementation among the black community. This insensitivity was starkly revealed following the death of Steve Biko and the inquest into his death when no government spokesman was prepared to raise his voice against the inhuman treatment meted out to Steve Biko, and by necessary implication to other detainees.

Internal and external opposition to South Africa's policies is focusing more upon political repression and less upon racial discrimination. It should be recalled that one of the major causes of the continued unrest of 1976 was the detention of large numbers of school children. Although the initial protest was sparked off by Bantu Education, the emphasis soon shifted to protests against the security laws and their implementation. On the international front, it should be recalled that it was not the laws of apartheid (that is, the laws of racial discrimination) that finally led the Security Council of the United Nations to impose a mandatory arms embargo against South Africa in November 1977, but the Internal Security

Act, under which organisations, newspapers and individuals were silenced, and the Terrorism Act, under which Steve Biko was held at the time of his death. The law is increasingly seen among blacks as an instrument of repression designed to maintain white supremacy. In its efforts to suppress extra-constitutional political dissent by all means the Government has given the value of effectiveness chief place of honour. The security laws may have saved lives and have led to the suppression of subversion. But at the same time the enforcement of these laws has lost the sympathy of a large section of the black community.[67]

Conclusion

Racial discrimination and political repression have marred the South African legal order throughout the past fifty years. The National Party Government did not introduce these features into the South African legal system in 1948. But since then, as the international community, and the Western world in particular, have aspired to higher standards of behaviour in respect of individual liberty and racial equality and have sought to use the law both in the international community and in domestic societies as an instrument of enlightened social change, the South African legislature has preferred to put back the clock. It has remained unconcerned about the cause of human rights as it has grown in strength as a factor in international politics. The failure of the South African legislature to respond to the idealism of the post-World-War period and its steadfast adherence to an unjust legal order have resulted in apartheid being likened to slavery or the legal system of Nazi Germany. However exaggerated these comparisons may be, they are not comparisons that can be ignored by South Africans. Seen in the perspective of decolonisation and the human rights movement, South Africa's legal system presents a unique target for international concern and, now, coercion. Only a complete dismantling of the present laws of apartheid will restore the reputation of the South African legal system.

1. For a full account of these laws, see Arthur Suzman 'Race Classification and Definition in the Legislation of the Union of South Africa' in *Acta Juridica* (1960), p. 339.
2. Immorality Act, 5 of 1927, sections 1-3.

3. In 1809 the Governor of the Cape, Earl Caledon, issued a proclamation prohibiting 'Hottentots' (Khoi Khoi) from moving from one district to another without a pass issued by a magistrate.

4. *House of Assembly Debates*, vol. 104, col. 4549 (31 March 1960).

5. See Ellison Kahn 'The Pass Laws' in *Handbook on Race Relations in South Africa*, ed. Ellen Hellmann (Cape Town, 1949), p. 275.

6. See, for example, the Mines and Works Act 12 of 1911, re-enacted as Act 25 of 1926, which permitted the granting of certificates of competency for a number of skilled mining occupations to whites and Coloureds only.

7. Industrial Conciliation Act 36 of 1937, section 1.

8. Act 27 of 1913.

9. Act 18 of 1936.

10. 1911 AD 635.

11. The term black is used in this essay to include Africans, Coloureds and Indians.

12. See *The Open Universities in South Africa and Academic Freedom* (Cape Town, 1974).

13. 1911 AD 635 at 643–4.

14. 163 US 537 (1896).

15. *Williams and Adendorff* v. *Johannesburg Municipality* 1915 TPD 106; *R* v. *Plaatjes* 1910 EDL 63. See further, Alfred Avins 'Racial Separation and Public Accommodations: Some Comparative Notes between South African and American Law' in *South African Law Journal*, 86 (1969) 53.

16. 1934 AD 167.

17. While South African courts may not pronounce on the validity of Acts of Parliament, they may set aside subordinate legislation where it is 'unreasonable'. In essence, therefore, in *Rasool*'s case the Appellate Division held that the reservation of separate facilities for different racial groups was 'reasonable'.

18. Under the Natal Code of Native Law and the Native Administration Act 38 of 1927, which permitted the Governor-General to authorise the detention for three months of any African who in his opinion might be 'dangerous to the public peace, if left at large'.

19. This provision now appears in section 3(5) of Act 17 of 1956.

20. Section 5(1)(b) of the Bantu Administration Act 38 of 1927.

21. Section 29 of the Bantu Administration Act 38 of 1927 and the Riotous Assemblies Act 27 of 1914, as amended by section 1 of Act 19 of 1930.

22. A. S. Mathews, *Law, Order and Liberty in South Africa* (Cape Town, 1971), p. 209.

23. *The Law and Custom of the South African Constitution* (Oxford, 1935), pp. 435–6. See too David Welsh, 'The State President's Powers under the Bantu Administration Act' in *Acta Juridica* (1968) 81.

24. Riotous Assemblies and Criminal Law Amendment Act 27 of 1914.

25. War Measure 13 of 1942, Proclamation 29, *GG* 2995 of 4 February 1942.

26. This new approach is particularly apparent in the writings of Lon L. Fuller. See, in particular, *The Morality of Law*, 2nd ed. (New Haven, 1969).

27. 347 US 483 (1954).

28. Act 46 of 1959.

29. Act 30 of 1950.
30. Section 5(1) of Act 30 of 1950.
31. Act 55 of 1949.
32. Immorality Amendment Act 21 of 1950, section 1.
33. 1934 AD 167.
34. *R.* v. *Abdurahman* 1950 (3) SA 136 (AD); *R* v. *Lusu* 1953 (2) SA 484 (AD).
35. Act 49 of 1953.
36. Act 25 of 1945, section 10; inserted by section 27 of the Bantu Laws Amendment Act 54 of 1952. See further on the history and effect of this provision, *Mtima* v. *Bantu Affairs Administration Board, Peninsula Area,* 1977 (4) SA 920 (AD).
37. Act 67 of 1952.
38. Act 64 of 1956.
39. Act 41 of 1950. This Act was consolidated by Act 77 of 1957 and later by Act 36 of 1966.
40. *Minister of the Interior* v. *Lockhat* 1961 (2) SA 587 AD at 602.
41. For example, the Bantu Buildings Workers Act 27 of 1951. The Industrial Conciliation Act was re-enacted in 1956 to allow the Minister of Labour to reserve specified classes of work for specified races as a 'safeguard against inter-racial competition' (section 77 of Act 28 of 1956).
42. Section 1(1) of Act 28 of 1956.
43. Act 48 of 1953.
44. Act 47 of 1953.
45. Act 45 of 1959.
46. *House of Assembly Debates,* vol. 55, cols. 382–83 (7 February 1975). This statement was later endorsed by the Prime Minister, Mr B. J. Vorster: *ibid.,* col. 383.
47. Section 18 of the Bantu Labour Relations Regulation Act 48 of 1953 as amended by Act 70 of 1973.
48. By section 51 of the General Law Amendment Act 94 of 1974.
49. Act 44 of 1950.
50. Alien Registration Act, 18 U.S.C. § 2385. This Act of 1940 was named after its sponsor congressman, Howard W. Smith.
51. Subversive Activities Control Act 50 U.S.C. §§ 781–94, 811–26.
52. See, for example, *R* v. *Sisulu* 1953 (3) SA 276 (AD).
53. By 1974 1 280 persons had been banned in this way. Usually a banning order remains in force for two or five years, but an order is often renewed.
54. Act 8 of 1953.
55. Act 3 of 1953.
56. Act 34 of 1960.
57. *House of Assembly Debates,* vol. 106, cols. 699–700 (3 February 1961).
58. Section 17 of the General Law Amendment Act 37 of 1963.
59. Section 215 *bis* of Act 56 of 1955 as inserted by section 7 of the Criminal Procedure Amendment Act 96 of 1965.
60. Act 83 of 1967.
61. Act 17 of 1956 as amended by Act 30 of 1974.
62. Act 42 of 1974.
63. Section 47(2) of Act 42 of 1974.

64. Section 21 of the General Law Amendment Act 76 of 1962.
65. Section 2 of Act 83 of 1967.
66. See generally on this subject, John Dugard, *Human Rights and the South African Legal Order* (Princeton, 1978), chapter 8.
67. This consequence of the rigorous enforcement of security laws was one of the reasons advanced by Lord Gardiner for opposing 'in-depth' interrogation of detainees in Northern Ireland. See his Minority Report in the Parker Committee Report, Cmnd No 4901 (1972).

5 The Changing Face of the Economy*

SHEILA T. VAN DER HORST

The fifty years 1929 to 1979 have seen the transformation of South Africa from a poor, simple economy in which only the mining of gold, diamonds and coal rivalled agriculture in the creation of income, to a modern industrial economy. The face of the economy has literally been transformed by the growth of the older and the creation of new towns linked by all weather roads, air services, an electric power grid and relatively effective telecommunications, in addition to the earlier railways. Farming too, in much of the country, has been developed from a largely pastoral base to a modernised, mechanised one.

Population has increased 3½ times from an estimated 8 million in 1929 to 27 million in 1978. National product has increased over tenfold from R3 000 (at today's prices) to R38 077 million in 1978. Thus over the whole period, real average product per head has more than doubled, having grown at an annual rate of between 2 and 3 per cent. However, South Africa's success story of development has been uneven and had, and still has, marked deficiencies. Since 1974 the rate of growth of the economy has fallen steeply and in 1976 and 1977 was too low to maintain per capita real income.

The distribution of income was, and has remained, very uneven and over some parts of the fifty-year period this inequality increased. Although since 1970 the black share of income has risen, pockets of great poverty and economic backwardness remain, especially in the African areas.

The period under review begins just before the great crash of October 1929 on the New York Stock Exchange precipitated long years of economic depression in most of the world. South Africa was relatively fortunate

*I am much indebted to Dr Ellen Hellmann and Mrs Myra Mark for helpful criticism.

because, although farming was severely affected, the world-wide fall in prices raised the relative value of gold, to which in 1933–4 was added the rise in the dollar and South African price. The sterling price had risen when Great Britain left the gold standard in September 1931. The consequent expansion of gold mining brought about a period of development in manufacturing from the mid-thirties during which 'real' national income rose at a rate of 7,5 per cent per annum.

The most outstanding feature of the whole period has been the growing industrialisation accompanied, inevitably, by the growth of towns. Urbanisation is discussed in a separate chapter but no study of the economy can fail to mention the growth of towns and the increase in the proportion of the population living in them. In 1970 the towns of the southern Transvaal had a population of over 3,25 million compared with just over 0,5 million in 1921. The three major coastal cities had a population of 2,5 million compared with less than 0,5 million in 1921.[1] No statistics are available for the years 1928 and 1978 but at the time of the nearest censuses (1921, 1936 and 1970) the percentages of the members of different racial groups living in towns and villages were recorded as follows:

	White	Asian	Coloured	African
1921	60	60	52	14
1936	68	69	58	19
1970	87	87	74	33

Some of the increase in the concentration of the population in urban areas has been the direct result of the development of new mines and new mining areas. Welkom in the Orange Free State and Carletonville in the Transvaal are examples. But a large part of the movement of population has accompanied and been the result of the growth of manufacturing industry and ancillary commercial and financial services.

Manufacturing industry (together with construction) in 1975 accounted for 28 per cent of national production. In 1928 it was responsible for 13 per cent. With the recession since 1975, the contribution of manufacturing and construction has fallen to 25 per cent. Mining of all types now accounts for 8 per cent, whereas in 1928 it was responsible for 18 per cent. Agriculture has fallen from first place with 19 per cent to 8 per cent. The development of manufacturing has not, however, been independent of mining. It was, for example, the mine and railway workshops which laid the foundation for the heavy engineering industry.

Gold and diamond mining made South Africa known on world capital markets and made it easier for both government and private industries to raise capital abroad. To a large extent the exports of gold and diamonds enabled interest and dividend payments to be met. They also helped to pay for imports of both capital goods and consumer goods which accustomed the urban population to a wide range of products not then manufactured locally. Until the 1970s the gold-mining industry also acted as a counter-cyclical stabiliser and thus allowed South Africa to maintain a higher and steadier rate of growth than most developing economies.

At the beginning of the period the 'Poor White' problem was causing much concern. The Carnegie Commission on the Poor White Problem estimated that in 1929–30, before the Great Depression had had much impact, nearly one fifth of white families in South Africa, some 300 000 people, were 'very poor', either largely supported by charity in the towns or living 'in dire poverty on the farms'.[2] During the thirties and the Second World War the 'Poor White' problem virtually disappeared as a result of increased employment in mining, growing industrialisation, special measures to assist this disadvantaged section and, not least, a rise in the educational level of the white population. It has been replaced by an increasingly recognised poor black problem which, like the 'Poor White' problem, has been thrown into relief by rising standards and differential increases in income.

In the case of both white and black, the basic cause was, and is, the familiar third world problem of a rapidly increasing population on a limited area of land, combined with a failure to adopt new types and methods of production sufficiently fast to absorb those ill-equipped either to modernise agriculture or unable to be absorbed into profitable employment in the towns.

The situation of the 'Poor Whites' in the twenties and early thirties has left a legacy which still has a potent effect on the economy, namely the belief which has dominated political policy and much of white trade union policy, that it is necessary to protect white workers from the competition of blacks. This belief was powerful when the industrial legislation of the twenties was framed. The most important statutes, the Apprenticeship Act of 1922, the Industrial Conciliation Act of 1924, the Wage Act of 1925 and the Mines and Works Amendment Act of 1926, were already operative at the beginning of our period.

Neither the Apprenticeship Act nor the Wage Act contained any racially discriminatory clauses. In fact they, as did the Industrial Conciliation Act, specifically stated that there should be no discrimination or differentiation on the ground of race or colour. This provision was to protect 'the rate for the job' and to prevent undercutting of the wages of skilled white workers by those customarily paid lower wages. The *operation* of these acts, however, led in practice to the exclusion of Coloured and Indian as well as African workers from most skilled jobs. In the first place, for thirty years (even in the Western Cape, where Coloured persons had customarily done much of the skilled work especially in the building and furniture trades) few Coloured, even fewer Indian and no African youths were apprenticed. Apprenticeship was then required for most skilled trades.

The Industrial Conciliation Act specifically excluded most African men from the system of collective bargaining it established, in that pass-bearing Africans were excluded from the definition of 'employee' and trade unions registered in terms of the Act were not permitted to have African members. In 1953 the Native Labour (Settlement of Disputes) Act extended this exclusion to all Africans, men and women. This meant that where closed-shop provisions were included in industrial council agreements made in terms of the Act, Africans were excluded from the categories of work to which the closed shop applied. The Industrial Legislation Commission, reporting in 1951 (U.G. 62, 1951, p. 116), found that of 88 industrial council agreements then in operation, 51 contained closed-shop provisions.

Such provision has been eliminated (June 1978) from the industrial council agreement for the metal and engineering industries. In these industries the categories of jobs from which Africans have been excluded have been much reduced over the years. In terms of the new agreement[3] the advancement of Africans to artisan status is permitted for the first time. Such advancement is to be negotiated with a 'shop floor' committee representing employers, trade unions and black works and liaison committees. The security of employment of trade union members currently holding jobs and preference for those recently retrenched is guaranteed. Those workers advanced will have to meet specific skill requirements to allay trade union fears of 'job fragmentation'. It is unlikely that many Africans will be advanced to artisan status in the near future as few have the necessary training.[4] Nevertheless this agreement represents a great breakthrough as artisan status has been the jealously guarded preserve of the white man.

The post-war years were to bring certain changes and additions to industrial legislation. The Bantu Building Workers Act of 1951 made provision for the training of African building workers but confined skilled African builders to working in African townships. The Native Labour (Settlement of Disputes) Act of 1953 made separate and different provision for African workers. Other measures were introduced in recurrent attempts

100

to halt the growth of the urban African work force, particularly in manu-facturing. But basically the four statutes referred to above provided the legal framework for industrial relations throughout the period.

At the time of writing this labour legislation is being reviewed by the Wiehahn Commission whose terms of reference – broadly, the adjustment of labour legislation to changing needs – suggest that it has been found in-appropriate to the changes that have taken place in industry and in the demand and supply of labour.

Growth of manufacturing

Over the period under review employment in manufacturing industry increased nearly tenfold from 157 000 in 1928 to a peak of 1 273 400[5] in 1976 while at the same time the work force changed its racial and sex com-position. The percentage of whites in the labour force dropped from 35 per cent in 1928–9[6] to 22 per cent in 1976. In 1928–9 the most important indus-

Table 5.1

EMPLOYMENT IN MANUFACTURING AND CONSTRUCTION
INDUSTRY[7]

| Year | Total | Racial Group: Numbers | | | |
		White	African	Coloured	Asian
1928/29	156 893	55 016	69 719	22 709	9 449
1938/39	268 392	103 720	120 969	30 350	13 353
1948/49	462 781	150 505	228 059	65 841	18 376
1958	645 561	171 602	351 062	94 315	28 582
1968	988 921	247 708	527 678	157 567	55 968
1976	1 273 400	276 900	717 900	205 700	72 900
1977	1 242 400	276 500	697 700	197 900	70 300
		Percentage			
1928/29	100	35	44	15	6
1938/39	100	39	45	11	5
1948/49	100	33	49	14	4
1958	100	27	54	15	4
1968	100	25	53	16	6
1976	100	22	56	16	6
1977	100	22	56	16	6

tries in terms of numbers employed were food, beverages and tobacco (30 000), clothing and footwear (16 000), basic metal and metal products (14 000). In terms of the value of net output, the processing of food, beverages and tobacco accounted for nearly a third, 32 per cent; metal products, machinery and transport equipment for 17,8 per cent; paper and printing for 11,5 per cent; chemicals for 10,9 per cent and textiles for 10,6 per cent.[8] By the outbreak of the Second World War the metal products group had reached first place, accounting in 1938–9 for 25,8 per cent of the net value of output followed closely by food and drink (25,1 per cent) with textiles and clothing in third place (12,5 per cent).

The growth of manufacturing industry in South Africa has been marked and indeed made possible by the increased employment of blacks, particularly African men and the employment of women of all racial groups. It is noteworthy that the fall in employment in 1977 affected all racial groups and the proportions of the different groups remained the same.

Over the period 1928 to 1970 the number of women in manufacturing increased tenfold, rising from 21 000 to 213 560 and increasing from 13 to 21 per cent of the labour force. The increase in the number of black women has been particularly noticeable as the following table shows.

Table 5.2

EMPLOYMENT OF WOMEN IN MANUFACTURING[9]

Year	Total labour force	Total Women	White	Racial Group African	Coloured	Asian
1928/29	161 349	21 010	12 971	655	6 853	532
1938/39	275 852	39 325	27 872	1 154	9 793	506
1948/49	556 779	73 075	39 683	4 756	27 509	1 127
1958	645 561	104 128	30 913	12 366	42 969	2 800
1970	1 109 784	213 560	52 260	70 080	71 660	13 530

PERCENTAGE OF TOTAL MANUFACTURING LABOUR FORCE

1928/29		13	8	0,4	0,4	0,3
1938/39		14	10	0,4	3,5	0,2
1948/49		13	7	0,8	5	0,2
1958		16	5	2	7	0,4
1970		19	5	6	6	1

The main reason for the slow participation of African women in manufacturing arises from the fact that in the early years of this period it was overwhelmingly men who made their way to the urban areas, while their families remained in the rural areas. In 1921 the ratio of African men to women was 3:1 in the towns. In 1936, when African women numbered 357 000, the ratio had fallen to 2:1. By 1970 their number had risen to 2 165 000 and they constituted 40 per cent of the urban African population – a percentage that would undoubtedly have been higher were it not for the increasingly stringent influx control, which stemmed the inflow of women to an even greater extent than that of men. Moreover, the main area of employment for women was in domestic service, at first almost exclusively and still predominantly.

During the Second World War South Africa was isolated by lack of shipping and at the same time called upon to provide munitions and other supplies both for her own army and to contribute to those of her allies. This led to the introduction and development of new types of production which laid the foundation for the post-war development of many new types of manufacturing, especially in the metal and engineering industries.

Up to the outbreak of the Second World War, the engineering industry in South Africa was essentially a jobbing and repair industry and did not, except in a few establishments, manufacture engineering supplies. Its main customer was the gold-mining industry. Precision engineering of repetition work with semi-automatic machines was pioneered during the war in South Africa by the South African Mint's armament factories.[10]

The changes in the racial and sex composition of the labour force have, in part at least, been the result of changes in the methods of production. The development of factory production, particularly in the metal and engineering industries, has resulted in the replacement of the artisan assisted by unskilled labour by the machine operative and the increasing employment in such jobs of black workers and particularly Africans. According to the Manpower Survey for 1977 of 298 278 artisans and semi-skilled and skilled workers (other than artisans) employed in the metal, plastics, machinery and motor industries, only 26 per cent were artisans. Of nearly 220 000 skilled and semi-skilled workers in these industries, 74 per cent were Africans (including 4 per cent women), 12 per cent were Coloured, 11 per cent were white and 3 per cent Asian.

Of the 78 563 classified as artisans in the metal and engineering industries (excluding the motor trades) 92 per cent were white, 6 per cent Coloured, per cent Asian and 0,5 per cent African. Of 25 763 artisans in the electrical trades 97 per cent were white, 2 per cent Coloured, 0,3 per cent Asian and

0,5 per cent African. In the motor trade of 27 957 artisans, 86 per cent were white, 8 per cent Coloured, 3 per cent Asian and 2 per cent African.

These figures illustrate the extent to which artisan work has remained a white preserve while African, Coloured and Asian workers undertake the skilled work (not classified as artisan) and the semi-skilled work.

Clothing manufacturing and textiles

Although the nature of the industry has not changed in the way that the metal and engineering has, there have been interesting and revealing changes in the racial composition of the labour force as the following table shows.

Table 5.3

CLOTHING MANUFACTURING AND TEXTILES

PERCENTAGE RACIAL AND SEX DISTRIBUTION

Year	Total	White		Coloured		African		Asian	
		M	F	M	F	M	F	M	F
1928/29[11]	14 526	17	35	10	17	13	8	6	0,3
1977[12]	171 025	0,8	0,8	5	24	23	31	5	11

In 1977 of 171 025 skilled and semi-skilled employees in clothing manufacturing, textiles and dry cleaning, whites comprised less than 2 per cent. In 1977 the largest group of employees were African women (31 per cent) followed by Coloured women (24 per cent). There were only 1 438 white women in this group of industries.

In manufacturing as a whole in 1970 (the last date for which this breakdown is available) there were 48 790 white women of whom only 12 228 (25 per cent) were engaged directly in manufacturing production. 36 562 were administrative and clerical staff, whereas of 157 946 black women workers only just over 7 000 (4,5 per cent) were administrative and clerical workers.[13]

White women were the first group of women to enter the manufacturing labour market, their numbers increasing from 12 971 in 1928-9 to 44 976 in 1953-4 of whom 47 per cent (21 014)[14] were clerical and administrative workers. Thereafter the total number of white women fluctuated between 37 000 and 45 000 but within this fluctuating total the proportion of administrative and clerical workers grew steadily. During the sixties there was a great increase in the number of black women entering the labour market, the number of Coloured women nearly doubled, increasing from 39 200 in 1960 to 76 820 in 1970; the number of African women more than trebled, rising from 16 600 to nearly 59 000; the number of Asian women, although relatively small, rose nearly fivefold from 3 500 to 15 116.

During the decade 1960 to 1970 some other interesting changes have taken place in the occupational structure of the labour force. Although the numbers concerned are relatively small, there has been a great increase in the number of black clerical and sales workers as is shown in the following table.[15]

Table 5.4
CLERICAL AND SALES WORKERS, MALE AND FEMALE, 1960 AND 1970

	White		African		Asian		Coloured	
Male	*1960*	*1970*	*1960*	*1970*	*1960*	*1970*	*1960*	*1970*
Clerical	131 530	150 390	18 276	84 700	7 728	22 760	6 707	24 880
Sales	61 681	87 850	25 522	92 200	21 343	26 750	8 027	17 900
Female								
Clerical	144 922	241 570	1 000	7 260	475	2 730	2 264	10 630
Sales	35 850	54 840	3 372	18 000	1 600	4 040	2 396	8 960

Whites continue to predominate in the professions and in semi-professional, technical and administrative work. One unusual feature of the occupational structure is that African and Coloured women outnumber men in the professional group, which is due to the predominance of teachers and nurses in the black professional group.

The great increase in the number and type of manufacturing and mining establishments has been accompanied by changes in the financial and organisational structure. At the beginning of the period the group system was in operation with regard to gold and some coal mines. According to this system, a number of mining companies constituted a group which provided financial, consulting engineering, and buying services and a sufficient shareholding to ensure control. Some groups, for example, Anglo-American, included diamond-mining companies and indeed had extended from control of diamond mining to gold and coal mining. Some groups owned farms and forests in addition to mines. Since the Second

105

World War groups have amalgamated and diversified and become great conglomerates, controlling a wide range of manufacturing in addition to mining companies. One of the most notable of such firms is Thomas Barlow and Sons, which grew from a small family business distributing at first blankets, then steel rubber belting and nuts and bolts and, in 1927, Caterpillar Tractors, to become a great manufacturing and mining concern comprising more than 500 separate companies, many of which are wholly owned. These companies include gold, uranium, chrome and coal mining; steel manufacturing; heavy engineering; electronic and electrical apparatus; telecommunications equipment and systems; paint and allied products; household appliances (T.V., radio and sound products, electric stoves, refrigerators and other household equipment); engineering supplies; earthmoving equipment; mechanical handling equipment; packaging; paper and printing; heavy vehicles and truck manufacture; cement and lime; machine tools; agricultural machinery; building materials; forestry and timber; property development. Barlow's mining activities grew when, in 1971, it took over Anglo-American's shareholding in Rand Mines to become Barlow Rand. In 1977 the Barlow Rand turnover exceeded R1 245 million.[16] The growth of this conglomerate epitomises the growth of manufacturing in South Africa.

Retailing too has changed from small independent shops and a handful of old established department stores with branches in the major cities, to chains of modern supermarkets and hypermarkets, with branches in most towns specialising in food, household equipment and clothing, or a combination.

In many sectors – manufacturing, wholesale and retail trade, construction and transport – there is a high degree of concentration. In these four sectors 10 per cent of firms are responsible for 75 to 80 per cent of the turnover. In no less than 58 of 181 manufacturing industries (classified according to the internationally used Standard Industrial Classification) three firms or less, manufacturing from condensed milk to blankets, fertilisers and tyres and tubes, were responsible for 70 per cent or more of the turnover. In 17 groups there was only one manufacturer, in 25 groups only two.[17] The degree of concentration in manufacturing is, in part at least, the result of the relatively small size, in terms of purchasing power, of the South African market.

Mining
Although mining has fallen in relative importance in its contribution to the

106

national product, it nevertheless remains very important, especially in its contribution to exports. The mining industry has expanded in terms of numbers employed from 306 792 in 1928 to 776 457 in 1977 and in value of output from R122 million to R5 500 million. Gold mining has continued to be pre-eminent, in 1977 employing 55 per cent of those working in this sector of the economy and being responsible for 51 per cent of the value of mineral output. In 1928 it had employed 64 per cent of those in mining and allied concerns and had been responsible for 66 per cent of the value of output.[18] As in the latter part of the nineteenth century the discovery and development of new gold and coal fields and of new minerals have led to the creation of new towns, new railways and new ports.

Although African mineworkers in recent years have been given access to some operations previously closed to them, the structure of employment on the gold and coal mines has remained basically the same. Constrained by the statutory colour-bar and the attitude of the mineworkers' trade unions which have jealously guarded the preserves of the white miner and artisan, constrained also by the Government's refusal to allow married quarters for African employees on new mines to exceed 3 per cent, mine managements have adhered to the policy of employing low-wage African labour housed in compounds. As a result the mines had to go further afield to obtain labour and the proportion of labour from the Republic sank from between 40 and 50 per cent to as low as 20 per cent in 1973, a trend which has since changed markedly. There have been several reasons for this change. In 1974 an accident to an aircraft flying mineworkers home led to an interruption of the supply from Malawi. Fear of political instability in Mozambique, following the institution in 1974 of a Frelimo-dominated government, led to concern regarding future supplies of labour from that source. At the same time increasing supplies of black labour were forthcoming from South Africa as a result of substantial increases in wages from 1973 onwards; the increasing number of Africans of working age combined with a decline in the rate of growth or actual reduction, from 1975, in the numbers employed in manufacturing and construction as a result of economic depression. In March 1978, 53 per cent of African labour on mines affiliated to the Chamber of Mines came from South Africa (including 25 per cent from Transkei).[19]

Whereas in the twenties wages on the gold and coal mines were comparable with those in manufacturing industry, the real wages of Africans on the mines remained almost the same until the early seventies,[20] after which there was a dramatic rise in African wages. The gap between white and African earnings on the mines and between African earnings on the mines and those in manufacturing industry increased markedly during the major part of this period. Between 1971 and 1976, while white wages on the gold mines increased by 91 per cent, black wages increased by 397 per cent. Nevertheless the absolute gap between white and black wages widened.[2]

Although with changes both in mining techniques and in the supply of labour, there have been some fluctuations, the proportion of Africans to the total labour force has been relatively stable. In 1977 the percentage of Africans employed varied from 68 per cent (copper) to 72 per cent (iron), 75 per cent (diamond), 88 per cent (coal), 89 per cent (manganese), 91 per cent (gold), 92 per cent (asbestos).

Coal comes after gold in numbers employed (average 1977: 93 000) and in value of output (1977: R755 million), and is followed by diamonds in number employed (average 1977: 17 451) and value of output (1977 R258 million).

	No. employed 1977	Value of output 1977 (R million)
copper	13 200	179
asbestos	21 600	138
chrome	12 600	99
manganese	9 600	120
iron	9 400	206

In 1977 minerals contributed 28 per cent of merchandise exports (i.e. exports other than gold).[22]

Central government employment

Concurrently with the growth in numbers employed in manufacturing industry, the number employed directly by the central government has grown nearly eightfold, increasing from nearly 39 000 in 1928–9 to 306 000 in 1977. The racial composition of the central government's employees has also changed, 76 per cent having been white in 1928–9 as compared with 40 per cent in 1977.[23]

Similarly, state enterprises, the South African Railways and Harbour and the Post Office, have grown in numbers and changed in the racial composition of their labour force; the Railways from 95 000 in 1928–9, of whom 60 per cent were white, to 262 000 in 1977, of whom 44 per cent were white; the Post Office from 13 000 in 1928 to 70 000 in 1977 (61 per cent white).

It will be noticed that in all these sections of government and state-enterprise employment, the proportion of white employees is higher than in private employment. Notable changes have, however, taken place in the training and use of black labour. Coloured, Indian and African workers are now being trained by both the Railway and Post Office administrations to do work hitherto reserved for white workers. Very few are, however, apprenticed and admitted to the ranks of the skilled artisan, although they may do the same work under another name. In February 1978 the Minister of Transport[24] stated that 21 372 Coloured, Indian and African workers were doing jobs on the Railways and Harbours previously done by whites.

In addition to running the Railways, Harbours and Airways, the Government has sponsored public utility corporations, the first of which, the Electricity Supply Commission (Escom), established in 1923, has since the Second World War established a national grid and the beginnings of an international one. Escom has taken over the generation of most of the electric power used from municipalities and from the Victoria Falls and Transvaal Power Company, which despite its name, ran thermal power stations and supplied most of the southern Transvaal. The greater part of the power is generated from coal but Escom is constructing a sea-water-cooled nuclear power station at Koeberg on the Western Cape coast and has established two hydro-electric power stations on the Orange River in conjunction with water-storage dams and irrigation schemes and a pumping power scheme on the Tugela River in the Drakensberg. Two hydro-electric schemes, one at Cabora Bassa in Mozambique, already linked to the South African grid, and one being constructed at Ruacana in Angola, may provide useful economic links in the future but have become risky ventures in the present climate of international relations.

The generation of electric power has increased more than twenty times from 2 454 kWh in 1930 to 64 390 kWh in 1974;[25] per head of population it has increased nearly tenfold from just under 250 kWh to 2 235 kWh.

However, although South Africa's generation of power per head is similar to that of France and Italy, is eight times that of Ghana and ten times that of Egypt and Zambia,[26] only one fifth of Soweto, the sprawling African township of one million inhabitants bordering Johannesburg, has electricity and the remaining areas are only now being provided with electricity for domestic purposes and street lighting. This illustrates the unevenness of South Africa's development. There are literally black patches beside large modern cities.

The changes that have taken place in the economy are illustrated by the fact that whereas in 1935 mining consumed twice as much power as the industrial sector and more than twice that of the household sector, in 1968 industry used nearly twice as much as the mining and household sectors combined.[27]

In 1928, at the beginning of our period, the Government established the South African Iron and Steel Industrial Corporation (Iscor) near Pretoria, taking up the shares itself when private investors looked askance at the project. This undertaking, much criticised in the thirties, justified its existence during the Second World War and has continued to expand. A second plant was established in 1948–50 at Van der Byl Park, a third is being built at Newcastle in Natal. Steel production rose tenfold between 1946 and 1977, although up to 1975 it did not keep pace with consumption.[28] Iscor owns its own coal mines in the Transvaal and Natal and also iron mines at Thabazimbi and Sishen. A railway has been constructed from Sishen to Saldanha Bay for the export of iron ore.

The Industrial Development Corporation (I.D.C.) was established in 1940 in order, as its name implies, to encourage the development of industries. The most notable industrial undertakings begun and financed by I.D.C. have been the South African Coal, Oil and Gas Corporation (Sasol, 1950), which produces petrol and a wide range of petro-chemicals from coal; and the Aluminium Corporation of South Africa (Alusaf) at the port at Richards Bay, which produces the country's entire requirements of aluminium from imported bauxite.

The growth of enterprises directly controlled by the Government and public corporations has been such that their external debt rose from R192 million in 1965 to R936 million in 1973.[29]

The importance of public corporations in domestic investment has grown from 3 per cent in 1946 and 6 per cent in 1955 and 1960 to 17 per cent in 1975 and 16 in 1976.[30] In 1975 public corporations alone borrowed abroad long-term capital of R718 million, more than the long-term foreign borrowings of the whole private sector (R697 million).[31]

It has been estimated that in 1960, 30 per cent of economically active white persons were employed in the public sector and that by 1966 this had grown to 35 per cent. In 1974 of a total labour force of 5 613 000 persons, 1 157 000 (21 per cent) were employed in the public sector, excluding public corporations such as Iscor and Sasol.[32]

The growth of the public sector and public corporations has not been without its critics. It is, however, now acknowledged that Iscor and later I.D.C.-established industries have proved to be of great strategic value and that, at least at the stage when they were initiated, private enterprise was not prepared to invest in these ventures.

110

Agriculture

During the period under review agriculture outside the homelands has changed immensely, especially since the Second World War. An agricultural revolution has been taking place, starting somewhat later than, but accompanying the industrial development. One indication of this revolution is the more than fourfold increase in the physical volume of output since 1928. Much of this increase is the result of increased mechanisation. The number of tractors, which was under 4 000 in 1930, increased more than eightfold between 1946 and 1973, from 20 000 to 164 000. Moreover, tractors also increased in size and power. The number of combine harvesters increased from under 2 000 (1946) to 20 000 (1973). At the same time farms increased in size. Whereas in the early 1950s more than one quarter of the farms were over 1 000 *acres*, in 1975 nearly one quarter were over 1 000 *hectares* in extent. While the area farmed remained much the same, the number of farms, which was 93 972 in 1928 and rose to a peak of 119 526 in 1952, fell to 77 591 in 1975.[33]

The increase in output has not been accompanied by an increase in employment as in manufacturing industry or mining. Indeed, although there was an increase in total employment up to 1971, since then there has been a decline. This generalisation masks significant changes in the racial composition of the labour force. With 1960 as a base, white employment in agriculture has fallen absolutely since 1936, Asian since 1921, Coloured since 1960 and African since 1971.

The following table summarises employment in agriculture including casual workers.[34]

Table 5.5

CHANGES IN EMPLOYMENT IN AGRICULTURE

Index 1960 = 100

Year	Total	White	Coloured	Asian	African
1921	42	143	59	168	29
1936	63	153	73	158	52
1946	71	142	77	117	62
1960	100	100	100	100	100
1971	109	83	98	59	110
1973	98	76	98	54	98

The census number regularly employed in 1975 was 715 863 of whom
12 633 were white, 602 325 African, 97 395 Coloured and 3 490 Asian. In
addition there were 615 111 casual employees, of whom 1 064 were white,
507 294 African, 105 261 Coloured and 1 492 Asian.

External economic relations

Throughout the period South Africa has been among the world's 'open'
economies, that is to say she is heavily dependent on international trade
and much of her mining and industrial development has been based on
foreign capital and technology. She has consistently derived between 25
and 30 per cent of her national income from exports, her principal export
being gold, which has normally contributed around 30 per cent to foreign
receipts, although in the late thirties the contribution of gold rose as high
as 70 per cent in 1938 and 73 per cent in 1939. Despite the rapid growth of
manufacturing industries, South Africa's main exports continue to be
primary and processed goods each contributing 36 per cent of the total in
1975. In the years 1969 to 1975 both capital goods and consumer goods

Table 5.6

IMPORTS AS A PERCENTAGE OF TOTAL SUPPLY[36]

Product	1926–27 %	1963–64 %
Clothing	76	8
Textiles	89	43
Footwear	40	3
Furniture	15	1
Paper	91	23
Rubber products	88	9
Petroleum and Coal	87	32
Basic Metals	92	22
Machinery	96	62
Electrical Machinery	90	37
Transport Equipment	73	37
Motor Vehicles & Repairs	83	36
Total Secondary Sector	57	24

exports declined in importance (from 7,3 per cent to 5,4 per cent and from 8,7 per cent to 7,1 per cent respectively).[35]

Industrialisation has led to great changes in the nature of South Africa's imports. Between 1926–7 and 1963–4 imports as a percentage of total supply fell greatly in almost every type of product but particularly in consumer goods.

The (Reynders) Commission of Enquiry into the Export Trade of South Africa considered that by the early 1960s import replacement opportunities in the light consumer goods industries and in processing had been largely exhausted and that considerable replacement of imports by locally produced intermediate and capital goods had taken place. Manufacturing industry, however, remained heavily dependent on imported capital goods. Consequently, it was essential to promote exports.

South Africa, like most trading countries, has experienced considerable fluctuations in her balance of payments. In part this has been the result of her dependence on primary product exports; although up to the seventies gold was a stabilising factor. Thereafter, fluctuations in the price of gold led to it becoming a source of instability. An even more important cause has been fluctuations in the supply of foreign capital and, at times, reversals of the flow.

During the expansion of the thirties, South Africa had begun to finance a much greater portion of investment from domestic savings. The external public debt was also much reduced, falling from £151 m. in 1928 (63 per cent of the total public debt) to £101 m. in 1938 (38,5 per cent of the total).[37] During the war years most of this external public debt was repatriated when Great Britain mobilised her capital resources to pay for imports. South Africa paid £80 m. in gold to repatriate debt. By 1945 the external public debt had fallen to £18 m. (3 per cent of the total). After the war the external public debt continued to fall until 1949 when it reached £13 m. (2 per cent of the total).[38] Thereafter it began to rise, although showing marked fluctuations, and by 1975 the central government and banking sector's long-term liabilities had risen to R1 672 m.[39]

There has also been a large inflow of foreign capital into the private sector (and into the public corporations) during the years 1946–76 although, as in the public sector, there have been periods of reverse flow. In the years 1946–54 the average annual inflow of private capital was R176 m.[40] Thereafter, there was a marked falling off and a net outflow in 1957, in the years 1959–64 and again in 1973 and 1977, when the net outflow amounted to R1 096 m. as compared to an inflow of R1 110 m. during 1976.[41]

The predominant cause of these sudden reversals of the flow of capital

113

has been political uncertainty. An outflow of short-term capital began in 1976 after the Soweto disturbances as it had after the Sharpeville crisis.

The source of South African borrowing has changed; in the thirties and earlier post-war years the chief source was Great Britain.

The chief sources of South African borrowing in the period 1956–76 are shown in the following table.[42]

Table 5.7

FOREIGN LIABILITIES 1956, 1973, 1976 (R000)

Year	Total	Percentage Present European Community Countries	(Great Britain)	Rest of Europe	Americas	Africa
1956	R2 794	71	(64)	5	13	1
1973	R10 380	65	(44)	9	17	4
1976	R19 929	57	(37)	10	24	3

Changes in the structure of the South African economy have been accompanied by changes in the supply of capital. As has been indicated, the internal supply has grown and the economy has developed a much more sophisticated money market which, taking into account the size of the economy, is comparable to those of the mature economies of western Europe and North America. The growth of a local short-term money market has, of course, made South Africa more subject to movements of short-term funds.[43]

Financial institutions, long-term insurers, pension and provident funds and building societies expanded greatly in the period since the Second World War. Between 1946 and 1977 the assets of long-term insurers and building societies increased twentyfold from R276 m. to R6 505 m., and from R282 m. to R6 249 m. respectively. Private pension and provident funds increased from R393 m. in 1958 to R5 235 m. in 1977.[44] Despite the more than fourfold increase in consumer prices from 45,6 in 1946 to 193,2 in 1977 (base 1970 = 100), there was a very great increase in real saving and investment through these institutions.

They have become an important source of finance both for the private sector and in recent years increasingly, because of 'prescribed investment' requirements, for the government and public corporations. In 1977 the increase in assets of these institutions was equal to 25 per cent of gross domestic fixed investment. In the same year corporate saving was equal to 16 per cent.

The Government and the economy

To what extent have the developments outlined been the result of deliberate policy and to what extent have they resulted from reactions to internal and external economic and political pressures? It is, of course, impossible to answer this question categorically and the answer can only be a matter of judgment. One can, however, indicate some of the pressures which have operated. To do this it is useful to subdivide the period. The first decade 1928–38 witnessed first the depression years of 1929–33 and then a period of great development led by the expansion of gold mining. During this period the value of gold output doubled, rising from R88 m. in 1928 to R173 m. in 1938. The value of other mining output *fell* from R45 m. to R24 m., largely because of the cessation of the mining and sale of diamonds during the depression years. The number of manufacturing establishments increased by nearly a third from 6 238 to 8 614 and their gross and net output nearly doubled, increasing from £81 m. and £34 m. respectively to £141 m. and £64 m.[45] During this period there was a *fall* in the consumer price index from 36 in 1928 to 34 in 1938 (base 1970 = 100).[46]

The enhanced profitability of gold mining attracted investment of large sums of capital from abroad and, as the national income grew, domestic savings became a greater proportion of the national income than ever before.

The increased profitability and expansion of gold mining increased the tax revenue and enabled the government to repay large amounts of external public debt and also to finance public works without borrowing.

At this time 50 per cent of all raw materials used in manufacturing industry were imported and, as manufacturing supplied only 2,5 per cent of the Union's exports, expansion in manufacturing was dependent on exports, mainly of minerals. It is a moot point how much of the expansion of manufacturing was the result of the policy of protection adopted in 1925. Certainly, the expansion was very dependent on that in the gold-mining industry and this was almost certainly the stronger force.[47]

Meanwhile agriculture, severely affected by the world depression, lagged behind. The gross value of arable and livestock production did not regain its 1928 level (R129 m.) until 1937 (R130 m.). This was largely achieved by the isolation of agriculture from world markets and the creation of agricultural control boards designed to raise the prices of the staple farm products through centrally controlled marketing and, in some cases, the compulsory export of products not absorbed by the local market at the prices set by the control boards. Here official policy was a dominant force.

The next decade covers the Second World War and the immediate aftermath up to the National Party's accession to power in 1948. This period was dominated by the exigencies of war which led to new development in manufacturing to meet war requirements, especially in the metal and engineering industries.

The war also generated new thinking, at least among that section of the white population directly involved and among large sections of the black population. For a war which emphasised opposition to an ideology of racial superiority and whose leaders enunciated the 'four freedoms' had implications at home. Increasingly, during the war and immediate postwar years Africans were accepted as part of the urban industrial work force.

Blacks in South Africa, 125 000 of whom had been mobilised and many of whom fought abroad, at least in a support capacity, cherished high hopes of participating in the democracy in defence of which the war was purported to have been fought. Expectations of higher wages, greater social welfare benefits and relief from the pass laws were aroused. The Reports of the Social and Economic Planning Council encouraged such hopes.[48]

In 1944 old age pensions had been extended to Africans and Asians and there were signs immediately after the war that the (United Party) Government was prepared to take some steps towards officially incorporating the African into the modern economy. It introduced a Bill into Parliament providing for the recognition of African trade unions and also had accepted in principle the recommendations of the Native Laws Commission (U.G. No. 28, 1948). This report accepted the permanence of an urban African population but confirmed the principle of residential segregation and the desirability of central control of African administration. It did, however, recommend the amelioration of the pass laws.

But when the National Party came into power in 1948, committed to implement a policy of apartheid, later to be renamed first separate and then multi-national development, it followed a very different path.

On coming into power in 1948 it appointed an Industrial Legislation Commission, one of the outcomes of which was, from 1956, the prohibition of the establishment of any further mixed trade unions, that is, unions of white, Coloured and Asian workers, Africans already being excluded. Existing trade unions were to form separate uni-racial branches, and the executive committees were to be all-white. Furthermore, provision was made for the introduction of statutory job reservation outside the mining industry where it had been operative for many years.

The period of National Party Government since 1948 in regard to labour policy falls into three phases, which inevitably overlap.[49] The first, 1948–57, was one of attempting to provide the legal framework for separate development; the second, 1957–71, the attempt to implement it; the third period, 1971–9, has been one of back-tracking on many of the previous policies. It is impossible in the space at my disposal to elaborate the details of these phases, but the experience of job reservation is indicative of the trend.

In 1956 a new clause (Section 77) in the redrafted Industrial Conciliation Act enabled the newly created Industrial Tribunal to make Reservation of Work Determinations, reserving particular categories of work in firms or industries for members of particular racial groups. In 1959 the Act was amended to make it possible for such reservation to be made on a percentage basis. This measure was an attempt to protect the white worker by halting and in some cases reversing the changes in the racial composition of the labour force that were taking place. Although work reservation determinations never applied directly to large numbers of the labour force, they created uncertainty among employers as to what changes in the pattern of employment the Government would permit and so retarded change. Moreover, work reservation orders were applied to many occupations in very important industries, including the metal and engineering industries, clothing manufacturing, motor assembly and mining.

In the field of education and training, official policy has moved from Dr Verwoerd's statement in 1954 that Africans outside the Reserves must be trained only for 'certain forms of labour', with the implicit assumption that these were to be the lowest categories, to the creation in the major urban areas of training institutions to provide industrial and technical skills and the encouragement of employers to provide training.

These changes have been the result of the pressure of circumstances. The rapid rate of economic growth in the sixties demonstrated the scarcity of skilled labour. The analyses of the requisite number of skilled workers which accompanied successive Economic Development Programmes and the acceptance of target rates of growth demonstrated the inability of the white population to provide sufficient higher grade manpower. The older division of the labour force into a white skilled section and a black unskilled one was clearly no longer applicable nor tenable. In fact it was already becoming outdated in the thirties.

The modification of policy in the face of economic imperatives has many facets. The first, chronologically, was in regard to immigration. On coming

117

into power the National Party Government reversed the policy of its predecessor, which had been one of encouraging immigration.[50] Subsequently, however, in November 1955 the Government appointed a Director of Immigration and in May 1956 South Africa joined the Inter-Governmental Committee on European Migration.[51] In October an agreement was reached whereby employers might share the cost of subsidising the fares of Dutch settlers. This reversal of policy did not involve a movement away from separation: the objective was to increase the supply of white skilled labour and to 'keep South Africa White'.[52]

Subsequently, more strenuous steps were taken to recruit immigrants and the Government itself, the provincial administration and some of the largest employers' associations organised recruiting campaigns overseas. Moreover, the Government now subsidised immigration.[53] In the sixties and seventies up to 1977, in which year there was a net loss, 600 000 immigrants came to South Africa.[54]

Economic aspects of the 'homeland' policy

The 'homeland' policy is the core of the National Party Government's political policy and has had important repercussions on its economic policy both within and outside the homelands. Outside the homelands it led to greater emphasis on preserving and even extending the system of migrant labour by increasing restrictions on the use of African labour in the major industrial areas and the tightening of influx control.

From 1968 there was an attempt to freeze African employment in all the larger industrial areas, with the exception of those in Natal, by limiting the establishment of new factories and the extension of existing ones, where this required additional African labour.[55]

Within urban African townships outside the homelands, restrictions were imposed on the development of education, on the growth of commerce and industry and on residential and welfare institutions, such as homes for the aged. In theory the upgrading of African life was to take place in the homelands.

The uncertainties and unrest which these policies caused have seriously affected economic development. The increasing severity of influx control measures in the fifties led to growing unrest and pass burnings culminating in the Sharpeville crisis in 1960. The consequent outflow of capital led to the introduction of severe exchange restrictions on the withdrawal of capital. Discontent with wages in the early seventies led to a series of strikes which caused the Government to revise its policy in regard to labour

118

legislation affecting Africans. Discontent with educational policy led to intermittent student unrest at black colleges and in 1976 to widespread riots springing from school children's protests in Soweto and Cape Town. These disturbances, which continued in 1977 and early 1978, stimulated external political and economic pressures on South Africa which have increased and are prolonging the only serious economic depression since that of 1929–32. Since 1975 the growth of the real domestic product has failed to keep up with the growth rate of population, consequently real income per head has fallen.[56] Fears concerning the stability of the internal situation in South Africa are undoubtedly a force retarding the inflow of capital and the speed of economic development. They constitute an important factor contributing to the growth of unemployment which affects Africans particularly severely and results from a rising rate of growth in the supply of labour combined with a falling rate of growth of employment opportunities.

In the face of these pressures, both internal and external, the Government has modified its economic policy, particularly with regard to the use of black labour. As early as 1971 it explicitly stated in a White Paper on the decentralisation of industry that it approved the training of Coloured and Indian workers for both skilled and semi-skilled work and of Africans for employment in the homelands and border areas,[57] always subject to the approval of trade unions.

Since that date it has, itself, embarked on the training of black workers for skilled and semi-skilled work in the Railways and Harbours administration and the Post Office. It has also, as mentioned above, established training institutions in African townships outside the homelands and made provision for expenditure on approved 'in-service' training schemes established by employers to be tax-deductible. (Section 11 of Income Tax Act taking effect from 1 April 1974.)

By the end of 1977, 18 of 25 work reservation orders in force had been cancelled and a further two, in the important metal and engineering industries, had been suspended, with the concurrence of the trade unions concerned.

Although reservation of work orders, according to the Government, had never applied to more than 2–3 per cent of the total work force, their withdrawal, together with the official encouragement given to the training of Africans outside the homelands, encouraged employers to train and promote Africans for supervisory and management positions. The actual withdrawal of job reservation orders did not have a large effect on the employment pattern, because in most cases Africans were already working in the reserved jobs in terms of exemptions from the orders or because employers had found it impossible to comply with them.

The apparent change in government policy has encouraged a widespread movement among employers to remove discrimination in employment. In December 1976 the Cape Town Chamber of Commerce issued a 'Manifesto for Change' and asked its members to commit themselves to a policy of 'total and genuine non-discrimination' within the provisions of the law, in regard to the selection, employment, training and promotion of staff, the determination of salaries and wages and fringe benefits.

In December 1977 the Urban Foundation and the South African Consultative Committee on Labour Affairs jointly published a code of employment practice providing, 'within the evolving South African legal framework', for the elimination of discrimination based on race or colour from all aspects of employment and 'the recognition of the basic rights of workers of freedom of association, collective negotiation of agreements or conditions of service, the lawful withholding of labour as a result of industrial disputes and protection against victimisation resulting from the exercise of these rights'. This code has been accepted by 90 per cent of the Republic's organised industry and commerce.[58]

Thus there has been some dismantling of the official apparatus of restrictive controls on the use of African labour outside the homelands and a perceptible loosening of the conventional colour bar with a commitment on the part of many employers to its elimination.

There has also been a reversal of official policy in regard to home ownership in urban African townships outside the homelands. In 1976 home ownership on 30-year leasehold land, which had been discontinued in 1968 was restored. Two years later, in 1978, the Government introduced legislation providing for 99-year leaseholds and made it possible for the first time for building societies to make loans to individuals in these African townships. It steadfastly refused, however, to accede to the African demand for freehold rights to land in these townships.

There has also been a significant relaxation of restrictions on trading in urban African townships.

Following the now famous statement of Mr R. F. Botha at the United Nations[59] that 'we shall do everything in our power to move away from discrimination based on race or colour', the Government has repeatedly stated that it intends to move away from salary discrimination in the government services and that there is nothing to stop other employers raising black wages. The Government has taken some small steps in this direction.

Economic development within the homelands

The need for the economic development of the African areas has been generally recognised. The neglect they have suffered was pointed out by the Native Economic Commission of 1930–2, and has been restated repeatedly. Their economic development is crucial for the success of the National Party Government's policy, political and economic. The Tomlinson Commission, which the Government appointed in 1952 'to report on a comprehensive scheme for the rehabilitation of the Native areas with a view to developing within them a social structure in keeping with the culture of the Native and based on effective socio-economic planning',[60] outlined a strategy for the economic development of the Reserves, the land set aside for Africans by the Native Trust and Land Act of 1936. The Government, however, although alarmed by its population forecasts, turned down three of the Commission's major recommendations, namely the encouragement of industry within the Reserves, the reform of the system of land tenure and the scale of spending required, which in itself was undoubtedly an underestimate. Instead, a policy of encouraging industries in the areas bordering the Reserves, renamed homelands, was embarked on from 1961. This has had only limited success. In 1970 the Permanent Committee for the Location of Industry estimated that during ten and a half years (July 1960 to December 1970) 68 500 industrial jobs were created in border areas, an average of less than 7 000 a year.

Later, the policy originally recommended by the Tomlinson Commission was adopted and has had some success in establishing industrial townships. By 1975, 973 000 Africans were living in towns in the homelands but the largest of these towns, Umlazi in KwaZulu (149 230), Mdantsane in the Ciskei (98 289) and Ga-Rankuwa in Bophuthatswana (73 926), were dormitory townships supplying labour to Durban or to the border industrial areas of East London and Pretoria (Rosslyn).[61] By 1977, excluding Transkei, 19 028 Africans were employed in the homelands in undertakings established by homeland development corporations and 15 843 in undertakings established on an agency basis.[62]

According to calculations of national income by the Bureau for Economic Research of the Department of Bantu Administration and Development (now the Department of Plural Relations and Development) the gross domestic *product*[63] of the nine homelands in the period 1954/5 to 1973/4 was between 2 and 3 per cent of that of the whole of the Republic of South Africa inclusive of the homelands. The contribution to the national *income*[64] of these homelands by migrant workers and commuters who work outside the homelands rose from 52 per cent in 1960 to 73 per cent in 1974, that is to say almost three-quarters of the income of the homelands was earned outside. Of the domestic product generated within the homelands, the contribution of different sectors has changed markedly. The contribution of agriculture, for the most part subsistence farming, fell from 46 per cent in 1959–60 to 24 per cent in 1973–4; that of mining (nearly all in Bophuthatswana and Lebowa) rose from 7 to 14 per cent; manufacturing, electricity, gas, water and construction rose from 7 to 16 per cent; trade and transport remained the same in their percentage contribution; financial insurance, fixed property and business services rose from 3 to 8 per cent; public administration rose from 8 to 11 per cent; education fell from 12 to 11 per cent and health services rose from 4 to 6 per cent.

Domestic *product* per head (that is excluding the earnings of commuters and migrant workers) rose (at current prices) from R28 in 1960–1 to R3. in 1970–1 and R49 in 1973–4, an increase of 75 per cent at prevailing prices but, as over the same period the consumer price index rose by 62 per cent in real terms the increase was very small. *Income* per head, however (that is including the earnings of commuters and remittances of migrants), rose, at current prices, from R57 per head in 1960–1 to R175 in 1973–4, that is by 207 per cent, an average yearly increase of 9 per cent, 6 per cent in real terms.

One noticeable change over this period was the increased share of national income arising from commuters. This was especially important in Bophuthatswana where they contributed 45 per cent of the national income the Ciskei, 29 per cent and KwaZulu, 28 per cent.[65]

After a very slow start the decentralisation policy appears to have had some success. In the years 1973 to 1975, that is before the depression bit deep, of the potential average annual increase in the supply of African labour in the homelands of 100 000, 28 per cent was estimated to have been absorbed in jobs in the homelands, 37 per cent in areas within commuting distance, leaving 35 per cent (35 000 persons per annum) as the potential growth in the number of migrant workers.[66]

African agriculture has made little progress. Maize remains the staple crop and is grown almost entirely for subsistence purposes. Yields per hectare are extremely low, even if one makes allowances for the consumption of green mealies.[67]

Between 1960 and 1972, the yield of maize was on average one fifth or less than that on white-owned farms. Ten per cent or less of agricultural production is marketed and production has not kept pace with the increase in population.[68] Agricultural production is hampered by lack of capital credit and labour, because in present circumstances it remains more profitable to work in other industries. The system of land tenure also creates difficulties for the innovator.[69]

There has been widespread land 'stabilisation' which involves regrouping homesteads, re-allocating individual arable plots, re-allocating and fencing grazing camps, making and planting grass contour ridges to prevent further soil erosion, sinking bore-holes and making small dams. Between 1960 and 1974 the total length of grass strips, contours, weirs and fencing increased from 248 992 km. to 414 509 km.; the number of equipped bore-holes and dams from 3 627 and 3 037 to 8 768 and 4 809 respectively in 1974.[70] Not an enormous achievement when one considers that in 1970 there were 7 000 000 persons in the African homelands and that a relatively small proportion, less than one million, lived in homeland towns.

Since 1972, to improve the productivity of agriculture and make better use of the agricultural potential of the homelands, the Bantu Investment Corporation and the Xhosa Development Corporation (part of which has become the Transkei Development Corporation) have established agricultural divisions to run large-scale commercial farming projects, to grow, process and market industrial crops, to use irrigated land more effectively, to manage and combat the deterioration of farms bought to fulfil the promised acquisition of land in terms of the 1936 Trust and Land Act.[71] Provision has also been made for farming on an agency basis. By 1974–5 there were a few such projects in most of the homelands. A total of 6 294 workers were employed.[72]

In 1975 mining in the homelands gave employment to 78 600 Africans, the great majority of whom (62 500), largely from the Transkei, were employed on platinum mines in Bophuthatswana. Asbestos mines in Lebowa and Bophuthatswana employed 10 000.

African unemployment

The low productivity and lack of employment opportunities in the homelands and adjacent areas, allied with the high rate of population growth, have resulted in a steady increase in the number of Africans available for work in the industrial areas. In spite of the relatively high growth rates which prevailed through most of the period (1946–57 5,1 per cent per annum; 1957–61 3,2 per cent; 1961–9 6,5 per cent; 1969–74 4,7 per cent), the expansion of employment in manufacturing, mining and services and the acute shortages of skilled labour, African unemployment has increased throughout the post-war period. Although there are no comprehensive and reliable official statistics of African unemployment, a number of highly

123

qualified research workers have made valiant and thorough efforts to estimate the extent of African unemployment. All these estimates show a rising trend, even before the downturn in the economy in the latter half of 1974.

Current estimates of African unemployment range from Professor van der Merwe's low of 528 000 (10,9 per cent of the economically active) outside the homelands (924 000 if unemployment and under-employment in the homelands is included)[73] to a high of over two million (Simpkins). Van der Merwe's study shows a rising trend and the 'startling' fact that, over the period 1970–6, 57 per cent of the *increase* in the potential supply of African labour had not found employment nor had 51 per cent of the Coloured. Simpkins gives a *total* of unemployment (all race groups) in 1976 of 2 139 000 (21,4 per cent) and in 1977 of 2 301 000 (22 per cent). The great majority of those unemployed are Africans but a sizcable number and proportion of the potential Coloured labour supply is un- or under-employed. The Theron Commission estimated that in 1973 100 400 Coloured men (nearly 20 per cent of the potential labour supply) were in this category. Simpkins estimates that to stabilise the current unemployment *rate* of 22 per cent of the potential labour supply, a growth rate of 5,3 per cent in the gross national product is required; stabilising the present *number* of unemployed and under-employed requires a growth rate of 6,7 per cent.[74] The attempts to quantify unemployment and under-employment have brought into prominence the gravity of the problem which faces South Africa.

The wage gap

In 1925 the Economic and Wage Commission drew attention to the large gap or differential between white (skilled) and black (unskilled) wages which it characterised as £1 a day and £1 a week respectively. Despite all the changes which have taken place in the economy and the movement of blacks up the industrial ladder, a large differential remains. The differential has not remained constant over time. It varies between industries and between members of different racial groups. It is greatest between white and African, usually followed by that between white and Coloured and least between white and Asian.

Statistics are available over the whole period only for manufacturing industry and mining. These show that in manufacturing industry the differential in average earnings decreased markedly during the Second World War, in the case of Africans from 20 per cent of white earnings in

124

1940–1 to 25 per cent in 1945–6; for Coloured workers from 36 per cent to 42 per cent; for Asians from 30 per cent to 40 per cent. Thereafter the differential widened again and for Africans the relative as well as the absolute differential exceeded that prevailing before the war. Moreover, whereas from 1941 to 1945 African real wages in manufacturing industry rose at an average rate of 10 per cent per annum, to be followed by three years of relative stability, real wages of Africans fell from 1948 to 1953 (at an average rate of 1 per cent per annum), whereas those of white workers rose at an average rate of 2 per cent per annum.[75] Until 1958 white wages rose slowly but at a faster rate than African. As a result, in 1957–8 African average earnings in manufacturing industries and construction averaged 18 per cent of white. An important cause of these changes was that during the war compulsory cost of living allowances were proportionately greater at lower rates of wages and, as part of anti-inflation policy, wage increases at the upper end of the scale were frowned upon. Subsequently, in 1953 cost of living allowances were frozen and the Wage Board was inactive until 1956–7.

The Alexandra and other bus boycotts in 1957 and the Sharpeville crisis focused attention on the wages of urban Africans. The operation of the Wage Board was speeded up and influential employers on the Witwatersrand took the lead in forming a voluntary association (the Bantu Wage and Productivity Association) for the improvement of the wages and productivity of African workers. In 1959–60 and 1960–1 the (real) wages of Africans in manufacturing and construction industries increased by 4,5 and 4,9 per cent as compared to increases of 2 and 1,9 per cent in the wages of white employees.[76] Over the whole decade 1960 to 1970, however, the average wages of white employees rose faster, from R1 942 in 1960 to R3 599 in 1970, an increase of 85 per cent in current prices (54 per cent when adjusted for the 31 per cent increase in the consumer price index); those of Africans from R362 to R624, an increase of 72 per cent (41 per cent in real terms), those of Coloured and Asian workers from R569 and R604 to R853 and R919 respectively, increases of 50 and 52 per cent (19 and 21 per cent in real terms). Consequently the 'gap' or differential between African and white earnings increased once more, African earnings in 1970 being 17,3 per cent of white. Coloured and Asian earnings were then 24 and 25,5 per cent of white.[77]

In the seventies and especially since 1972 the real wages of Africans have increased greatly. The most dramatic increase has occurred in the mining industries where between 1973 and 1975 the wages of blacks (nearly all African) doubled, rising from R288 per annum to R586. The ratio between white and African wages on mines fell dramatically from 20:1 in 1971 to 7:1 in 1977.[78] In 1977 average annual African mine wages were R1 275 (current Rand).[79] This increase was made possible by the rise in the prices of gold and other minerals.

In manufacturing industry between 1970 and 1977 the real earnings of Africans rose from R572 per annum to R872, an average rate of 7 per cent per annum.[80] In 1977, African annual earnings were R1 695 (current Rand), 23 per cent of white earnings.[81]

In the period 1970 to 1976 in all sectors excluding agriculture, the average real earnings of Africans rose at a faster rate than those of any other racial group, the rate of increase having been: 1970–1 3 per cent; 1971–2 4,5; 1972–3 7,4; 1973–4 11,5; 1974–5 11,7; 1975–6 5,1. Over this period the ratio of average white to average African wages fell from 6,8 to 4,7.[82]

Sample estimates indicate that from 1970 to 1976, excluding farm workers and professional services, the real earnings of Africans increased 51,3 per cent, of Asians 29,4 per cent, of Coloureds 15,7 per cent and of whites 3,8 per cent. Black spending power is now a considerable force in the economy, so much so that a number of chains of retailers have established parallel chains directed particularly to appeal to black customers.

There can be little doubt that the wave of strikes in 1973 which, although technically illegal, did not lead to prosecution of the strikers, together with the focus of foreign attention on wages and conditions of employment in South Africa, were important factors leading to the wage increases.

The Government reacted to the strikes by amending the Bantu Labour (Settlement of Disputes) Act, renamed the Bantu Labour Relations Regulation Act, to increase the size of works committees. Provision was also made for liaison committees of an equal number of workers' and employers' representatives. The prohibition of strikes by Africans was also repealed (except for those employed by local authorities and those in essential services), provided prescribed procedures were followed, including a thirty-day cooling-off period. These conditions correspond to provisions applying to workers of other racial groups in terms of the Industrial Conciliation Act.

Since 1973 there has been a big increase in the number of works and liaison committees, the number of the former rising from 18 at the time of the 1973 strikes to 207 in 1974 and 305 in 1977. The number of liaison committees, introduced in 1973, rose to 2 552 in 1977.[83]

There can be little doubt that employers in South Africa, as a result of both internal and external pressures, are committed to a policy of upgrading Coloured, Asian and African labour and to a policy of non-discrimination 'within the law'. In 1976 employers of differing political outlook, including some of South Africa's most prominent and influential entrepreneurs, organised a multiracial conference at which it was resolved to establish the Urban Foundation, a non-profit association, pledged to raise R25 million over five years in order to improve the quality of life of the urban African population.

It appears likely, too, that the Government will amend industrial legislation in such a way as to eliminate overt racial discrimination. It is unlikely that attempts to control the movements of Africans into towns will be abandoned. The creation of homelands, whether they have opted for political independence or not, has not and is not likely to fragment the South African economy into economically independent sectors. Despite the growth of manufacturing in a few centres in the now politically independent Transkei and Bophuthatswana, their economies remain essentially dependent on the export of labour. Their economic development is linked to and dependent upon that of the Republic, even though they may be able to attract some capital and technical skills from abroad.

The problems facing the Republic by the threat to the supply of capital from abroad and by the possibility of economic sanctions are very serious. For, although South Africa may in the short run be able to withstand such eventualities and her exports, particularly of gold and other minerals, could probably continue, short of a blockade, she needs foreign capital to maintain a rate of growth sufficient to absorb her rapidly increasing population. Moreover, she needs imports of technology and modern machinery – for example, the now widely used computer.

Despite its great economic progress, modern industries, affluent cities and prosperous farms, South Africa remains a very mixed economy with great wealth side by side with poverty. Apart from the African areas where economic modernisation has made little impact on subsistence-farming practices, the economy is essentially a modern industrial one. But the inequality in the distribution of income, although recently a little diminished, and the general linkage between income and racial group, create very real problems in extending on a non-discriminatory basis the social services expected of such a state.

1. *Official Year Book of the Union of South Africa*, No. 12. 1929–1930 p. 871; *South African Statistics* 1976, 1.23.

2. *The Poor White Problem in South Africa*, Carnegie Commission, vol. 1, vii. Pro Ecclesia-Drukkery (Stellenbosch, 1932).
3. Government Notice R1112, *Government Gazette* No. 6036, 2 June 1978.
4. *Financial Mail*, 2 June 1978, p. 697.
5. *S.A. Statistics*, 1978, 7.4.
6. *Union Year Book*, No. 12, 1928–9, p. 523.
7. *Statistics for Fifty Years*, G-6; *S.A. Statistics* 1968 H36, 1976, 7.4.
8. *Union Statistics for Fifty Years*, 1910–1960, L4.
9. *Statistics for Fifty Years*, G–6.
10. H. M. Robertson, 'The War and the South African Economy', *South African Journal of Economics*, vol. 22, No. 1 (March 1954), pp. 101–2.
11. *Year Book No. 12*, 1929–30, p. 522.
12. *Manpower Survey* No. 12, 1977.
13. *S.A. Statistics*, 1976, 7.9.
14. *Statistics for Fifty Years*, G–8.
15. *South Africa 1974*, pp. 533–4.
16. *Barlow Rand Limited Annual Financial Statement*, 30 September 1977, pp. 10–12.
17. *Report of the Commission of Inquiry into the Regulation of Monopolistic Conditions Act*, 1955, R.P. 64/1977, pp. 32–41.
18. *Year Book No. 12*, 1929–30, p. 468; *Mining Statistics*, 1977, Tables 1, 6.
19. *Financial Mail*, 23 June 1978, p. 988.
20. F. Wilson, *Labour in the South African Gold Mines*, 1911–69 (Cambridge Univ. Press, 1972), p. 43.
21. *Survey of Race Relations*, 1977, p. 261.
22. *S.A. Statistics*, 1976, 16.5–9; *Mining Statistics*, 1977, Table 1.
23. *Union Year Book*, No. 12, 1929–30, p. 83; *S.A. Statistics*, 1978, 7.19.
24. *Cape Times*, 25 February 1978.
25. *S.A. Statistics*, 1976, 14.3.
26. *South Africa: an appraisal*, Nedbank Group, 1977, p. 33.
27. *Ibid.*, p. 35.
28. *South African Reserve Bank Quarterly Bulletin*, March 1978, S–88.
29. A. B. Dickman, 'The Development of the Financial System', *S.A. Journal of Economics*, vol. 42, no. 3 (September, 1974) p. 33.
30. *S.A.: an appraisal*, pp. 97, 98.
31. *S.A. Reserve Bank Quarterly Bulletin*, March 1978, p. 14.
32. A. D. Wassenaar, *Assault on Private Enterprise*, 1977, pp. 72, 73.
33. *Agricultural Census* No. 48, 1975, p. 50.
34. J. Nattrass, 'Migration flows in and out of capitalist agriculture' in *Farm Labour in South Africa*, ed. Francis Wilson, Alida Kooy and Delia Hendrie, p. 53.
35. *S.A.: an appraisal*, p. 199.
36. *Commission of Enquiry into Export Trade of South Africa*, R.P. 69/72, p.35.
37. *Union Year Book*, No. 21, 1940, p. 609.
38. *Union Year Book*, No. 26, 1950, p. 686.
39. *S.A.: an appraisal*, Table 96.
40. D. Hobart Houghton, *The South African Economy*, 3rd ed., 1973, p. 181.
41. *S.A. Reserve Bank Quarterly Bulletin*, March 1978, p. 14.

42. S.A. Reserve Bank, *The Foreign Liabilities and Assets of the Union of South Africa, 1956–59; Census of Foreign Transactions,* 31 December 1973; *Quarterly Bulletin,* March 1978, S–64, 65. Figures for Great Britain in 1973 and 1976 from Arnt Spandau, *Economic Boycott against South Africa* (Labour Research Programme, University of the Witwatersrand Report No. 17 (May 1978) Table 22).

43. A. B. Dickman, 'The Development of the Financial System', *S.A. Journal of Economics,* vol. 42, no. 3 (September 1974), p. 278.

44. S.A. Reserve Bank, *Selected capital market and government finance statistics 1946–1970; Quarterly Bulletin,* September, 1978 S-35, 37, 41. Figures for 31 December.

45. *Statistics for Fifty Years,* L–2,3.

46. *S.A. Statistics 1976,* 8.18.

47. S. Herbert Frankel and H. Herzveld, 'An Analysis of the Growth of the National Income in the period of Prosperity before the War', *S.A. Journal of Economics,* vol. 12, no. 2 (June 1944), pp. 126–34.

48. The Social and Economic Planning Council was appointed in 1942. Its reports included Report of the Social Security Committee and Report No. 2, *Social Services and the National Income,* U.G. 14/1944; No. 7, *Taxation and Fiscal Policy,* U.G. 48/1945; No. 9, *The Native Reserves and their Place in the Economy of the Union,* U.G. 32/1944.

49. S. T. van der Horst, 'Labour policy in South Africa (1948–76): A Sketch', in *Public Policy and the South African Economy,* ed. M. L. Truu (O.U.P., 1976).

50. *Survey of Race Relations,* 1955–56, p. 161.

51. *Survey of Race Relations,* 1956–57, p. 151.

52. *Assembly Hansard* 1 (27 January 1959), col. 55–6 cited *Survey of Race Relations,* 1958–59, p. 207.

53. *Hansard* 1, 1964, col. 239.

54. *Cape Times,* 1 June 1978.

55. This was in terms of the Physical, Planning and Utilisation of Resources Act, No. 88 of 1967, now the Environment Planning Act.

56. *Statistical/Economic Review Budget* 1979–80.

57. *White Paper on Decentralisation of Industry,* 1971.

58. *The Urban Foundation,* Information Sheet No. 3, January 1978.

59. Statement by Ambassador R. F. Botha, then Permanent Representative of South Africa to the United Nations, in the Security Council on 24 October 1974. Reproduced in *Southern Africa Record* No. 1, March 1975 (The South African Institute of International Affairs), p. 21.

60. *U.G. 61,* 1955, xviii.

61. Statistics from *Black Development in South Africa,* Benbo 1976, Tables B, 10, pp. 1–11.

62. *Hansard* 5, 1978, col. 299.

63. *Gross domestic product* is the value of goods and services *produced within* the area.

64. *National income* is domestic product plus the earnings of factors of production (in the case of the homelands almost entirely labour) *outside* the area.

65. *Black Development, op. cit.,* pp. 67–9.

66. *Ibid.*

129

67. See Merle Lipton, 'South Africa: two agricultures?' in *Farm Labour in South Africa*, ed. F. Wilson, F. A. Kooy, D. Hendrie, p. 73.
68. *Black Development, op. cit.*, p. 82.
69. G. L. Rutman, 'The Transkei: An Experiment in Economic Separation', *S.A. Journal of Economics*, vol. 36, No. 1 (March 1968); G. Westcott, 'Obstacles to the Development of Transkei Agriculture', Southern African Labour and Development Conference, September 1976, pp. 28–33.
70. Figures from *Black Development in South Africa, op. cit.*, p. 34.
71. *Ibid.*, p. 84.
72. *Ibid.*, III, Table B.9.5.
73. P. J. van der Merwe, 'Unemployment Statistics'; paper presented at Workshop on Unemployment and Labour Reallocation, Development Studies Research Group, Department of Economics, University of Natal, Pietermaritzburg (March 1977), p. 52.
74. C. Simpkins and D. Clarke, 'Structural Unemployment in Southern Africa, *Development Studies*, Series 1, University of Natal Press (1978) 34, 40; N. Bromberger, 'Unemployment in South Africa: A Survey of Research', *Social Dynamics*, University of Cape Town, vol. 4, No. 1 (June 1978); *Verslag van die Kommissie van Ondersoek na Aangeleenthede Rakende die Kleurlingbevolkingsgroep*, RP 38/1976, 84.
75. W. F. J. Steenkamp, 'Bantu Wages in South Africa', *S.A. Journal of Economics*, vol. 30, no. 2 (June 1962) p. 96.
76. *Ibid.*
77. *S.A. Statistics*, 1976, 7.9.
78. *S.A.: an appraisal*, pp. 67–68.
79. *Survey of Race Relations*, 1977, p. 261.
80. *S.A.: an appraisal*, p. 75.
81. *Survey of Race Relations*, 1977, p. 234.
82. *Afrikaanse Handelsinstituut*. Cited *Survey of Race Relations*, 1977, p. 206.
83. *Hansard 4*, 1977, col. 660. Cited *Survey of Race Relations*, 1977, p. 302.

6 Urbanisation in South Africa: 1929—1979

DAVID WELSH

Like all developing countries South Africa has undergone a massive process of urbanisation. In 1979 some 50 per cent of the total population live in towns and other urban areas; by the year 2000, according to various projections, nearly 80 per cent will be urbanised. Most of the new migrants to the cities and towns will be Africans.

This essay is concerned with a fifty-year span, from 1929 to 1979, that takes in a major part of some of the crucial social and economic processes that have shaped and will continue to shape modern South Africa. It is in this period that secondary industry developed on a large scale, gaining momentum in the war years of 1939–45 that succeeded the depression of the early 1930s. It was also the time when the movement of rural people to the cities and towns assumed unprecedented and massive proportions, and created social, political and economic issues that are still very much with contemporary South Africa. It is no over-simple judgment to remark that the dynamics and thrust of South Africa's development have exceeded the capacity and will of its present political leaders to accommodate to and cope with the problems that have arisen.

In dealing with urbanisation in South Africa certain themes stand out, and, apart from the general account, they will be emphasised in what follows. The major theme is the racial and ethnic diversity of the peoples who moved off the land and sought to establish new lives for themselves in the towns. A great deal of recent scholarship in America has demonstrated that the assumption that the city was to be a 'melting pot' of immigrants of varying origins is unfounded;[1] so it is in South Africa as well, where the social and cultural distances separating urban communities have mostly been wider than in the typical American case involving the interaction of white ethnic groups. For all of the period with which I am concerned segregation, of one kind or another, has been the official policy of the

131

State, and one of its major concerns has been to ensure the preservation of the towns as places of undisputed white hegemony. As the Transvaal Local Government Commission, better known as the Stallard Commission, put it frankly in 1922, 'it should be a recognised principle of government that natives – men, women and children – should only be permitted within municipal areas in so far and for so long as their presence is demanded by the wants of the white population'.[2]

The Stallard Commission's views on the status of urban Africans have remained the basis of official policy up to the present day, although in recent times there have been indirect affirmations of the sociological reality that there is a substantial number of Africans who are not 'temporary sojourners' (the official designation), but rooted townspeople, often with only limited ties with rural communities.

This official approach to African urbanisation has profound ramifications throughout urban communities, and it points to a further major theme: the endeavour to halt, thwart, or limit the strong drive by Africans living in deteriorating rural areas and on white-owned farms to move to the towns where there are better economic and educational opportunities. The present urban African population, which now numbers over four million, has grown in spite of these efforts to curb it.

For most rural people coming from decaying and impoverished communities the transition to urban life is a painful process, often marked by fantasies about a future return to the countryside. No less than other groups did Africans experience these pains, but for them the process was greatly exacerbated by the impact of official policies that not only bound them in a maze of bureaucratic regulations but also served to underline to them their pariah status in the cities and towns of the white people.

There would be substantial agreement among commentators of varying political persuasions that the status of urban Africans is the major unresolved issue in modern South Africa. Their exclusion from full membership in the urban communities of which they are part (and in most areas of South Africa the numerically preponderant part) is in my judgment the greatest source of conflict. For the society as a whole it becomes difficult to talk of progress as a countervailing trend if the society remains riven by an exclusion of so great a magnitude.

A further theme in the urbanisation of South Africa is the development of local government. Especially in the areas of English settlement sturdy traditions of local autonomy and initiative were transplanted from the English tradition; but the imperatives of co-ordination and national planning, particularly in the vast field affected by considerations of race relations, have stunted this autonomy, in many spheres reducing local authorities to being mere creatures of the all-powerful central government.

The term 'modernisation' has been criticised by a number of scholars for its ambiguities and its hidden value assumptions,[3] but it remains a useful catch-all concept for the body of changes that fundamentally affect a society in the process of development. The period 1929 to 1979 was one of modernisation for South Africa, during which time its economic centre of gravity shifted decisively away from agriculture, its urbanisation was greatly and irrevocably increased, and the major focus of political conflict became the town.

The dimensions of urbanisation can be gauged from the following table:

URBAN POPULATIONS AS PERCENTAGES OF THE TOTAL POPULATION

	1921	1936	1946	1951	1960	1970
Whites	55,8	65,2	74,5	78,4	83,6	86,8
Africans	12,5	17,3	23,7	27,2	31,8	33,1
Coloured	45,8	53,9	60,9	64,7	68,3	74,0
Indians	30,9	66,3	71,3	77,5	83,2	86,8
	25,1	31,4	38,4	42,6	47,0	47,9

It has been emphasised that with the large-scale movement of people to towns the site of most conflict in the society became the urban environment. It was here, for example, that the mass-based African political movements had their major following; it was in urban factories, mines and other enterprises that class issues were fought over. Even in white politics, with its built-in bias in favour of the rural areas, it can be seen that the urban areas dominate. Historically, the National Party was primarily a rurally based party, representing Afrikaner farming and other rural interests. By the 1970s the Nationalists had become a predominantly urban party in terms of the seats they held, although of course they dominated every rural area (with limited exceptions in Natal) as well.[4]

Historically, the towns of South Africa were, with few exceptions, the political, economic and cultural strongholds of English-speaking whites. As a demographic phenomenon urbanisation among the English-speakers has been of limited significance because they were the most highly urbanised of all the South African groups, and to a large extent they constituted the urban 'establishment' of the cities and towns. Echoes of the

133

American situation, of old-established Yankee or Wasp (White, Anglo-Saxon, Protestant) resentment against newcomers to the towns, have frequently been heard in South Africa as well. In a number of cases the increase in Afrikaner urban residents has effectively taken control of local government out of English hands or reduced very substantially the influence that they formerly enjoyed.

People usually move to the towns when their traditional rural life-styles become economically insupportable. Urbanisation is one aspect, admittedly the key one, of a process of social change that involves a new occupation, an adaptation to different social mores and different residential patterns. From each of these changes profound implications flow for the individuals and families caught up in the process. Afrikaner literature is filled with fictional but true-to-life accounts of the transition, with the town being regarded as the destroyer of rural virtues and the seat of sin. From early in this century Afrikaner leaders have inveighed against the dangers of urban life, and have deplored the haemorrhaging of platteland communities. An elaborate series of myths was invented to portray the rural past as a 'golden age' of the Afrikaner people, glorifying the farming way of life and its stability and conservatism.[5]

Even in the face of considerable poverty among rural whites, and the discovery by the Carnegie Commission in 1932 that 300 000 whites were 'very poor', many leaders hoped that the dislocation was temporary and that displaced rural people could be repatriated from the towns and resettled on the platteland. If any one slogan (and it was little more than a slogan) dominated thinking on the topic of the depopulation by whites of the rural areas it was 'Back to the land!'. But such a call was purely chimerical: very few in fact were ever resettled on the land, and the white exodus from the land has continued so that by 1979 there are probably no more than 75 000 white farmers in South Africa and perhaps 90 per cent of Afrikaners are urban. (The latter figure must be an estimate because the census no longer distinguishes between the white ethnic groups.)

For any student of Afrikaner nationalism urbanisation is a major theme. When it is recalled that in 1906 only six per cent of all Afrikaners were urban and the present figure is compared, the magnitude of the demographic revolution is apparent. The break-up of rural Afrikaner communities and the diversification of Afrikaner society presented challenges to those Afrikaner leaders who were committed to preserving the unity of Afrikaners as an ethnic group and to attaining and maintaining their political hegemony. For them, the prime danger of urbanisation was its denationalising effect, by which was meant that the English-dominated town would have a strongly acculturative impact on the poor, unskilled (in urban terms, at least) and vulnerable Afrikaner newcomer. The leakage of Afrikaners through this process would so weaken Afrikaner nationalism that its prospects of assuming control of the political system would be seriously diminished.

The strategy of Afrikaner nationalism, in the face of this assumed threat, was to seek to encapsulate Afrikaners even in the urban environment in which they were forced to interact with non-Afrikaners, both black and white. Encapsulation meant essentially creating environments that were supportive of and protective to Afrikaners in the various spheres of life. A notable example of this process is provided by the role of the three Dutch Reformed Churches in reaching into the urban areas, establishing congregations for the newly urbanised flock and creating congenial environments for Afrikaners. The largest of the churches, the Nederduitse Gereformeerde Kerk, had been long concerned with the problem of poor whiteism; its concern continued into the twentieth century and embraced also the problems of the urban Afrikaner.

As an organised force possessing considerable political resources, Afrikaner nationalism set out to 'conquer the cities'. From the 1930s onward, and especially when the Broederbond focused its attention on urban problems, the task was tackled with formidable organisational zeal in all the spheres in which Afrikaners were active.[6]

By the 1940s poor whiteism had been substantially eliminated – ironically, by an economic boom occasioned by South Africa's participation in the war, to which Afrikaner nationalists were bitterly opposed. The cries of 'back to the land' grew fainter in the face of palpable evidence that thousands of Afrikaners were adjusting to urban life, were becoming moderately prosperous and showed little or no inclination to return to the vagaries of rural life and its poverty.

If the adjustment of whites to town life was facilitated by their possession of political power and the active concern on their behalf of powerful pressure groups, the lot of black migrants to the towns was greatly exacerbated by their powerlessness and extreme vulnerability to egregious forms of exploitation at the hands of employers, officials and other agents of white authority.

In his study of local government in Johannesburg, published in 1938, John P. R. Maud pointed out the underlying structural features that rendered Africans powerless:

There are few occasions in history when a privileged section of any community has succeeded even in knowing what are the needs and just demands of the unprivileged, still less in satisfying them. Certainly it would be difficult to name a city in any part of the world in which the governing class has either known or done what justice demanded for the poorer or more needy sections of the community, so long as those sections have had no effective say in the government of the city. Where such a miracle has happened, it has usually been brought about by the central government insisting, in the interests of the country as a whole, that slum conditions, and the danger to public health which they represent, should not be allowed to continue. It is hardly surprising, therefore, if the white enfranchised section of Johannesburg, unassisted by any large measure of encouragement from the central government, has not succeeded altogether in understanding or doing justice to the needs of the unenfranchised. The very breadth of the franchise given to Europeans has made it harder for the council. For example, on various occasions when the council has planned the establishment of a native or coloured location in some quarter of the area, the white constituents of councillors representing that area have raised such a storm of protest that the plan has been dropped. Nor has the task of slum-clearance been made easier for the council by the fact that European owners of slum property lucratively overcrowded with native tenants, have had political power.

At the time when these words were written local authorities still had a great deal of power over urban African affairs, even if they were chronically short of funds for expenditure on housing, welfare and amenities for Africans. Yet the situation described by Maud was a microcosm of the power relationship between white and black in the society as a whole.

The African masses that surged to the towns came primarily in search of economic opportunity. In the nineteenth century land alienation by whites, the imposition of taxes and other instruments had been applied to traditional African societies to prize Africans out to work on farms, mines and other enterprises. Initially most of the people who came out were migrants, intending to work for a particular period and then return to their rural homes. But gradually in all of the major urban centres of South Africa a core of urban-rooted Africans developed, whose descendants today are in no sense 'tribal' or 'temporary'. But, given the tenet of official policy, they were anomalies who ought not to exist, in spite of mounting evidence from the 1920s and even earlier of their permanence.

In one of the early sociological studies of urban Africans carried out in the late 1930s Ray E. Phillips gives a striking account of Witwatersrand

136

Africans' grievances. They complained of low wages; the colour-bar in industry; high taxation; the inability to buy land in urban locations for building purposes; school fees; lack of business facilities; pass laws; pick-up vans; differential treatment in the courts; lack of direct representation on the municipal councils; insanitary slums and lack of knowledge of hygiene in the home; lack of school facilities for children and of education along business and technical lines; immorality in locations; evil practices of other tribes; illicit liquor buying and selling; the drift away from the churches and the breakdown of parental discipline. Commenting on this long list, Phillips wrote:

> For the average African worker there is little prospect for advancement or promotion in his work. His is a 'blind alley' or 'dead end' job which is never secure in the face of Governmental insistence on the employ-ment of Europeans by employers. Outside of three Townships in Johannesburg, and Alexandria, the African householder on the Reef has no security of land tenure. He is a renter on a thirty-day lease. His house is not his, consequently he generally takes little pride in it. His low wage means increasing debt, the entrance into service of his wife and older children, or embarking upon illegal ventures for recouping himself.[8]

The views thus recorded, and the many comparable ones to be found in other sources, form a convenient benchmark to enable an informed judg-ment to be made as to whether by 1979 progress has in fact been made. It may be noted here, however, that with one or two exceptions the recitation of African grievances has a curiously contemporary ring about it. South Africa is notable for its continuities in questions of race policy, and ac-cordingly the response of the people affected will also show continuity.

Only a few years before 1929 the relative absence of any systematic and co-ordinated structure for urban African administration had been tackled by national legislation in the form of the Natives (Urban Areas) Act of 1923.[9] This Act sought to require municipalities to take appropriate mea-sures for the housing, welfare and administration of the African popula-tions within their areas of jurisdiction. Provision was also made to enable local authorities who requested it to restrict the right of Africans to enter or remain in an urban area. It was also laid down that the finances relating to African affairs be kept in a separate Native Revenue Account and that the officials responsible for enforcing the law and regulations in terms of it be licensed by the central government's Department of Native Affairs.

The latter provision was intended as a measure of protection for Africans against unqualified or unscrupulous local authority officials.

It was this Act that laid down the framework within which urban African administration was to develop. There can be little doubt that it marked an improvement over the *laissez-faire* conditions prior to 1923, in which white South Africa had had to be shocked into action by revelations of appalling health and housing conditions in the slums in the towns themselves and in locations adjacent to white areas. The legislation embodied segregationist principles, notably in its requirement that Africans be accommodated in segregated areas, and in the crucial area of financing. Moreover, the legislation implied (and administrative practice confirmed) that urban Africans were to be the objects of control, rather than full partners with whites in the municipal enterprise. Provision was made for the ratification (where they already existed) or creation of urban advisory boards that would enable the local authority to consult with African opinion on municipal matters of concern to them, but the system was a failure as the boards were powerless, their advice was often disregarded, and people became disillusioned with them, as was reflected in the near-universal low-percentage polls in elections.

If the underlying premise of racial policy was that urban Africans were temporary sojourners, little else could have been expected from the provisions of the Act, which attempted to straddle the gulf between ideology and social reality. Through the 1930s lip-service continued to be paid to the premise and to the notion that Africans were to 'develop along their own lines'. It was only in the 1940s that real signs became apparent that the premise was being doubted. The most notable of these was Prime Minister Smuts's famous speech to the Institute of Race Relations in Cape Town where he declared of African urbanisation: 'Segregation has tried to stop it. It has, however, not stopped it in the least. The process has been accelerated. You might as well try to sweep the ocean back with a broom.'[10] Similar testimony to the permanence of an urban African population was offered by the Smit Committee in 1942[11] and the Social and Economic Planning Council in 1946[12], but the major statement of the case for a change of policy was made in 1948 by the Native Laws Commission under the chairmanship of Judge H. A. Fagan.[13]

The Fagan Commission concluded that 'the idea of total segregation is utterly impracticable; secondly, that the movement from the country has a background of economic necessity – that it may, so one hopes, be guided and regulated, and may perhaps also be limited, but that it cannot be stopped or be turned in the opposite direction; and thirdly that in our urban areas there are not only Native migrant labourers, but there is also a settled, permanent Native population.' The truth was, as the Commission underlined, that 'back to the land' solutions were as chimerical for urban Africans as they had proved to be in the case of urban Afrikaners.[14]

The fate of the Fagan Commission's recommendations was their repudiation by the newly elected Nationalist Government in 1948. The Stallard Commission's conclusions were not to be dislodged from their status as official policy and white farmers were to benefit from the renewed impetus to limit the entry of Africans into urban areas, thus forcing them more and more to seek work on farms and mines to which influx control measures did not apply.

This policy has not fundamentally changed, even if the terms in which the ideology is presented have been modified. Urban blacks remain, in the theory of separate development, people who are not entitled as of right to expect full citizenship as the equals of whites in the urban communities of white-ruled South Africa: their citizenship rights are to be exercised in one of the homelands, and the policy is to ensure that all Africans become homeland citizens. We may note here that despite these policy statements, certain indirect affirmations of the Government's inability to ignore the claims of urban Africans for the security that should accompany sociological town-rootedness have been made in recent years.

The major instrument for restricting the movement of Africans to the urban areas, and inhibiting (but not preventing) the growth of fully urbanised communities, has been the pass laws, or in its modern designation, influx control. Passes have a long history in South Africa: they have provided a means of white control over black movements, a means of identification, a method of directing labour to particular categories of employers and, so some have argued, a source of revenue to the State. A detailed history of the pass laws, even confined to the period under consideration, is not possible in the allotted space, and accordingly I can note only the briefest of salient details. Between 1923 and 1952 the application of influx control was optional for local authorities, and in some cases, notably the city of Port Elizabeth, no restrictions were applied. By comparison with the severity of later legislation, the pass laws in this earlier period were relatively lax, although they were a source of bitter grievance to Africans. Between 1942 and 1946 the operation of the pass laws was suspended in all the major towns of South Africa, in response partly to the economy's boom conditions and the need for labour and partly to remove an immense source of irritation from Africans whose loyalty was needed in the tense circumstances of the war years.

In 1952 the first of a series of drastic amendments to the Natives (Urban Areas) Act was passed, and in succeeding years right up to the present, highly restrictive controls apply to both African men and women. A brief summary of the existing legislation covering influx control gives only a bare indication of the immense scope of the bureaucratic maze that envelops Africans seeking employment or residence in prescribed urban areas. The law provides that Africans may not be in an urban area for longer than 72 hours unless they can prove qualifications under one of the following headings: (1) continuous residence since birth in the particular area; (2) continuous employment for the same employer for ten years, or lawful residence in the area for fifteen years, without incurring criminal convictions carrying fines exceeding R100 or imprisonment exceeding six months; (3) the wife, unmarried daughter or son under 16 years of age of a person qualified under (1) or (2); and (4) permission of the labour bureau to be within the area.

A few modifications in the application of the pass laws have been made (such as the reference of arrested persons to aid centres), but their essential force and rigour remain undiminished. Their effects in exacerbating African opinion and in disrupting African family life are of incalculable magnitude.[15] During 1976 a total of 216 112 males and 33 918 females were arrested for pass-law offences throughout the country, and over 9 000 persons were repatriated from the major metropolitan areas to homelands.[16]

It would be difficult to estimate how many persons are prevented from entering urban areas by the operation of influx controls. Some reports have suggested that the number is considerable, but against this it must be noted that large numbers of people come to the towns illegally, ignoring the provisions of the law and reckoning that the cost of the periodic conviction is less than the economic gain to be derived from a better chance of employment. The extent of illegal entry can only be estimated, and it varies from area to area. In greater Cape Town, for example, where influx controls are enforced with peculiar severity in view of the Government's insistence that the Western Cape be regarded as a Coloured labour preference area, the number of 'illegals' probably equals the number of 'legals'. In Soweto, the largest African urban area in the country, the discrepancy between the official figure for the population, of 657 860 in 1977, and the more realistic unofficial estimate is possibly of the magnitude of half a million or even more. Comparable discrepancies occur in the other urban centres of South Africa, representing a situation that call into question the efficacy of the entire influx-control situation.

Equally striking is the immense cost of operating the pass-law system. In a detailed effort to compute the actual figure for a particular year (1974), Professor Michael Savage arrived at the annual sum of over R112 m. which he emphasised was a conservative estimate and could be regarded as only some fraction of the total sum involved in running the pass-law system.[17]

The obverse of the refusal to recognise fully the implications of permanent African communities in urban areas in the white-controlled sectors of South Africa has perpetuated the migrant labour system, which involves in the region of two million Africans from South Africa and neighbouring countries in southern Africa. This system has a long history in South African labour experience, and it was first utilised on a large scale by the mining industry, in which it survives despite the efforts of more enlightened mining houses to reduce its scope. In the 1950s, during the debate on the Tomlinson Commission Report, it became clear that the Nationalists were intent on extending migrant labour on the pattern of the mining industry. Their plan crystallised into the notion of the contract worker, who ideally was to be male and would be recruited from the homelands through official labour bureaux for periods not exceeding one year, after which he would be required to return to his homeland.

To a very limited extent the need for migrant labour has been mitigated by government attempts to locate industry near the borders of homelands, a policy that was expressed by the enactment in 1967 of the Physical Planning and Utilization of Resources Act which sought to control the establishment of new factories and the expansion of existing factories in urban areas if they required additional African workers.

Where possible, townships for Africans were located in homelands close to their places of employment. Notable examples of the latter phenomenon are Umlazi and Kwa Mashu (near Durban), Mdantsane (near East London), and Ga-Rankuwa (near Pretoria). Official policy lays down that if a white town is close to a homeland the black workers must commute to and from the homeland on a daily basis. It has been claimed that workers can travel up to 120 km (1,5 hrs) in one direction per day before their productivity is adversely affected.[18] In recent years various suggestions have been made to establish rapid transit systems for daily and weekend African commuters.[19] Less consideration, it would appear, has been devoted to the impact which these lengthy travel times make on the home life of the Africans involved.

The administrative responsibility for urban Africans was, for much of the period under review, a matter of some contention between local authorities and the central government. Both had been given responsibility in terms of the South Africa Act of 1909 and, as was indicated, in terms of the legislation of 1923 an attempt was made to strike a balance between the claims of the local authorities for autonomy and the requirement of overall supervision by the central government in the interests of ensuring that official policy was carried out. Collectively, the local authorities could mobilise a good deal of influence to oppose the introduction of legislation or drag their feet over its implementation. In 1937, for example, friction arose when the Fusion Government armed itself with powers to require local authorities to carry out biennial censuses of African populations under their control to determine if numbers were surplus to labour requirements. At a specially convened meeting in Pretoria in September 1937 Smuts, as acting Minister of Native Affairs, carefully explained to the municipal representatives why his Government had assumed these powers:

> Where the situation is getting out of hand, where the Natives are accumulating in the locations far beyond the urban requirements, the Government takes power to itself to step in and to act for itself to impose restrictions on the ingress into towns. That is one of the most important provisions in this Act. You can understand, gentlemen, that no Government likes to interfere with the job which in the first instance is that of the Municipalities, and as long as we are satisfied that you are reasonably doing your best we are not going to interfere. We do not want to make trouble for ourselves and we would be quite prepared to leave the matter in your hands, and I hope that as a result of this new power which the Government has taken but does not want to use if it can avoid it, the towns will develop a sense of responsibility to themselves and to the country and deal with this question themselves; make use of the power which they have to restrict ingress and so make it unnecessary for the Government to intervene.[20]

In response to Smuts's velvet glove there was some grumbling, allegations that 'we have to carry out impossible laws made by the Government', but overall acquiescence.

Tensions between some of the municipalities and the central government increased dramatically in the 1950s as the Nationalists' blueprint for apartheid unfolded and local authorities were required to co-operate in its implementation, often against their will. In terms of official policy, for example, Africans as 'temporary sojourners' could not be allowed to own urban land in freehold and pressures were exerted upon a reluctant Johannesburg Municipality to abolish its African freehold areas. When this pressure failed to produce results the Government forced the issue by enacting in 1954 the Natives' Resettlement Act which abolished the freehold 'Western Areas' of Sophiatown, Martindale and Newclare, and created two new non-freehold townships, Meadowlands and Diepkloof, which were to be controlled by a Resettlement Board established by the Government.

Similarly the enactment of the Group Areas Act of 1950, which aimed at the racial zoning of every town and village in the country, was, in one dimension, a massive usurpation of local authorities' powers in the interests of having the racial configuration of towns conform to an ideological blueprint.

In other respects local authority powers in the area of African administration declined or were increasingly circumscribed. As the severity of influx-control laws increased, so the discretionary powers of local authorities decreased until they became, in this sphere at least, mere creatures of the central government.

The conclusion of this process was the enactment in 1971 of the Bantu Affairs Administration Act in terms of which the Minister of Bantu Administration and Development could create Bantu Affairs Administration Boards over any designated area outside the homelands. These areas might include one or more local authorities, and provision was made for consultation with them and for their representation on the boards. Despite these provisions the legislation represented the assumption of total control of urban African administration by the central government. Moreover, it has been the practice that only whites may serve as members of the boards even though this is not stipulated in the legislation. By the end of 1978, 22 boards had been established and their gridlike controls covered the entire country outside the homelands. This number is being reduced to 14 in 1979.

The boards are required to operate their finances on a self-balancing basis, i.e. their expenditure must balance their revenue garnered by the boards, which comes mostly from rents, profits on the sale of liquor and labour bureaux fees. The self-balancing principle is a continuation of an old local authority tradition, whereby Native Revenue Accounts were also made to be self-balancing. In 1938 a survey showed that:

> the vast majority of Urban Local Authorities . . . attempt to arrange the services which they perform for the benefit of the Natives within their area in such a manner that (a) in no case is there a serious deficit on the

Native Revenue Account; (b) a deficit when incurred can often be charged against an accumulated revenue surplus; (c) if a small regular deficit has to be incurred and it is decided to meet this out of the general rate fund, then this charge (which partakes of the nature of a subsidy), must be kept as small as possible; and (d), if possible a regular profit should be made on the Native Revenue Account from which a contribution towards the cost of the purchase of capital assets can be made.[21]

The authors concluded that the expansion of social services for urban Africans was limited by the inelastic revenue base and, therefore, that 'no real solution to the problem can be obtained, so long as it is attacked from the angle of ability to pay rather than from the viewpoint of what are the *needs* of the urban Native'.[22] Nothing in the legislation required the self-balancing principle to be maintained. Indeed, there are some indications that suggest that the architects of the original legislation of 1923 had no such views, and expected that the Native Revenue Accounts would be subsidised from General Revenue. But this implied that white rate-payers would have to bear the burden, and few municipal councils were prepared to do this, confirming Maud's point (see p. 136). In 1971 it was officially stated that only 21 out of more than 450 local authorities were subsidising their Bantu Revenue Accounts. Johannesburg had long done so and in 1971–2 it had done so to the tune of about R2 500 000.[23]

In establishing the boards the Government required them to be financially self-sufficient in the sense of not looking to the Treasury for recurrent subventions. Repayment of housing loans, services and maintenance, welfare, recreational and other amenities were all expected to be financed from revenue obtained from within each of the respective administrative areas. The boards were, however, to be permitted to raise loans and to obtain overdrafts from commercial banks. A major problem in their operation thus far has been their chronic shortage of funds, in spite of repeated raising of rentals and of the compulsory contributions by employers, and the boards' monopoly of the sale of traditional or sorghum beer and of hard liquor in the urban African townships which yielded substantial profits.

As indicated, a major source of revenue for the boards is derived from the sale of liquor. This, too, is a tradition with deep roots in urban African administration, and it incorporates the principle that the profits from such sales shall be devoted to expenditure on welfare. In the initial period, prior to the legislation in 1961 which removed restrictions on the sale of hard liquor for Africans, this applied to the then so-called 'Bantu Beer'. In

1942–3 the Native Affairs Commission of Parliament criticised the tendency for municipalities 'to exploit beer-hall profits to meet recurring expenditure on ordinary municipal services' which, in the Commission's opinion, ought to have been charged against the municipalities' General Revenue Accounts.[24] In 1945 the Social and Economic Planning Council reckoned that Bantu beer profits amounted to almost one-fifth of the cost of services and amenities for townships and that net profits of 100 per cent were often made. The Council criticised these profits as 'a highly regressive concealed tax [which] in no way conforms to the norm of equity.'[25]

There is deep resentment on various grounds in the African townships of the liquor monopoly exercised before 1973 by the then existing local authorities and since then by the boards. Why, it is asked, in a free-enterprise economy are Africans not permitted to obtain licences to sell liquor as do members of other racial groups? Many of the African youth leaders, bitterly aware of excessive African expenditure on liquor, accuse the boards of deliberately siting beer and liquor outlets near to the railway stations to encourage workers to stop there on their way home. It is little wonder that in the unrest of 1976 the various official liquor outlets, together with the administrative centres of the boards, were the prime targets of the rioters.

Given the failure of the advisory board system and the refusal of the central government and most municipalities to consider the direct representation of Africans on town councils, other representative devices have been attempted. In 1961 legislation was enacted to establish Urban Bantu Councils which were to comprise elected and nominated members. These Councils were to perform broadly the same functions as advisory boards but, in addition, provision was to be made for their being vested with additional administrative powers. In practice hardly any such powers were delegated to the Councils and they remained largely advisory. Accordingly, their credibility among the communities they were intended to serve remained low.

In 1977 the Nationalist Government again attempted to address itself to the (by now) crisis proportions that the urban impasse had reached. The Community Councils Act seeks to establish Councils in urban areas elected on a non-ethnic basis, and enables them to be vested with more powers and duties than the Urban Bantu Councils. Indeed, during 1978 official spokesmen were promising 'full autonomy' for Soweto and other urban African townships. These promises should be evaluated against the actual terms of the legislation, which at numerous points is studded with overriding Ministerial controls, including a provision that the Minister

145

of Plural Relations and Development may, after consultation with the particular Bantu Affairs Administration Board and Community Council, withdraw any power or duty vested in the Council. The real power, in other words, that a Community Council can exercise is seriously circumscribed, and the fate of the Councils is likely to be similar to that of their predecessors. A substantial number of Soweto residents, for example, have completely rejected the innovation and called for a boycott of the elections held in 1978. The result, a six per cent poll, indicated the strength of popular feeling on the issue.

In the circumstances, it has been impossible for the Government to secure the participation of many authentic community leaders in government-initiated bodies. In Soweto there can be little doubt that the Committee of Ten, under the chairmanship of Dr N. Motlana, does represent community feeling, but it has consistently refused to be a party to what it considers to be sham representative bodies.

The crisis of the urban Africans' situation remains unresolved. They remain uninterested in proposals that offer the shadow, but not the substance of real power. The palliatives that may be offered are unlikely to succeed until a real accommodation with urban African leaders is achieved, and by 1979 it was clear that the price which white South Africa would have to pay for such an accommodation would be no less than the abandonment of separate development. From the 1920s onward it has been clear that the flashpoint in South African race relations has been among the millions of urban Africans, who confronted a harsh system of control that they could do little to change or even mitigate in its impact. Whether the issue was passes, housing, or education they were the objects of administration, rather than citizens who fully participated in the making of policies. Although by the time of writing the report of the judicial commission of inquiry into the unrest of 1976 had not been made public, it is quite apparent that the root cause of those events, and of earlier ones like Sharpeville and Langa in 1960, was the rejection by Africans of their powerlessness in the face of white power channelled through authoritarian bureaucratic structures. It is this theme which pervades the evidence given by the S.A. Institute of Race Relations to the Cillié Commission. In one of its conclusions the Institute states:

If the Government does not accept the permanency of urban Africans, fails to grant legal relief from the discriminatory pass laws, and continues to force millions to become foreigners in the places where they live and work, in order to enjoy the most elementary human rights, then it is

146

virtually certain that South Africa is entering a long period of further and increasing civil unrest.[26]

It is apparent that a number of leading members of the Government have been seriously concerned with the question of how urban Africans are to be accommodated within the framework of separate development. In the 1960s there were some advocates for the idea that urban townships far removed from homelands should be declared homeland territory, but this was unacceptable to the Government. Others have toyed with ideas such as 'city-states' or 'cantons', but none of those proposals has found favour with policy-makers who, on the face of things, remain committed to established dogma.

Until this issue is resolved to the satisfaction of both Africans and whites it is hard to write of progress in the sphere of urban communities. Whatever achievements particular local authorities or groups of Africans or individuals may have attained, they have all been within the context of an overriding failure fully to integrate substantial segments of the urban population into the life of the towns and cities. Integration in this context means more than the fact of economic interdependence, which all but the most die-hard of segregationists accepts as a fact; it refers also to the acceptance of urban Africans as equals in the urban enterprise, as people whose needs and aspirations are as deserving as those of other urban groups.

The residential configuration of South Africa's towns has been determined by a combination of economic and racial forces. Even where no racial or ethnic considerations have been involved, economic and status considerations are significant factors in shaping the residential ecology of towns in all urban societies; and even where there have been no legal compulsions, economic forces and ethnic ties have joined together to give cities a kind of mosaic pattern. The visitor to New York City, for example, cannot but notice how particular ethnic and racial groups are dominant in particular neighbourhoods or zones of the city. Some have given this phenomenon the label 'natural' or 'voluntary' segregation.

Comparable forces have been at work in the development of residential patterns in South African towns, and even without the application of legal restraints it is very likely that a substantial degree of *de facto* segregation of neighbourhoods would have occurred. This was certainly the pattern in Cape Town, which was, in these terms, the most polyglot and unsegregated city in South Africa. A similar pattern prevailed in a number of other towns and villages of the Western Cape. Penumbral areas, where a significant degree of interspersal of different ethnic groups was present, did exist, but mostly these came about as white expansion enveloped Coloured residential areas. Little or no friction was ever reported of these situations. A comparable absence of friction was reported by Margo Russell in her study of a mixed white/Indian neighbourhood in Durban.[27]

In all countries the residential configuration of towns is, of course, not static: changes in status and economic well-being enable whole groups to move to more desirable areas, the vacated parts of the town are filled by other groups as the price of property declines. This phenomenon, known as 'succession and invasion' has had its counterparts in South Africa and, as Justice F. C. Broome declared in one of the several reports on so-called 'penetration' by Indians in Natal in the 1930s and 1940s, it was a universal urban phenomenon 'but in South Africa because of the colour varieties of her population, it is obvious and easily becomes a focus of racial antagonism'.[28]

From the latter part of the nineteenth century onwards numerous attempts were made to segregate Indians both in Natal and in the Transvaal. The segregation of Africans was also attempted, in the first place by local authority decisions to establish locations on the peripheries of towns (and to move them when the towns expanded), and in the second place by the requirements of the Natives (Urban Areas) Act of 1923. The massive influx of Africans in the 1930s and 1940s overtook the segregationist requirements, and in 1942 the Smit Committee estimated that if residential segregation were to be fully applied, one-third of the urban African population would have to be rehoused.[29] In the same period numerous efforts were made to effect the residential and business segregation of Indians in Natal.

In 1950 the Nationalist Government enacted the Group Areas Act, which was aimed at being a comprehensive scheme for the racial zoning of every town and village in the country. Its intended scope and actual enforcement made all previous efforts at racial division seem puny. By 1977 6 960 whites, 349 616 Coloureds, and 163 770 Indians had been moved, and a further 1 287 whites, 91 427 Coloureds, and 66 655 Indians were still to be moved. A number of other 'racially disqualified' persons, including 1 482 Indians (with 3 576 still to be moved) had been moved out of business premises.[30] Few of the measures enacted since 1948 have caused more dislocation or resentment than this. When it is appreciated that nearly one-third of all Asian families and one-fifth of all Coloured families have been affected by Group Area proclamations, the scale of its operation can be seen. The discriminatory aspect of its implementation can be gauged by the fact that less than one per cent of white families have been affected. This occurred, despite assurances given by the legislation's political architects that it would be carried out justly.

A recent, detailed study of the Group Areas Act by Maasdorp and Pillay has graphically documented its effects on Indians. The authors conclude that far from validating the segregationist contention that racial separation reduces racial friction, the Group Areas Act has increased racial friction. They show also that the uncertainties generated by the legislation have caused otherwise house-proud people to let their homes deteriorate. Moreover, in spite of serious housing shortages, a large number of adequate houses that might have been renovated have been demolished. The economic consequences for displaced traders have been serious, and many people have sustained serious losses:

> The artificial shortage of land for homes is the major complaint among the rising Indian middle class; dispossessed families pay inflated prices for land in new areas, compensation is often below the market value of their previous properties, and the sense of injustice is heightened by profits made by the Department of Community Development on the resale of properties.[31]

For the most part, implementation of the Group Areas Act and other measures incorporating the principle of residential segregation has pushed blacks further and further to the peripheries of cities. As Anthony Lemon has noted 'the poor live at high densities, but further from the city than do Whites. This is the reverse of the income gradient normally associated with Western European cities, which also applies within the White sectors of South African cities.'[32]

The Group Areas Act is another example of how white political power has been mobilised against voteless and vulnerable communities in furtherance of the enforcement of a racial ideology. In a number of cases, such as Cape Town, the local authorities were opposed to the application of Group Areas to their towns, and gave evidence in this vein at the hearings convened prior to the making of proclamations by the Group Areas Board. But their opposition was of little avail, and local authorities had to surrender significant powers over their own town-planning to the central government.

A critically important aspect of urban environments is housing and accommodation. In South Africa's twentieth-century urban history this has been a perennial, even chronic, problem, beset by lack of funds, lack of co-ordination between concerned authorities, racial restraints, and above all a lack of will to ensure that the poor should be decently accommodated.

The uncaring, *laissez-faire* attitude towards housing and the associated range of urban problems that characterised the first two decades of this century, was partially halted by the Natives (Urban Areas) Act of 1923, which placed the responsibility for housing urban Africans on local authorities. Their response, however, was tardy, and even the availability of State loans for housing for all races did not do much to alter their indifference. This indifference stemmed partly from the official policy of regarding urban Africans as 'temporary'.

By 1946 the housing shortage, especially for Africans, had reached critical proportions. The massive influx occasioned by the war-time demand for labour, and the restriction on the use of building materials for residential purposes, had led to the creation of huge shanty-towns near all the major urban centres of South Africa. Emergency camps were established by many municipalities in which rough shelters and rudimentary services could be provided.

In December 1951 it was calculated that there was a shortage of 167 328 houses for urban Africans, and 185 813 more would be needed to meet the anticipated increase in the urban population between 1951 and 1962.[33] It was perhaps ironic that the Nationalist Government, which had reiterated its adherence to the Stallard doctrine on urban Africans, tackled the urban housing shortage with unprecedented vigour, and by 1960 the backlog had been substantially reduced. Heavy reliance was placed on the 'site-and-service' scheme, under which Africans were provided with a serviced site in a demarcated township upon which they could build a temporary dwelling that was to be replaced by a more permanent structure within five years.

However considerable the achievement in building new houses, aesthetically the new townships were a disaster. Row upon row of box-like houses were difficult to make into an attractive suburban setting and difficult for the occupants, many of whom were, and are, house-proud people, to endow with beauty, although as any visitor notices numerous attempts have been made to establish gardens or to paint designs on the walls to break up the bleakness and aridity of the typical township. In a very few places, such as Dube in Soweto, the pattern is broken and substantial, even elegant, houses have been built by middle-class townspeople.

The question of freehold land rights for urban Africans has long been an issue and it can be mentioned only briefly. The segregationist land legislation of 1913 and 1936 did not apply to urban areas, and many Africans acquired land in freehold in townships near Johannesburg, Durban, Pietermaritzburg and elsewhere, especially in the Eastern Cape. To the Nationalist Government of 1948 these rights were a symbolic affront to their policies concerning urban Africans, and they moved decisively against many of these freehold areas, using a variety of legislative and administrative instruments in the process. Furthermore, in 1968 the hitherto existing right of qualified Africans to build their own houses on thirty-year leasehold plots or to buy houses from the local authority was revoked.

In 1975, however, the official policy thawed somewhat with the announcement by the Government that the right of qualified Africans outside the Western Cape to build or buy houses on thirty-year leasehold plots and to sell and bequeath them to qualified persons was to be restored. In 1978 the Government introduced a 99-year leasehold scheme for qualified Africans, again with the exception of the Western Cape, together with new provisions enabling building societies to grant the equivalent of mortgage bonds to leaseholders. As before, the land remains the property of the relevant Administration Board and only Africans qualified under the influx-control laws may occupy such houses. Both restrictions diminish the attractiveness of the scheme. Moreover, an amendment to the Bantu (Urban Areas) Act in 1978 deprives children born to urban Africans after homeland independence (since they automatically become *de jure* citizens of independent homelands from the date of independence) of influx-control qualifications they might otherwise have had. While the Minister of Plural Relations and Development gave an explicit undertaking in the parliamentary debate about home ownership contained in a further amendment that 'citizens in South Africa of a homeland which becomes independent will not be worse off than before' and that this applied to 'not just one generation but also the descendants',[34] at the time of writing there was still considerable public uncertainty as to the precise effects of the new legislation.

The lack of freehold rights remains a source of bitter grievance to Africans who object to being able to buy only the house and not the land: 'Rather like a man selling you a shirt, but retaining the right to its pockets.'[35]

The housing shortage for Africans, especially, has reached massive proportions once again. The exact figure for the urban areas of 'white' South Africa is not known with any precision, but may well be of the magnitude of 175 000. A projection of the number of houses needed for low-income urban Africans between 1975 and the year 2 000 puts the figure at 3,3 million.

The Government's refusal to allocate money for sub-economic housing for Africans, its reluctant foot-dragging on the building of family housing units, and its evident preference for large barrack-like hostels for accommodating single, contract migrants (such as those in Alexandra, near Johannesburg) do not augur well for the emergence of stable and peaceful urban communities.

For many Africans, the unavailability of official housing and the legal restrictions on having their families live with them, illegal squatting has become the only option, in spite of government disapproval and stern legislative steps to eliminate it. In the area of Greater Cape Town squatter camps such as Unibell, Modderdam and Crossroads have become famous names as the symbols of people who wished to establish stable, family based communities – and substantially succeeded in doing so – and met with demolition orders and bulldozers. Perhaps in no other country in the world could men be charged with 'illegally harbouring their wives and children': yet this has been done to people in the squatter camps of Cape Town.

In 1979 only an optimist could deny that South Africa gave every indication that it was moving steadily into a chronic urban crisis. The projections for urban population growth in the next twenty years and the evident incapacity of the Government to cope with urban problems point to an intensification of conflict. There can be little doubt that South Africa will have to endure serious and intense conflict for a long time to come, whatever changes are made in its policies. If an accommodation cannot be reached with the millions of urban Africans, then the hopes of attaining peace and stability for South Africa as a whole are slender indeed.

1. See, for example, Nathan Glazer and Daniel P. Moynihan, *Beyond the Melting Pot* (M.I.T. Press, Cambridge, 1963).
2. *Report of the Transvaal Local Government Commission*, 1922, para. 267.
3. Reinhard Bendix, 'Tradition and Modernity Reconsidered', in *Embattled Reason – Essays on Social Knowledge* (Oxford University Press, New York 1970), pp. 250–314.
4. David Welsh, 'Urbanisation and the Solidarity of Afrikaner Nationalism', *Journal of Modern African Studies*, 7 (1969), pp. 265–76.

5. David Welsh, 'The Growth of Towns', in the *Oxford History of South Africa, II* ed. Monica Wilson and Leonard Thompson (Clarendon Press, Oxford, 1971), pp. 202–5.
6. D. O'Meara, 'The Afrikaner Broederbond 1927–1948: class vanguard of Afrikaner Nationalism', in *Journal of Southern African Studies* 3(2) 1977.
7. John P. R. Maud, *City Government: The Johannesburg Experiment* (Clarendon Press, Oxford, 1938), pp. 209–10.
8. Ray E. Phillips, *The Bantu in the City: A Study of Cultural Adjustment on the Witwatersrand* (Lovedale Press, Lovedale, 1938), pp. 379–80.
9. T. R. H. Davenport, *The Beginnings of Urban Segregation in South Africa: The Natives (Urban Areas) Act of 1923 and its background* (Institute of Social and Economic Research, Rhodes University, 1971).
10. J. C. Smuts, *The Basis of Trusteeship* (S.A. Institute of Race Relations, Johannesburg, 1942), p. 10.
11. *Report of the Interdepartmental Committee on the Social, Health and Economic Conditions of Urban Natives*, 1942, para. 8.
12. Social and Economic Planning Council, Report No. 9, *The Native Reserves and their place in the Economy of the Union of South Africa*, para. 11.
13. *Report of the Native Laws Commission*, 1946–8.
14. *Ibid.*, paras. 8, 25, 28.
15. The monthly reports of Black Sash advice offices are an invaluable source of material, derived from case-studies, illustrating this point.
16. Loraine Gordon *et al.*, *A Survey of Race Relations in South Africa 1977* (S.A. Institute of Race Relations, Johannesburg, 1978), p. 386.
17. Michael Savage, 'Costs of Enforcing Apartheid and Problems of Change', *African Affairs*, 76, 1977, p. 299.
18. T. Malan and P. S. Hattingh, *Black Homelands in South Africa* (Africa Institute of South Africa, 1976), p. 68.
19. P. J. Hugo, 'Migratory Labour in South Africa: Illusion and Reality', in *South African Journal of African Affairs*, Nos. 1 and 2, 1976, pp. 65–71.
20. *Notes on Conference between Municipalities and Native Affairs Department held at Pretoria on 28th and 29th September, 1937, to discuss the provisions of the Native Laws Amendment Act (No. 46 of 1937)*, p. 3.
21. P. R. Guénault and R. J. Randall, 'Some Financial Aspects of Urban Native Segregation in South Africa', in *Race Relations*, 4 (7), 1940, p. 96.
22. *Ibid.*
23. Muriel Horrell *et al.*, *A Survey of Race Relations in South Africa, 1971* (S.A. Institute of Race Relations, Johannesburg, 1972), p. 139.
24. *Native Affairs Commission, Report on Kaffir Beer* (1942–3), para. 93.
25. Social and Economic Planning Council, Report No. 8, *Local Government Functions and Finances*, para. 109.
26. S.A. Institute of Race Relations, *South Africa in Travail: The Disturbances of 1976/77* (Johannesburg, 1978), p. 49.
27. Margo Russell, *Study of a South African Interracial Neighbourhood* (Institute for Social Research, University of Natal, 1961).
28. *Interim Report of the Commission of Enquiry into Matters affecting the Indian Population in the Province of Natal*, 1945, para. 14.
29. Smit Committee *Report, op cit.* para. 155.

30. Muriel Horrell, *Laws Affecting Race Relations in South Africa* (S.A. Institute of Race Relations, Johannesburg, 1978) pp. 75–6.
31. Gavin Maasdorp and Nesen Pillay, *Urban Relocation & Racial Segregation: The Case of Indian South Africans* (Dept. of Economics, University of Natal, Durban, 1977), p. 180.
32. Anthony Lemon, *Apartheid: A Geography of Separation* (Saxon House, Westmead, 1976), pp. 75–6.
33. Cited in Welsh, 'Growth of Towns' p. 235.
34. *Hansard*, 19 of 1978, col. 9234.
35. Makgare Sekoto, 'Telling it as it is', *The Nation*, 17 October 1978.

7 Conflict and Progress in Education

E. G. MALHERBE

Poor Whites and Poor Blacks[1]

Fifty years ago, when the Institute of Race Relations was established, the big problem that exercised white South Africans was the so-called 'Native Question'. This did not stem from concern for the welfare and development of the South African Native. The Native Question which people, and mainly politicians, then had in mind was in essence little more than the Poor White problem. To call it the Native Question was one of those tricks of human nature that psychologists call 'projection'. It grew out of the fear that a considerable portion of the white population, mainly the poor whites, were sinking below the level of civilised standards of economic efficiency and would in course of time lose out in competition with the Native. The Native Question at the time was little more than the obverse of the Poor White Problem. This was clearly demonstrated by the Carnegie Commission on the Poor White Problem which published its findings in a five-volume report in 1932. It showed that measures which would check the development of the African and at the same time coddle and give an unfair advantage to the ruling white race, would in the long run rob the latter of its virility, bred from the buffetings of stern competition and would render it soft and weak when the real nemesis came. The only permanent remedy for the poor white problem lay in education, through which the poor white would learn to adapt himself more successfully to the demands of a modern industrial society. The Commission warned that the same causes that had produced the drift of landless poor whites to the cities and created slums, would cause a similar drift of landless poor blacks to our cities. This would bring about a poor black problem, which would far exceed in seriousness the poor white problem.

At the time there was a general economic depression. The poor black problem seemed too remote to warrant serious attention. Instead the Government, prodded by the Dutch Reformed Church, concentrated on the poor whites. A State Department of Social Welfare was established. A poor white slum-clearance campaign was embarked upon. Special educational facilities for indigent children were provided in rural as well as in urban areas. Special job opportunities were created for poor whites. One of these was roadmaking in the hitherto neglected areas of the North-west Cape; for this the wage was five shillings per day. A ruse that a number of these poor whites resorted to was to hire Coloureds to do the pick-and-shovel work at two shillings and sixpence per day, while they sat beside the road in a supervisory capacity!

It was in this type of attitudinal climate that the South African Institute of Race Relations was founded fifty years ago. It acted as a clearing house of information and as a forum for discussion on race relations. It stimulated constructive thinking about South Africa's educational problems, in particular those facing the black section of the population under the rapidly changing conditions of a rural people moving into an industrial urban society.

In addition to the fear on the part of whites about job competition, there was the prevailing doubt as to the educability of the Africans beyond a certain level. This doubt has persisted in many quarters, despite outstanding examples of brilliant achievements by Africans in the academic field. The logically contradictory nature of these doubts and fears did not prevent the Government from imposing regulatory measures reserving certain jobs for whites only. As regards education of the blacks, the prevailing attitude of the whites was aptly summarised by Professor Edgar Brookes as: 'Too humane to prohibit it, and too human to encourage it'. The statistics and diagrams that follow show clearly the retarding effect which this attitude had on the amount of money made available by the State for the education of Africans during the last fifty years. To a lesser extent this happened also in the case of the education of the Coloureds and Indians.

During the first fifty years of its existence, the Institute of Race Relations contributed to stimulating rational and constructive thinking amongst the public, mainly about the need for developing the education of the black section of the population. This it did through the holding of multiracial conferences, the creation of bursary funds and the publication of the results of factual research to show how the ultimate survival and prosperity of South Africa were dependent upon the development of skills and general education of *all* the racial groups in the country.

156

Contributions by missions

When it came to paying for the education of the Africans in the early days, it was not undertaken by the commercial and industrial concerns that employed them. Whatever the State contributed was small and given rather reluctantly. The missions bore the brunt of the burden. It is probably true that about 80 per cent of the cost of African education up to the 1920s was borne by the missions. The Native Economic Commission in 1930 estimated that two leading missionary churches had spent over R2 million on black education in South Africa during the previous century.

Mission statistics are, however, so elusive in quality that even today it is not possible to obtain an adequate statistical survey of the contributions made in money or in kind towards African education by the various missions. Their success was undoubtedly far in excess of the statistical results. While the work of the Government was easily measurable in terms of taxes and grants and discernible in terms of laws, ordinances and codes, the contribution of the missionary lay mostly in the realm of service, devotion and sacrifice.

Dr C. T. Loram, who was the Inspector of Native Education in Natal and also served on the Native Affairs Commission in the twenties and thirties, sums up the missionary contribution as follows:

It is said that a certain wise old Bantu chief divided Europeans into two classes, namely white men and missionaries. The distinction is significant. To the thoughtful Native, the white man is the disintegrating force which has broken down his tribal customs and sanctions, and has replaced them with nothing but innumerable and vexatious governmental restrictions introduced for the benefit of the white man. On the other hand, he knows the missionary to be his friend. It is the missionary who educates his children, who writes his letters, who cares for him in sickness and sorrow, who acts as a buffer between him and the local storekeeper or governmental official and whose motives are always altruistic.

Dr Loram concludes: 'It would be difficult to find a nobler record of heroism than the history of missionary enterprise in South Africa.' However, as a practical worker in the field of African education, he was fully aware of the problems that denominational rivalry and inter-church jealousies caused for the African. Disturbing as they often were to the untutored African's mind, they did not distress him as much as the multifarious state regulations which increasingly conditioned his life. To him,

157

the white man's activities on behalf of his spiritual and economic welfare seemed often to be of a purposeless nature. They constituted a conflicting heterogeneity instead of a purposeful homogeneity.

The inadequacy of State support

The responsibility for running the schools for Africans, Coloureds and Indians as well as for whites fell on the shoulders of the four provincial administrations. In 1926 the provinces were absolved from the responsibility of financing the education of Africans from their own resources, yet they continued to be responsible for administering it. This situation in itself created problems. The chief anomaly, however, was the creation of a Development Fund by the National Government which, as events proved, was itself incapable of development.

It depended on an annual block grant of R680 000 (the total expenditure by the four provinces on African education in 1922) plus a gradually increasing proportion of direct taxes paid by Africans, the poorest section of the population. The basis on which this grant was arrived at was also unfortunate because it penalised from the start the African population of those provinces which had lagged behind owing to their parsimonious attitude in previous years towards African education.

Despite its restrictive nature, this system remained in force until 1945, when African education became a direct charge on the Consolidated Revenue Fund, thereby bringing African education into line with the system which applied to the financing of the education of the white, Coloured and Asian groups. During the following decade expenditure on African education increased three-fold.

But in 1955, after the control of African education had – in terms of the Bantu Education Act of 1953 – been transferred from the provinces to the then Department of Native Affairs, the Government reverted to the former practice. It created a Bantu Education Account into which an annual block grant of R13 million – the amount calculated to derive from general revenue for African education the previous year – was to be paid, the remaining expenditure to be met from four-fifths of the general tax paid by Africans, sundry other receipts from Africans and advances made by the Government. Despite increased rates of African taxation from 1958, the payment of the total amount deriving from such tax into the Bantu Education Account from 1963, transfer of the costs of the three African universities to consolidated revenue, a number of economies in administration and sundry other measures, African school education continued to be severely handicapped by the inadequacy of funds. The starvation of African education in those years is part of the price exacted from South Africa in the seventies for its past neglect.

In 1972 the Bantu Education Account Abolition Act was passed. It provided for scrapping the Bantu Education Account, writing off the outstanding R10 million it owed and financing the Bantu Education Department from general revenue.

Criteria of educational progress

It is impossible to assess the progress in education during the last fifty years without resorting to objective criteria in the form of statistics. However, for those who are allergic to statistics, the rate at which education progressed is illustrated by means of graphs and diagrams. These show also the differences in the tempo of progress during the last fifty years between the different racial groups: whites, Coloureds, Indians and Africans. Besides such quantitative criteria there are also *qualitative* criteria of progress. Some of these are of a subjective nature and cannot be expressed in numerical terms: for example, the spiritual and moral effects of the education given and the psychological atmosphere in which such education is administered by the authorities and received by the children. In an atmosphere of conflict, teaching is bound to suffer; and there can be little or no *real* progress in education.

During the last fifty years there have unfortunately been a number of periods of unrest, caused mainly by conflict between the Government and a particular race group inside as well as outside the school. While there cannot be the slightest doubt that such conflicts and the resulting general unrest impeded real progress in education, it will be difficult to assess the extent to which progress was retarded, or to state what the progress would have been during the last fifty years had these conflicts not taken place. Here and there during the fifty years the specific effects of unrest and conflict are reflected in the statistics and graphs. The main cause, however, of retardation in the rate of progress, particularly in the case of the education of Africans, lay in misguided government policies as a result of which conflict and unrest broke out from time to time.

In discussing educational progress during the last fifty years, we shall use the following criteria in the case of each of the four racial groups, white, Coloured, Indian and African, as well as their total.
  1. The growth in the number of children drawn into the school net in relation to the population.

159

2. The growth in the percentage of such pupils who go on to post-primary education.
3. The growth in the number of Matriculation and Senior Certificate passes in relation to the population.
4. The growth in the proportion of the population receiving higher education.
5. The growth in the amount of money spent on education in relation to the population. This criterion is the best single index of progress in the *quality* of education provided for each population group, because it determines the qualifications of the teachers and the general standard of facilities provided.

As a background for the consideration of these criteria, figures showing the rapid population growth from 1927–77 are given in the following table.

Table 7.1

POPULATION INCREASES 1927–77[2]

| | In 1000s | | Total Increase | Percentage Increase per year | |
	1927	1977	1927–77	1960–70	1970–77
White	1 710	4 375*	255,85	2,24	1,91
Coloured	638	2 441	382,60	3,29	2,35
Asian	188	765	406,01	3,04	2,54
African	5 478	19 140**	349,39	2,80	2,67
Total	8 014	26 721	333,43	2,75	2,51

Criterion 1: Growth of School Population

Table 7.2

SCHOOL POPULATION 1927–77

| | 1927 | | 1977 | |
	Number	Percentage	Number	Percentage
White	352 000	53,6	940 000	16,4
Coloured and Indian	78 000	11,9	890 000	15,5
African	225 000	34,5	3 900 000	68,1
Total	655 000	100,0	5 730 000	100,0

*Including immigrants
**Including Transkei

Fifty years ago 53,6 per cent of the school population was white. Now whites have dwindled to 16,4 per cent while Africans have increased from 34,5 to 68,1 per cent of South Africa's school population. (No separate statistics for Indians and Coloureds were kept fifty years ago.)

The progressive introduction of free and compulsory education for whites, and of free and partially compulsory education for Coloureds and Indians contributed to their large pupil increases. What is remarkable, however, is the fact that without free and compulsory education, the African pupils increased from 225 000 to 3 900 000. The Africans were late starters, but their rapid increase is clear evidence of the tremendous desire for education which has developed among the African population during the last fifty years. Many hundreds of would-be pupils were turned away each year, especially at the Standard III and Form I levels, because of lack of accommodation and of qualified teachers. Most of those who were accommodated still received their education under considerable disabilities. For example, by 1975, over 11 000 teachers and nearly one million African pupils, especially in the lower school classes, were involved in the double-session system, by which one batch of pupils attended in the mornings and another batch in the afternoons in the same school building. To introduce compulsory education under such conditions would have been self-defeating because the schools cannot even today accommodate those African pupils who are willing to attend without any compulsion; there were simply not enough qualified teachers and not enough school buildings. Even including poorly qualified teachers, the number of pupils per teacher in many cases was frequently more than sixty. In some larger homelands, for example KwaZulu, the *average* number of pupils per teacher (primary and secondary classes taken together) was 61,3 in 1972. In that year, the average number of pupils per teacher in all African schools was 58,5 as compared with 20,0 for whites, 30,8 for Coloureds and 27,0 for Indians.

In 1964 Coloured education was taken away from the provincial administrations and placed under the Department of Coloured Affairs. In 1968 education became free for all Coloured children and certain steps towards compulsory attendance were taken.[3] As a result, double sessions had to be introduced because of the lack of accommodation. By 1970, 420 schools involving about 40 000 Coloured pupils were conducted on this system.

As regards Indians, Act 61 of 1965 transferred all Indian education from provincial control to the Department of Indian Affairs. Though no general compulsory law was applied, nevertheless about 99 per cent of educable

161

Indian children between the ages of seven and thirteen were attending school by 1972. The education of white children was both compulsory and free by 1920, at least up to Standard VI. These upper limits were gradually extended, and in 1971 the Minister of National Education decreed that white children shall attend school 'until the end of the year in which any pupil attained the age of sixteen years, or until he has passed the matriculation or the school-leaving examination'. No school fees were charged and books were free.

The first step towards the eventually envisaged compulsory education

Figure 7.1

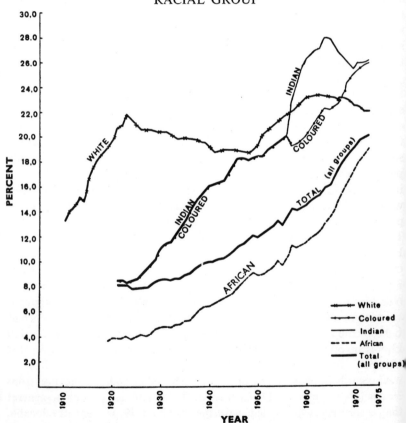

PERCENTAGE OF POPULATION AT SCHOOL FOR EACH RACIAL GROUP

for Africans was taken when parents of children attending school for the first time in January 1977 were required to sign an undertaking to keep the child at school until he had completed Standard 2, that is, after four years of schooling.

Much more significant than the increase in the absolute numbers that were drawn into the school net during the last fifty years is the increase in relation to the population, particularly in the light of the rapid population growth during this period, with the rise in the black population significantly higher than that of the white group. This is illustrated in the accompanying graph, Figure 1, where the percentage growth of school population is shown for each of the four population groups as well as for the four groups combined in relation to total population.

Figure 1 shows the rapid rise in the percentage of the black population attending school from 1920–75. Up to the 1950s, the school statistics of the Indians and the Coloureds were grouped together. Because the Indians were mainly urban, they had a greater percentage of their population at school than the Coloureds and even, due to their younger age composition, than the whites in recent years.

During the last fifty years, blacks had to make up tremendous leeway in comparison with whites who already had an established educational system, with institutions for higher education, at a time when hardly any of the black groups had got beyond the mere literacy stage. For example, fifty years ago the Africans had less than 4 per cent of their population at school. Today the proportion has grown to close on 20 per cent, and compares very favourably with other African countries. Indians and Coloureds increased at a faster rate, largely because of their much closer association with the whites and also on account of the higher birth rate of these two population groups until 1970, whereafter the African birth rate was higher. They have a larger percentage of children of school age in their population. For example, in 1970, the percentage of children of 6–19 years of age out of the total population was 27,8 for the whites, 37,2 for the Coloureds, 36,2 for the Indians and 35,6 for the Africans. So much for mere *quantitative* progress. We come now to the criteria of *qualitative* progress.

Criterion 2: Increase in Percentage of Post-Primary Pupils
Here, too, the whites have had a considerable start over the other population groups (Figure 2, overleaf). The percentage in Standards 6–10 of the white school population rose from a little over 20 per cent to nearly 30 per cent during the last fifty years. The Coloureds rose from a little less than 3 per cent to over 14 per cent, while the Indians grew from about

Figure 7.2

PERCENTAGE OF PUPILS IN POST-PRIMARY CLASSES
(STDS. 6–10) IN PUBLIC AND PRIVATE SCHOOLS

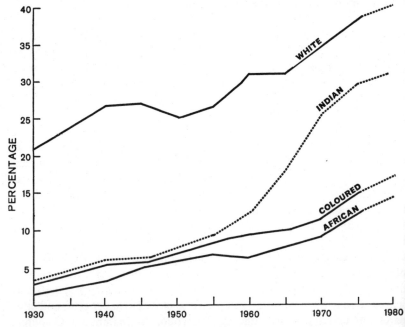

4 per cent to some 28 per cent. The Coloured and Indian lines on the graph run together because under the provincial system the Coloured and Indian pupil statistics were differentiated only in the 1950s. From then onward the Indian group advanced at a much faster rate than the other population groups in the country, and they now have a much larger proportion of high school pupils than, for example, the whites had during the 1950s.

The most backward group in this respect are the Africans, who had barely 2,5 per cent of their pupils in secondary classes fifty years ago. Only in the 1960s did the percentage rise to about 7 per cent. In the 1970s, however, there was a very rapid increase in the number of African pupils staying on in the higher classes of the secondary school. For example, in 1973 there were about 70 000 pupils in Form I (the first year of secondary school). By 1975 the number of such pupils had nearly doubled to 139 000. In 1976 it stood at 214 454. Today the total secondary class enrolment has

164

probably reached 12 per cent of all pupils in school. This progress has come about in spite of all the vicissitudes that befell African education during the last decade.

Recently, Dr K. B. Hartshorne, former Director of Planning, Department of Bantu Education, reported as follows on the situation:

Of the 30 129 pupils who passed Form III (Junior Certificate) successfully at the end of 1975, about 16 000 went on to Form IV, while 9 000 entered the teacher training colleges to train as primary school teachers. Many of the remaining 5 000 were taken up in nursing training and in trade and technical schools. Very few did not go on to some form of further education and training. In the light of the need for trained manpower, both in the homelands and in the rest of South Africa, this accelerated development in the field of secondary education, in spite of all the problems it is posing the Department, holds considerable promise for the future.

Criterion 3: Increase in Matriculation and Senior Certificate Passes

South Africa owes its great industrial and commercial progress in the last fifty years mainly to the unprecedented increase in the number of its population, white and black, that annually completed high school by passing matric and senior certificate. Fifty years ago the annual number (in round figures) of whites who passed stood at 2 000. In 1950 it increased to 10 000; in 1960 to 20 000 and in 1970 to about 40 000. (In 1976 there were 44 849, the latest figure available.) This rate of growth was more than eight times faster than that of the white population growth during the last fifty years.

Though the blacks made a late start for the reasons already indicated, their annual passes in matriculation and senior certificate increased very rapidly in later years, as the following table for the two decades 1955–75 shows.

Table 7.3[4]

PASSES BY BLACKS IN MATRICULATION AND SENIOR
CERTIFICATE

	African	Coloured	Indian	Total
1955	465	392	291	1 148
1965	1 143	956	1 100	3 201
1975	5 347	2 374	3 679	11 400

Relating these numbers to the size of the respective racial groups, the number of passes in 1975 per 1 000 of population was: 9,7 for whites, 5,1 for Indians, 1,0 for Coloureds and 0,3 for Africans.

In relation to the size of their population groups, the Indians had in 1975 reached the same proportion of passes that the whites had attained in 1956. The Coloureds had reached the proportion of the whites in 1922, but the Africans had as yet only reached the proportion of passes which the whites had in the early 1900s. Nevertheless, we have here evidence of considerable progress achieved in education despite many obstacles and shortcomings. These figures are important because they indicate the *relative* size of the annual sources from which South Africa has to recruit its skilled and professional manpower.

Criterion 4: Growth in Higher Education

During the last fifty years, the number of white university students grew from about 6 500 to about 76 000 (1977 figures). If one adds the number studying as external students at the University of South Africa (Unisa), which grew from about 8 000 in 1960 to nearly 31 000 in 1977, the total number of white students involved in university study in 1977 was over 107 000. The proportion of white university students rose from 2,2 to 24,5 per 1 000 of the white population from 1927–77, a proportion higher than that of any country in the world with the exception of the United States of America. Impressive as this growth may be, it is, however, a matter of concern that it has been proceeding at a faster rate than the *rate* of growth in the number of white high-school pupils. This is probably one of the causes of the increasing number of drop-outs from our universities. And it would seem that the time has come to consider seriously whether

Table 7.4

GROWTH IN THE NUMBER OF WHITE UNIVERSITY STUDENTS

Year	Number in Residential Universities	Per 1 000 of White Population	Total including Unisa	Per 1 000 of White Population
1920	2 946	2,0	3 150 (est)	2,1
1940	11 411	5,3	13 400 (est)	6,2
1960	31 739	10,3	39 662	12,9
1977	76 400	17,5	107 162	24,5

we are not sending too many white students to university in comparison to the number going in for higher technical training in which there is a great shortage in South Africa.

Until 1959, when strict ethnic segregation was imposed on all South African universities (as dealt with more fully later in the section on conflict), black students could attend the Universities of Cape Town and of the Witwatersrand on the basis of 'academic non-segregation' and of Natal where classes were at that time segregated but whenever possible taught by the same staff as white students. (In later years classes were integrated.) In addition Natal had – and still has – a medical school for black students, which had an enrolment of 621 students in 1978 (238 Africans, 355 Indians and 28 Coloureds). The University College of Fort Hare, the then only university existing solely for blacks, had in 1959 an enrolment of 489 students, of whom seventy were Coloured and one hundred Indian students. Then as now Unisa provided correspondence courses to all population groups.

In 1959 the number of Coloured students studying at the three open universities was 540, of Indians 815 and of Africans 300 (including students at the Natal Medical School but excluding those at Fort Hare), a total of 1 656. The enrolment at Unisa was 211 Coloured, 601 Indian and 1 252 African students, bringing the combined total of black internal and correspondence students to 3 719.

From 1960 onwards, no new student could enrol at a university other than that of his own ethnic group without obtaining ministerial permission, usually given only if the course to be studied was not available at the appropriate ethnic university. Fort Hare was designated to serve the Xhosa and Fingo groups. New university colleges, later to become autonomous universities, were established: the University College of the North (Turfloop) near Pietersburg in the Transvaal for the Sothos, Tswanas, Vendas and Tsongas; the University College of Zululand at Ngoye in Natal for the Zulus and Swazis; that of the Western Cape near Cape Town for the Coloured people; that of Durban-Westville for Indians. After the independence of Transkei, a University of Transkei was established at Umtata in 1977. The building of the Medical University of South Africa (MEDUNSA), a new medical school for Africans to train doctors, dentists and veterinarians, was started near Pretoria in 1977, for a planned annual intake of 200.

Despite deep resentment of these apartheid measures, but in the absence of an alternative, the number of black students grew rapidly as the figures in Table 5, overleaf, show.

Table 7.5

BLACK UNIVERSITY STUDENTS IN SOUTH AFRICA, 1977[5]

	African	Coloured	Indian	Total
(a) At black universities	4 695	2 637	3 628	10 960
(b) At white universities	494	720	763	1 977
(c) Total (a) plus (b)	5 189	3 357	4 391	12 937
(d) Unisa (correspondence)	6 320	2 000	3 477	11 797
(e) Total (c) plus (d)	11 509	5 357	7 868	24 734
(f) Per 1 000 of population	0,6	2,3	10,3	1,1

The number of black students at white universities, after decreasing from 1 728 in 1960 to 1 219 in 1968, began rising very slowly until recently when both the number of black students at white universities and the number of white universities admitting black students increased significantly. By 1977 there were 1 977 black students at white universities, both English and Afrikaans, though at this stage the number of admissions to the English universities far outnumbered that of the Afrikaans universities. By 1978 the only university in South Africa which had taken no steps to admit black students at any level was the Afrikaans University of Pretoria.

The fact that in less than two decades the total number of black university students increased from 3 719 to 24 734 is evidence of the strong desire that exists amongst blacks for higher education. There is no doubt that these numbers (especially of the Africans) would today have been considerably larger, had it not been for the way in which higher education for blacks has been restricted and administered by the Nationalist Government during the last two decades, causing unrest and general unhappiness. Moreover, the number of African high-school pupils has for many years warranted a higher intake into university. This number has now for the last two years been larger than the white high-school population.

If one relates the number of university students to the size of the respective population groups, one finds that the Indian group has 10,3 students per 1 000 of its population, a figure which is nearly five times as large as that of the Coloureds, and about twice as large as in India (5,4 per 1 000). The proportion of the Indian population in South Africa receiving university education is now the same as that of the whites in 1957 and the proportion of Coloureds is at the stage that the whites were in 1920.

Combining all racial groups, one finds that the number per 1 000 of the

168

Republic's population is 3,3 for internal students only, and 4,5 if one includes those who study externally under Unisa. Looking at the proportion of our total population (white and black) that receives university education to-day, one finds that, though South Africa still lags far behind the countries of Europe, North America and most of the countries in South America, it is far ahead of any country in Africa with the exception of Egypt, where the proportion is 5,8, as compared with South Africa's 4,5. Backward as the proportion of our Africans receiving university education may be when considered by itself, it is still ahead of that in Uganda, Nigeria, Kenya, Rhodesia, Ethiopia and Tanzania.

Criterion 5: Increase in the Financial Provision for Education

In comparing education of the various racial groups I prefer to use the expenditure per capita of population rather than the expenditure per pupil as a basis of comparison between racial groups, because of the wide divergence in scholastic attainment of pupils in the respective population groups. For example, more than 41 per cent of all Africans in school are still in the substandards, compared with 18 per cent of the whites, 23 per cent of the Indians, and 35 per cent of the Coloureds.

Figure 3, overleaf, reflects in an epitomised form the growth and relative size of the financial support by the state for education among each of the four racial groups from 1910 to 1975. These per capita figures are averages, and it must not be forgotten that averages conceal a wide diversity of conditions within the same racial group and within the same year. They do, however, indicate general trends over a period of time. Among these, several facts stand out clearly.

First, education has become much more expensive than it was at the beginning of the century, even in terms of real money, allowance having been made for depreciation. This is because we have moved into a technological age in which expensive equipment is required both for general teaching purposes and more especially for science teaching and research in the universities. Then, too, the salaries of teachers have increased, but not relatively so when compared with salaries in most of the other professions, and in commerce and industry.

The second and most striking feature of the diagram is the big difference between the four racial groups. These differences have persisted despite the great advances that have been made in the case of each individual group. These figures more than any other single measure reflect the *quality* of the educational facilities provided at particular times during the last fifty to sixty years of South Africa's educational history.

Figure 7.3*

STATE EXPENDITURE IN RAND ON EDUCATION PER HEAD
OF POPULATION OF THE FOUR RACIAL GROUPS (1910–1975)

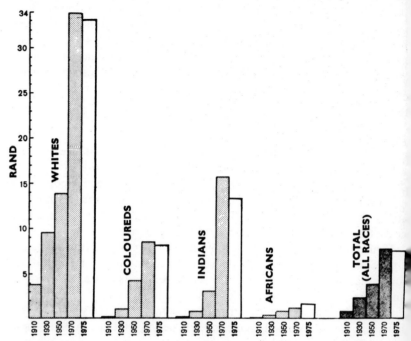

Among the black groups, the Indian group has shown the biggest advance
during the last twenty years, especially in the facilities available for technical and university education, which are the more expensive types of
education. Today their average position is actually ahead of that of
the whites in 1950 as regards the amount of *real* money spent on their

*The amounts of money spent per head of population shown by the height of
these columns have all been adjusted in terms of the Consumer Price Index in
order to eliminate the effect of inflation during the last forty years. They therefore reflect the *real* value of the money spent on education over the years. If
today's current value of the Rand had been used, the columns showing educational expenditure during recent years would have been four times as high on the
diagram. Such a picture would have been completely unreal.
  The decrease in 1975 is evidence of the fact that the Government in subventing
education did not sufficiently take into account the decrease in the value of
money due to inflation during the present decade.

education per head of population. The average educational facilities for Coloureds are now more or less at the level of the whites in the 1920s.

As regards the Africans, the average educational facilities provided for them have been, and still are, pitifully small in relation to the size of their population, when compared with those of the other racial groups. Despite the progress that has been made, these facilities are on an average still below those enjoyed by whites more than one hundred years ago. Even when we compare what is spent today per head of the African population with what is spent on other blacks, the difference is very great. The per capita figure for the Coloureds is almost seven times, and for the Asiatics thirteen times, as much as that spent per capita on the Africans.

The following are some of the main features of the poor situation of the African in comparison with the other racial groups in South Africa: (a) the high average pupil/teacher ratio (± 56), and the overcrowding of classes owing to a shortage of teachers and the inadequate school buildings and other facilities; (b) the low qualifications of most teachers; (c) the relatively low salaries paid to African teachers in general, reflecting the low earning power of the African community as a whole.

Table 7.6

GROWTH OF EDUCATIONAL EXPENDITURE ON DIFFERENT RACIAL GROUPS FROM 1925–75

| | 1925 | | 1975 | |
	Amount R	%	Amount* R	%
White	14 259 000	91,4	139 300 000	67,9
Coloured	454 000	2,9	21 071 000	10,2
Indian	79 000	0,5	9 257 000	4,5
African	805 000	5,2	35 629 000	17,4
Total	15 597 000	100,0	205 257 000	100,0

The above table makes a comparison between the total amounts spent fifty years ago with those spent in *real* money today on the education of

These amounts are comparable because they have been adjusted according to the Consumer Price Index in order to make the comparison valid in terms of the *real* value of money at two points of time fifty years apart.

the different racial groups. The fact that the effect of inflation has been eliminated makes the comparison valid. What is interesting to note is that whereas fifty years ago the expenditure on white education constituted 91,4 per cent of the total amount spent on education, today it has decreased to 67,9 per cent. At the same time the percentage spent on education of blacks increased from 8,6 per cent to 32,1 per cent. The overall total shows a thirteen-fold increase from R15 597 000 to R205 257 000, compared with a nine-fold increase in the school population during the same period. The biggest relative increase has been registered in the case of Indian education. Next comes the expenditure on Coloureds and Africans, and the smallest relative increase is in respect of white education, chiefly because fifty years ago the whites were already very far advanced in education compared to the other groups. The fact that South Africa had to deal with racial groups that are historically at different stages of development as regards adjustment to a modern westernised society is not generally realised by people in overseas countries. Gradualness is a characteristic of human progress, especially in Africa.

Limitation of space in this short chapter precludes me from dealing with all the diverse aspects in which there has been progress in the education of all the racial groups of South Africa during the last fifty years. This progress varied according to the financial provision made by the state every year. Private and local enterprise, however, also played a role in developing, for example, libraries, pre-school education, the training of physically handicapped children, adult and continued education as well as in-service training for industry and the provision of bursaries.

Technical and vocational education has, however, lagged behind academic education at the adult level in the case of all the racial groups. Recently Dr A. J. A. Roux, president of the Atomic Energy Board, drew attention to the fact that there was in the Republic a shortfall of 17 000 engineering technicians at all levels and that the annual output of 3 000 technically trained people was far short of the demand. 'Widespread efforts to attract suitable technicians from overseas have borne little fruit,' he said, 'and it is evident that South Africa will increasingly have to rely on its own resources . . . . One solution to the shortfall is to train blacks as technicians.'

Teachers' qualifications improved

Of all the aspects of education in which there was progress due to increased financial provision by the state, the most important one was the improvement in the qualifications of teachers. *Schools are as good as the teachers are.* The quality of persons attracted to the teaching profession is determined by: (a) the conditions of service and salaries offered, and (b) the training provided.

During the last three years, the numbers being trained at teachers' training colleges increased since 1975 roughly as follows: whites: from 12 000 to 14 000; Coloureds: from 4 600 to 4 700; Asians: from 650 to 950; Africans: 15 000 to 22 000. The biggest increase is in the case of the Africans, where the need has been the greatest, as was shown in connection with the impossibly large classes with which the African teacher has to cope.

These African teachers as well as the Coloured teachers still lag far behind the whites and Indians as far as their *general* education (apart from their professional training) is concerned. The position in 1977 was as follows in regard to *professionally qualified teachers:*

Table 7.7

QUALIFICATIONS OF TEACHERS

General Education	White	Indian	Coloured	African
Percentage with Degree	29,6	18,2	3,7	2,2
With at least Matric	64,9	63,9	24,0	12,1
	94,5	82,1	27,7	14,3

There is a positive correlation between the levels of education of teachers and the amount of money that the state spends per pupil on the four racial groups.

In the fifties and sixties it was government policy deliberately to mould a form of African education that would be different in kind (as described in the following section). In the seventies the emphasis changed. The threshold of 1977, six months after the onset of the Soweto disturbances, saw Mr M. C. Botha, the Minister of Bantu Education, attempting to allay public concern regarding 'the quality of Black education'. He stated that his department cherished the same basic goals of education as those of any other education department, that in academic terms it aimed 'to maintain the same *standards* as those of any other group', that curricula and syllabuses were those established on a national basis for all groups, with black youngsters writing the same senior certificate/matriculation examinations. Mr Botha outlined a number of important reforms already introduced or soon to be undertaken, among them the progressive provision of free textbooks so that by January 1979 all primary and secondary schools would be supplied, the establishment of twenty adult education centres in the major African townships to assist some 40 000 African adults, including many African teachers, to take junior and senior certificate examinations, building more teacher training colleges, state-run secondary schools in urban townships and industrial training centres, efforts to reduce pupil: teacher ratio and to eliminate double sessions.[6] In 1978 it was announced that building had started on a R30 million technical training college near Pretoria.[7]

Indicative of greater official sensitivity to African attitudes were certain amendments to existing legislation relating to nomenclature passed during the 1978 parliamentary session. These expunged the greatly disliked term 'Bantu' and replaced it, in the main, by the term 'Blacks'. 'Bantu Homelands' became 'Black States' and similar changes were made in other terms. The terms Minister, Secretary and Department of Bantu Education were replaced by the terms Minister, Secretary and Department of Education and Training. Measures such as these, together with other policy and administrative changes, give grounds for a guarded optimism for the future development of the admittedly vast, complex and financially demanding task of making adequate educational provision for a rapidly growing African population.

Issues of conflict

There were three main issues over which there was conflict and unrest which impeded the progress of education during the last fifty years: (1) Language medium in schools; (2) Separation on the basis of ethnicity; (3) Ethnicity versus academic freedom. Of course, there were other issues beyond the school which caused general unrest and affected the progress of education adversely in an indirect way.

1. *Language medium in schools*
Language, and especially the medium of instruction in schools, has been a source of conflict in white education since the days of Lord Charles Somerset, and later in the two northern provinces during the post-Boer War regime under Lord Milner. During the subsequent years under the leadership of Generals Hertzog and Smuts a generally accepted basis was arrived at, namely, (a) that the home language of the child should be

174

the medium of instruction at least at the primary stage, (b) that both English and Afrikaans should be taught as subjects, and (c) that English- and Afrikaans-speaking children living in the same community should be together in the same school rather than in separate schools. It was felt that this would not only facilitate bilingualism, through the informal learning of the second language by having at least both languages spoken on the playground, but it would also from early on foster a feeling of *common loyalty* to their school and also to their country, South Africa.

In 1925 Afrikaans, instead of High Dutch, became recognised as the second official language and as a medium of instruction together with English. This greatly facilitated the learning process of both English- and Afrikaans-speaking children in school.

Such, however, was the zeal engendered in certain Afrikaans circles by the advent of Afrikaans in government departments and in the schools, that a campaign was started to separate Afrikaans children into separate schools, lest they should become anglicised through contact with English-speaking children. As it turned out, this idea was politically motivated and actually implemented in those provinces where the Nationalist Party was in the majority. This matter became a very controversial issue especially during the late 1930s and 40s. During the Second World War our soldiers were fighting 'up North' together as English- and Afrikaans-speaking *South Africans* in the same regiments. They were incensed when they learned that their children at home were being kraaled off into separate schools. A survey made among the troops at the time showed that 93 per cent of them favoured keeping Afrikaans- and English-speaking children together in the same school.

During the war, in 1943, Mr M. C. Botha, in his capacity as secretary of the Afrikaanse Kultuurraad, secretly tried to organise a strike among all Afrikaans students and pupils throughout the country against being 'put into one kraal with the English'. The object of the strike was 'to bring the Smuts government to its senses'. He even enlisted the support of the Dutch Reformed Church to implement this strike. This project was, however, fortunately nipped in the bud by General Smuts's military intelligence department which intercepted the secret circulars calling the strike.

Incidentally, it must be mentioned here as a case of historical irony that years later, in 1976, this same Mr M. C. Botha was the Minister of Bantu Education when the fateful strike among the African pupils in the schools of Soweto took place. In this capacity he had imposed the compulsory use of Afrikaans on a 50:50 basis as a medium of instruction in

175

the Soweto schools, where hardly any of the children or the teachers knew the language. The quelling of the strike caused widespread rioting and even bloodshed. The general unrest which ensued proved a great setback to African education in those areas and even beyond. Another tragic consequence was that among many blacks a fine language like Afrikaans has become hated as 'the language of the oppressor'.

In 1948, when the National Party came into power, separate schools for English and Afrikaans children became part of the Party's general education policy. Apart from the greatly increased capital cost of education which the erection of separate school buildings involved, this policy resulted in the decrease in the level of bilingualism amongst English and Afrikaans pupils, a handicap that was perpetuated when those who became teachers were trained in separate English and Afrikaans teacher-training colleges. When these teachers went back into these separate schools, very few of them could use the second language with competence or confidence. The subject that suffered most was the teaching of the second official language. Of the two, English has suffered more than Afrikaans because nearly 70 per cent of the teaching profession is today drawn from Afrikaans institutions. Under the National Party Government regime most of the plums in the teaching profession have gone to the Afrikaans teachers, with the result that the profession has become less attractive to the English-speaking youth.

This policy of kraaling our youth off into separate institutions not only deprived a large proportion of our youth, during the most impressionable stage of their lives, of that cultural enrichment which comes from the teaching of English literature by one who is steeped in it and loves it; but what was even more serious from a national point of view, it prevented them from cultivating those friendships and that understanding of each other's point of view which comes from the interplay of ideas in an institution where English and Afrikaans youth study and play together.

It was an astute move on the part of the National Government to separate children at school according to their home language, because the proportion of Afrikaans-English home language was roughly in the ratio of 60/40, and any attitude towards other ethnic or racial groups which children bring from home tends to be perpetuated much more in schools where they are kept separate than where English- and Afrikaans-speaking children attend the same school. This was found in a survey made some years ago by the National Bureau for Educational and Social Research in order to compare children's attitudes to the other language group according to whether they were in separate schools or in the same school.

176

The survey, which included 18 000 pupils in a few hundred representative schools, showed that feelings of social distance and antipathy which children brought from home still remained with them by the time they reached Std X to the extent of 75 per cent in the separate Afrikaans-medium schools, 22 per cent in the separate English-medium schools and only 10 per cent in the schools where Afrikaans and English children were in the same school. We have no similar statistical evidence regarding white children's attitudes towards black racial groups. The chances are, however, that the effect of the school on home attitudes will be similar, except that since then there has been much greater inbreeding of Afrikaans teachers in the Afrikaans schools.

It is a fact that Afrikaans homes, which are in the majority, are predominantly exposed to government-oriented mass media. The chances are, therefore, that the attitudes thus generated in the home will not markedly be affected by the children's contacts in a homogeneously separate Afrikaans-medium school.

It must be appreciated that the National Government has created through the schools a self-perpetuating mechanism which operates according to what might be termed the 'Law of Circular and Reciprocal Motion'. Where, however, English- and Afrikaans-speaking youth, with possibly differing attitudes and points of view, are educated together in the same institutions there is, through the interplay of differing ideas, a far better chance of dynamic thinking about social relationships being stimulated than in unilingual institutions where stereotyped concepts and attitudes are simply perpetuated, if not actually reinforced. Obviously no hard and fast lines can be drawn between the attitudes of South Africans according to the language they speak at home. There are many exceptions. What it is intended to describe here are the general trends of the influences brought to bear on our youth and to indicate in what type of educational institution our hope lies for training our children to meet the rapidly changing and complex interracial situations which lie ahead.

2. Separation on the basis of ethnicity

The preservation of ethnic identity as one of the main functions of education found overt expression in the Bantu Education Act of 1953, which in turn gave expression to the ideas embodied in the Eiselen Report. Dr H. F. Verwoerd, Minister of Native Affairs, had at the time become head of the government department in control of African education. In his speech before the Senate on 7 June 1954, Dr Verwoerd made what was probably the clearest statement of the National Government's policy in connection with African education:

It is the policy of my Department that [Bantu] Education should have its roots entirely in the Native areas and in the Native environment and in the Native community. There Bantu Education must be able to give itself complete expression, and there it will have to perform its real service. The Bantu must be guided to serve his own community in all respects. There is no place for him in the European community above the level of certain forms of labour. *Within his own community, however, all doors are open* [my italic]. For that reason it is of no avail for him to receive a training which has as its aim absorption into the European community, while he cannot and will not be absorbed there.

What Dr Verwoerd did not seem to realise, or deliberately chose to ignore at the time, was that only 37 per cent of the Africans at that time were domiciled in their 'own communities'; that is, in the homelands where 'all doors would be open'. The other 63 per cent worked in the white areas (31,8 per cent in urban areas and 31,2 per cent on farms owned by whites), where they had to earn a living in the westernised context of the white man, and where they felt frustrated in functioning because they could not quickly enough acquire the white man's education and know-how. At the same time, they were frustrated because of the reservation that was made that only 'certain forms of labour' would be open to them in the white man's areas. As political events subsequently proved, the aim was that the African child should be taught that he is a foreigner while he is in 'white' South Africa. In short, African education would teach Africans 'from childhood that equality with Europeans is not for them'. Needless to say, these views were strongly opposed in Parliament by members of the opposition. For instance, Mrs Helen Suzman emphasised that it is 'quite futile to try and keep Natives in a perpetual intellectual twilight and lead them back to a tribal Eden'.

What Dr Verwoerd also seemed to ignore was that forces far more powerful than the education they had been receiving were fast changing their tribal ways through the rapid industrialisation of the country. Sheer economic pressures have caused them to adapt themselves to 'European ways', and they were doing so for their own survival. In fact, it has in recent years become a matter of concern for the National Government that tribal ways are still so uneconomically entrenched in the Africans' agriculture.

While Africans do not seem to be lacking in enthusiasm to maintain their own language and culture, and to develop the use of their own vernacular, even to the extent of excluding Afrikaans as an official language in Transkei, they feel the necessity of also having English as an official language to serve as an open window to the world beyond. This was well illustrated to me (while serving on the Native Education Commission in 1935) by what an old Zulu chief replied to Dr D. Malcolm (a great expert on the Zulu language, and author of the Zulu dictionary), who was also a member of the Commission. Dr Malcolm tried to impress on the old chief the importance and beauty of the Zulu language. 'Of course', he replied, 'I love my language. But you see, if I know only my own language, I am just like a chicken confined to a pen, where I can peck at my food and be quite well-fed. But when I can speak the white man's language [English], I can soar like an eagle!'

Since earliest times there has been an awareness of the differences between the various African tribes in southern Africa. At the same time, the missionaries tended to look upon the *Bantu* (the people) as all being children with the common Fatherhood of God, and gave them all more or less the same education based on the Christian religion and European culture. This the National Government regarded as bad for the Africans and during the 1950s became very concerned with the preservation of the ethnic identities and cultures of the various Bantu tribes, even to the extent of creating, at considerable cost, separate ethnic universities for them.

While in no way lacking in appreciation of their own language and culture, many Africans – especially the more enlightened ones – regarded with suspicion this sudden solicitude on the part of the white government over their cultural development and ethnic identity. They felt that this was a part of its apartheid policy designed to confine and isolate them from the broad stream of South Africa's socio-economic and political life.

3. *Ethnicity versus academic freedom*

So obsessed had the National Government become with ethnicity that it next proceeded to project it even into the field of university education, one of the last places on earth where it would seem to have significant relevance. In April 1957 it introduced into Parliament a Bill called The Separate University Education Bill. This elicited the most vigorous protest not only from the opposition in Parliament, but also from those English-speaking universities which had black as well as white students. It was felt that while the concept of ethnicity might be appropriate in education at that stage of

179

life where the family was of paramount importance for rearing the young and for their acquiring knowledge through the language of the family, it became decreasingly relevant, as the child grew to maturity and sought wider fields of experience, to confine him to the limitations of the tribe. It is to meet this need in the development of human civilisation that universities had their origin. The very word *universitas* implies contact with what is *universal* in human experience, and goes beyond the confines of the family, the tribe and even the nation. Athens became the great seat of learning in the ancient world because it was a place where scholars from many nations foregathered. The famous universities of Europe owed their growth to the wandering scholars from many countries. For the National Government, therefore, to have made ethnicity the basic principle and justification for creating ethnic universities showed a gross ignorance of the origin and nature of a university.

Just how irrelevant this concept was, in the event, was shown in the case of the two ethnic universities established for the Sothos and the Zulus respectively. To make them truly ethnic, these universities were sited in completely tribal areas where the students considered themselves superior to that rather primitive and largely illiterate environment. They had very limited contact indeed with the surrounding tribal inhabitants.

What the Government proposed in the Bill and eventually put into effect was formulated by the Minister as follows:

The necessity of maintaining ethnic ties in university institutions flows from the conviction that the future leader during his training, including his university training must remain in close touch with the habits, ways of life and views of members of his population group. What we envisage is to make provision for a separate university for the Xhosa population group at the existing university college of Fort Hare, as well as a separate university college for the Zulu group in Zululand, one for the Sotho group in Northern Transvaal, one for the Coloureds at Athlone in the Cape Peninsula, and one for Indians near Durban in Natal. The Coloured population is concentrated here in the Cape Peninsula, and their institution will therefore be in their midst, and that applies also to the Indians in Durban.

Apart from giving expression to the rather irrelevant concept of ethnicity this Bill had in it clauses which struck at the very roots of the academic tradition. It excluded blacks from existing teaching universities, and it made it a punishable offence (a fine of R200 or six months' imprisonment for a black to register at a white university without permission from the Minister. Another clause in the Bill made it an offence subject to the same penalty for a white to register at a university for blacks. Even the positive provisions of the Bill were anathema to anyone who valued the freedom accorded elsewhere to universities. These new institutions were to be controlled in a manner 'more fitting for a reformatory than an academic community', to use the words of Sir Eric Ashby in his book *Universities – English, Indian and African*.[8]

The Minister reserved to himself the right to appoint, promote, transfer and discharge members of the staff. These members of staff could be discharged by the Minister on any one of seventeen counts, which include:

> If he publicly comments adversely on the administration of any department of the government or propagates any idea or takes part in, or identifies himself with any propaganda or activity, or acts in a manner calculated (1) to cause or promote antagonism amongst any section of the population of the Union against any other section of the population of the Union, or (2) to impede, obstruct or undermine the activities of any government department.

In introducing this Bill, the Minister had said: 'These non-whites must be so educated that they do not want to become imitators of the whites.' However, matters such as the curriculum to be followed, the examination papers set, the examiners who marked the scripts and the pass marks for the award of the degree, were to be the same as those applying to thousands of white South Africans who were enrolled as correspondence students of the University of South Africa. This was the position for some years until they later became independent universities, awarding their own degrees.

Despite virtually three years of dignified dissent by the open universities, and desperate protests by students and all liberal-minded South Africans, this Bill, with minor amendments, became law under the ironical title of The Extension of University Education Act No. 45 of 1959.

As an illustration of the utterly unrealistic ideas which the Government at that time had about running a university, I may mention the fact that during the course of these proceedings the Government wanted to place the Medical School for blacks at the University of Natal under the direct control of the education department in Pretoria. To have placed the control of such a complex institution as a medical school, involving also a huge teaching hospital, under an administration in Pretoria 500 miles away, was such an unacceptable idea that the whole Medical School staff threatened

181

to resign. This would have put an end to an institution that had taken years to build up, and which had already produced a number of highly qualified black medical doctors who had become experienced in dealing particularly with those diseases to which blacks were prone in this country.

Luckily, however, the Government had second thoughts on the matter, and the University of Natal continues to administer its Medical School up to the present day. It was, however, not allowed (except by special permission of the Minister) to have black students in other faculties. Natal had at that time the largest number of blacks attending any South African university. Over the years, the University of Natal had gone to considerable expense in appointing additional staff and in providing additional accommodation for these students. For it, by government decree, to lose such a large number of students proved a serious financial loss to the university, in fees and in government subsidy. The University Council accordingly invited the then acting Minister for Education, Mr B. J. Vorster, to visit the University of Natal and see for himself the conditions under which we were training these black students. Despite our pleadings, the Minister remained unmoved, simply stating that 'it was government policy' to place these black students in separate institutions of their own. Thoroughly disappointed at the Minister's attitude, I made the following remark, which unfortunately proved prophetic, in the light of what happened during the next two decades: 'Mr Minister, you penalise the University of Natal financially for what it has done for the higher education of the non-whites, and yet you are prepared to spend millions on building separate universities for them. The blacks will think you are foisting something inferior onto them, and I won't be surprised if they burn those blooming places down!'

Shortly after I had taken the Minister to the airport, I started to write a pamphlet in Afrikaans, *The Autonomy of our Universities and Apartheid*. It was printed and published in 1957. As it throws light on the conditions that from time to time led to unrest in these separate, isolated universities for blacks, I take the liberty of quoting from it:

These isolated institutions in the Native areas may easily become centres of political disaffection, for, no matter how strict the supervision may be, it is impossible to isolate non-European students from outside influences. They read newspapers, and will undoubtedly be exposed to expression of discontent with the various disabilities under which their people suffer. This will not be avoided by placing the institution in the Native rural areas. A little yeast of discontent will soon leaven the whole lump.

In an isolated group of this kind there is a strong tendency for a grievance to be cherished, so that, sooner or later, there is an outbreak that may have disastrous results. These people are in many cases still close to the primitive mode of life; so that, as experience has shown, they may take to burning down buildings, just as they burn down each other's huts in tribal warfare. Experience in such separate institutions as Fort Hare, Adams College, Healdtown, Lady Frere, Lovedale, etc., has over and over again demonstrated that grievances degenerate into a kind of group neurosis. In such an isolated and limited environment there is little opportunity for pent-up feelings to be dissipated. They have no safety valve such as they would gain from contact with larger and wider institutions. They have no white contacts except with those put there by the government to discipline them.

It can be shown that in these isolated and separate institutions there have been bred more fanatically anti-European agitators than in the mixed universities. . . . The phenomenon is inherent in the situation, such as was evident from a report submitted to the Honourable the Minister of Education by a committee appointed some years ago to inquire into disturbances in Native educational institutions.

The mere fact that people who have a high-school and university education are more articulate than the untutored rural masses makes it more possible for them to ventilate their grievances and to become labelled as agitators. This is especially so among the blacks. Where, however, they attend mixed universities they are more likely to learn that there are limits beyond which one does not go, that certain things are 'not done' in a university. Association with the white students acts as a restraining influence as well as a means of dissipating the grievances of their race. I can testify to this as a result of twenty-one years of first-hand experience in handling the mixed university of Natal, with its large number of black students.

While one does not like to be dogmatic on these matters, one thing is certain: the future of this multiracial country of ours will depend largely on the type of white and black leadership that can be fostered in our universities.

The development of a black leadership which is self-reliant and free from inferiority complexes must go hand in hand with the development of a sense of responsibility towards the country as a whole. This, I believe, can most effectively be achieved where students, during their most formative years, can make contact and exchange ideas with the future leaders of the other racial groups. They must be given every opportunity of learning to understand each other's aspirations and to create a common set of values.

183

Thus far experience has shown that this is best achieved in a mixed institution of higher learning.

Conflict impeded progress

That there has been progress in education in the case of all racial groups during the last half-century cannot be denied. Of this, ample evidence has been given in the diagrams and tables already cited. What became clear also is that this progress took place at a different rate in the case of each of the four racial groups depending on the stage that each had reached at the beginning of this half-century, and also on the amount of leeway the black groups had to make up during this time. The rate at which they progressed was determined mainly by the amount of money that was spent on each group during the last fifty years.

What this progress would have been had this period not been marred by conflict, especially during the last decade, is difficult to show in statistical terms. What is certain, however, is that the material damage to school and university property, and the loss of life which these conflicts entailed, proved a great setback to education among certain population groups in several parts of the country, not to mention the loss in working hours on the part of the order-keeping forces of the Government.

However great this overt interference with the normal school procedure was, it is relatively small when compared with the incalculable psychological and moral damage which these conflicts caused in the field of human relations. In a subtle, but nevertheless real way, they created a hangover of unhappy instability among those who administered black education as well as among those who received that education. This was particularly so among the Africans, because, however hungry they were for education, this unhappy atmosphere affected the educational process adversely in the classrooms of the high schools and especially at university level in several parts of the country.

In conclusion, I emphasise again that the educator through the home and the school is the most powerful single attitude-forming agent in our society, particularly when it comes to the cultivation of attitudes towards other language and racial groups. These attitudes determine the way people will vote and in the end the laws under which we will live, learn and work in this complex country of ours.

. There has been considerable variation in the names designating the different ethnic groups in South Africa during the last fifty years. I sometimes use the terms current at the particular period of time under discussion, but wherever possible I have followed the Institute of Race Relations which refers to African, Asian and Coloured people collectively as 'blacks'. For detailed treatment see Ethnic Glossary in E. G. Malherbe, *Education in South Africa* (Johannesburg, 1977) vol. II, p. xiii.

. *Ibid.*, p. 700 for 1927 figures. Figures for 1977 kindly provided by J. H. Martins, Bureau of Market Research, University of South Africa.

. See *ibid.*, p. 252 *et seq.*, for a historical account of the provisions relating to compulsory school attendance for all four population groups.

. *Ibid.*, p. 295 for 1955 and 1965 figures, and Muriel Horrell *et al.*, *A Survey of Race Relations in South Africa, 1976* (Johannesburg, 1977) pp. 333, 342 and 348 for 1975 figures.

. Loraine Gordon *et al.*, *A Survey of Race Relations in South Africa, 1977* (Johannesburg, 1978) p. 522.

. Statement issued by Mr M. C. Botha on 29 December 1976, and published in full in *Bantu*, South African Department of Information, March 1977.

. *South African Digest*, 11 August 1978, p. 5.

. Sir Eric Ashby, *op. cit.* (Harvard University Press, Cambridge, Mass, 1966), p. 347.

8 Changing Racial Attitudes

HENRY LEVER

A base-line for the study of change

The scientific study of race attitudes in South Africa began at about the same time as the South African Institute of Race Relations was founded. The one event was not a cause of the other. It was rather that they both emanated from a common concern. MacCrone, a past President of the Institute, published the findings of his first study on race attitudes in 1930 based upon research that he had undertaken shortly before. His article[1] therefore, provides a suitable base-line against which changes in attitude can be assessed. MacCrone observed that: 'On all sides at the present moment in this country the problem of the relation between white and black is being subjected to an analysis from the historical, the economic, the political, the social and the religious points of view. Attempts are being made to diagnose the problem, to locate the difficulties and to propose solutions; and always the problem itself has been interpreted by those who have brought their minds to bear upon it in the light of their own special interests.'[2] These words, the opening sentences of MacCrone's early article, are as appropriate to-day as they were when they were first written.

MacCrone considered the attitude of whites towards blacks to be a complex one, being a compound of superiority, dislike, hostility, contempt and fear. There are now few social scientists who would dispute such a view. Public utterances by leaders representing most shades of political opinion to-day tend to discourage openly the notion of superiority or inferiority, although they may emphasise 'differences', especially differences in culture or value-orientation. Nonetheless, there is sufficient evidence to indicate that most whites tend to think of blacks as inferior. Thus nearly 90 per cent of a sample of voters in Durban agreed with the assertion that 'The Bantu is by nature a considerable way behind the whites in his level of civilisation'.[3] Even in an élite group of whites, nine in every ten believed

186

that: 'Even when a Bantu has a doctorate, Western culture is often a layer of veneer; deep down he remains a Bantu.'[4] The most authoritative finding on this issue comes from an opinion poll undertaken for the newspaper *Rapport* and is based on a large sample of white adults selected in such a way as to be representative of the electorate as a whole. In a study undertaken in March 1974 it was reported that nearly 90 per cent of the sample held the view that: 'It will still take many years before the Bantu will reach the same level of civilisation as the Whites'. There may be diverse views as to the causes of blacks 'lagging' behind whites in their level of 'civilisation', which would reflect differing attitudes toward blacks. Yet when whites make judgments as to the level of their own 'civilisation' they see blacks as being at a 'lower level'. This belief was held by supporters of all political parties, although there were differences in the extent to which the belief was held (nearly two-thirds of Progressives and more than 90 per cent of Nationalists held that view). When the differences between whites and Africans are regarded as 'inherent' it becomes a racist view. In the same study undertaken for *Rapport* two-thirds of the white voters supported the view that the differences were inherent (including one-third of Progressive supporters).[5] Despite official protestations, therefore, the notion of inferiority of blacks remains a significant and vital component in the attitudes of whites.

MacCrone pioneered the use of precise methods in the study of racial attitudes. His first study, however, was based on an analysis of essays written by 25 advanced students who were asked to describe their attitude to the black community and to give reasons for their answers. It will be helpful in attempting to assess the extent of changes in attitude to examine the racial situation as perceived by these students some fifty years ago.

In the first instance, MacCrone examined the influence of the past on then existing attitudes. He found that school textbooks emphasised violent conflict between the two groups. Massacres of unsuspecting whites by savage blacks formed the staple of the accounts of first contacts. This focus was especially strong among the descendants of the Voortrekkers. A trace of this influence was discernible in the prohibition of fire-arms to blacks. The rifle was the privileged possession of the white man and remained, in the last resort, 'that weapon which may be relied upon to settle any dispute between white and black'. Any outbreak of violence in South Africa produced emotional excitement in the minds of the whole white community. (Was the rush to purchase fire-arms and to emigrate from South Africa following the disturbances of 1976 an over-reaction on the part of whites?)

187

A second factor considered by MacCrone was the status of blacks. It was readily observable that all the menial and dirty work was performed by blacks. There was no question of comradeship since this implied equality; 'Kaffir work' was work which was below the dignity of whites to perform.

A third factor involved a consideration of crime. The impression was created that crimes were almost exclusively committed by blacks. The extensive burglar-proofing in South African houses was intended as a precaution against the black man. The convicts who were put to work in the streets and thus were exposed to the gaze of the public were always blacks. White convicts were never seen.

The perception of the black as inferior was considered as a fourth factor. A variety of factors which differentiate whites from blacks encouraged the image of the black as the opposite of the white.

MacCrone also considered certain psychological factors which had a bearing on understanding the attitudes of whites toward blacks. One such was the psychological significance of 'blackness'. The colour 'black' has a sinister connotation. 'It is the colour', says MacCrone, 'which always has been and still is associated with misfortune, ill luck, danger, witchcraft, evil or sin. Thus "black magic" is evil magic while devils and the ministers of evil in general are usually as black as the pit in which they have their dwelling place. The raven is a bird of ill-omen and, originally, the black cat was the familiar spirit of every witch.'[6] Black was identified with the savage who was free from the inhibitions found in civilised life. The sex impulse was particularly important. The black man therefore represented the unconscious with which the white man was in conflict. The white man experienced a hostility as well as an attraction to blacks which emanated from the same source. White men acted with resentment and jealousy at the thought of a black man coveting a white woman. White women reacted with fear. Yet, as most sexologists will confirm, black does elicit a strong sexual attraction. Thus we have a society which keeps the black man 'at arm's length and has no objection to embracing the black woman'.[7]

After a period of fifty years, South Africa remains the same society in a number of important respects. There have also been significant changes in the social climate described by MacCrone. Perhaps the most significant of these concerns the access to fire-arms. Blacks are still less likely than whites to obtain a fire-arm licence, although they are likely to be more successful in procuring one than they would have been years ago. The most significant change, of course, concerns the training of blacks in the use of fire-arms within the army. During the Second World War, blacks in the South

African army were generally relegated to service occupations such as cooking and the driving of trucks. Contemporary South Africa now witnesses the despatch of black soldiers to 'operational areas' and the preparation and training of 'homeland armies'. Almost daily there are exhortations on the national radio to the effect that the security of South Africa's borders is not the sole responsibility of the white population. Whites and blacks have to stand together in order to meet the common threat of Communism. Whatever the motivation may be, the salient fact is that fire-arms have been put in the possession of blacks and it is whites who are training them in their use.

A further important change is concerned with terminology. The term 'black' was originally used in a derogatory sense.[8] The terms 'Native', 'Bantu', 'African' and once again 'black' have been current at one time or another. At the time of writing the term 'black' has now been substituted for 'Bantu' in official documents. An interesting feature of South African society is that the terms used to describe racial or quasi-racial groups reveal something of the political orientation of the person using them. The political standpoint of the person using 'Bantu' or 'African' is easily recognisable. The return to the use of 'black' with a positive imputation as used, for example, by the 'Black Consciousness' movement is an attempt to redress the feelings of inferiority induced by white attitudes and behaviour.

This brings us to the question, is there a suitable base-line against which changes in the attitudes of blacks may be assessed? The study of the attitudes of blacks is far less satisfactory than the study of the attitudes of whites. Research undertaken before the 1970s is generally of an exploratory kind. The early study of the attitudes of blacks was undertaken at a later stage by whites who, of course, were in greater need of understanding such attitudes. For many years the resources at their disposal were inadequate for the task. It was only in the 1970s that a more satisfactory and systematic attempt at understanding the attitudes of blacks was undertaken.[9] Although there is no early social scientific appraisal of the attitudes of blacks, there is an important source which may be used. One of the most articulate spokesmen for Africans in South Africa was the late Dr D. D. T. Jabavu, a past vice-president of the South African Institute of Race Relations and a former leader of the African National Congress (originally formed as the South African Native National Congress). While he does not specifically describe the attitudes of blacks towards whites, he does present a graphic picture of South African society as viewed by Africans in the 1920s. In his book *The Black Problem*[10] he drew attention to the positive discontent existing amongst Bantu people. (Jabavu used the term 'Black', 'Bantu' and

'Native' interchangeably.) The blacks were awaking from their slumber and were beginning to make their voice heard. He expressed the view that unless something was done to heed that voice, 'it will not be very long before the whole white community must deal with a situation overwhelmingly beyond their control'.[11] The grievances of blacks could be summarised as follows:

1. The most immediate source of unrest was the financial pinch. Africans were living on pre-war wages (that is, First World War), plus a small increment, while the cost of living had increased considerably.
2. Successive droughts had made agriculture unprofitable and unpopular.
3. The political restrictions on Africans. The main sub-areas within this category were:
   (a) Taxation without representation is unjust. The time is past when Africans can be treated as children.
   (b) The greatest resentment is caused by the Native Land Act of 1913.
   (c) The pass laws are also a source of resentment. According to Jabavu: 'If ever one race in the world did ever seek the most original way to repress and humiliate one another, human invention could not have done it more effectually than the system of Pass Laws now obtaining in the Northern provinces.'[12]
4. The African has lost faith in the Department of Justice. The jury system is weighted against Africans and disproportionate sentences are imposed on racial lines.
5. The educated African is continually being harassed. 'Evening curfew bells restrict his freedom of movement among his friends and he is cut and snarled at throughout his life.'[13]
6. Africans are not properly treated on the railways.
7. Housing for Africans is inadequate. They live in squalid surroundings and in overcrowded conditions. The conveniences are distant and sometimes non-existent. Sanitation is bad.
8. The insecurity of land tenure. The possession of land is a natural ambition. In the locations (now called the 'townships') there are no facilities for the purchase of land and accordingly little incentive to improve houses.
9. The missionaries adopt a socially distant attitude.

10. Education for the Africans is in a chaotic condition.
11. The civil service is dominated by whites and Africans are placed on lower pay scales.
12. Bolshevistic and Nihilistic doctrines are gaining ground.
13. Agitators are able to exploit a situation where it is seen that whites have everything and blacks have nothing.

Jabavu cautioned that it was necessary to be familiar with the grievances of Africans in order to be able to make a positive contribution to their resolution. Such understanding is perhaps more necessary today than it was a half-century ago.

Many of the grievances enumerated by Jabavu in the early years of South Africa's history are still among the principal grievances of a broad cross-section of the African community. The financial difficulties of living in a period of rapidly rising costs is still of prime importance to the majority of Africans. This is clear from the *Quotso* report of 1973 based on a sample of 800 Africans in Soweto, the Markinor homelands study of 1974 and the *Quotso* 1975 study[14] based on a sample of 800 African women living in the major metropolitan areas of Johannesburg, the East and West Rand, Pretoria, the Durban/Pietermaritzburg area, Port Elizabeth and East London and the Bloemfontein/Goldfields areas.

The pass laws still remain a source of resentment. Approximately two-thirds of the African youths studied by Edelstein expressed resentment of influx control.[15]

From the point of view of the black man, some conditions have changed while others, especially the issue of political rights, have remained the same over the period of a half-century.

The importance of attitudes

There are divergent views on the importance of attitudes in social life. In terms of the Marxist theoretical perspective, for example, attitudes do not play a dynamic role in the shaping of a society. To believe the contrary would be regarded as 'idealistic' and hence unacceptable to a 'material-istic' interpretation of history. Marxists accordingly tend to regard atti-tudes either as non-existent or as 'irrelevant' or even 'superficial'. If they are none of these, then it is argued that attitudes simply 'reflect' the social class backgrounds of individuals. Of course, attitudes do not simply 'reflect' social class backgrounds, but it is hard to shake the faith of the adherents of this modern secular religion.

The importance of attitudes tends to be assessed differently by persons of different background, interest, occupation and experience. Church ministers and educationists, in particular, are likely to regard attitudes as crucial. Since they deal with the 'soul' or 'mind' of man their views are understandable. Members of minority groups react in different ways to attitudes and prejudice (a particular form of attitude). Thus members of the Jewish group tend to pay particular attention to attitudes and prejudice. Throughout the centuries, Jews have been the subject-matter of a number of outlandish beliefs. Thus, for example, they have been accused of 'torturing the holy bread'. This abomination was said to cause holy statues to shed tears. Whole communities of Jews were exterminated on the grounds of these beliefs.[16] Jews have also been accused of sacrificing Christian children as part of the Passover rites. Furthermore, in spite of their contributions to the arts and sciences, Jews were described by the Nazis as 'destroyers of civilisations'. The attempt to understand the thinking which underlies these bizarre beliefs is understandable in the Jewish group. On the other hand, many blacks in the United States are relatively unconcerned with the attitudes of whites. They maintain that institutionalised racism is their principal impediment to advancement in social life. In terms of this view, they are unconcerned if whites retain inaccurate and biased notions of blacks. What is important to them is that there should be no discrimination.

Attitudes refer to subjective states of the individual. Attitudes, accordingly, can never be seen, touched, heard or felt. Attitudes are always inferred from observable conduct. Most of the information on racial attitudes obtained by social scientists is based on statements of opinions from which an inference of an underlying mental state is derived, since opinions are regarded as the verbalised expression of attitudes. Attitudes may thus be regarded as a compound of beliefs, feelings and tendencies to react which are inferred on the basis of expressed opinions.

One of the difficulties concerning attitudes is that they (attitudes) often diverge from expected behaviour. Attention was drawn to this phenomenon as early as 1934 by the eminent social scientist Richard LaPière.[17] LaPière had occasion to travel extensively across the United States with a respectable-looking foreign Chinese couple. They booked into numerous hotels and frequented more than a hundred restaurants in areas known for their hostile attitudes toward Orientals. LaPière was puzzled by what he had seen. After completion of his travels he sent a questionnaire to the restaurants and hotels they had visited (and to a control group of similar restaurants and hotels in the same areas). He found that the overwhelming majority of the establishments visited said that they would not accept Chinese visitors. Yet these were precisely the establishments which had accepted them. LaPière used his very convincing data to embark on a polemic against the value of conventional attitude scales. To-day social scientists do not dispute LaPière's data. However, there are more satisfactory explanations for his findings. It is generally recognised now that behaviour itself can be inconsistent. Furthermore, behaviour like opinions, can be calculated to mislead. Attitudes can tell us a great deal about behaviour, but behaviour cannot be understood or 'predicted' simply from attitudes. If we are to understand behaviour, we must understand attitudes plus a number of other factors which are relevant in a given social situation. As one authority has put it: 'An attitude . . . is simply one of the terms in the complex regression equation we use to predict behaviour.'[18] Above all else, we need to understand the social context within which behaviour occurs. Thus a woman living in an integrated neighbourhood in the United States could take pride in being greeted by her first name by her black neighbours, 'but would faint if they did so in the main street in front of my friends'.[19]

During the 1960s and 1970s in particular, a great deal of progress was made in identifying the 'missing variables' which need to be fitted into the complex regression equation linking attitudes with behaviour. The role of leadership is important in affecting behaviour[20] and if leaders differ in their policies in different settings, then the behaviour of their followers is found to differ in such settings. Thus when a trade union opposed racial discrimination but a neighbourhood association debarred Negro residents, the majority of people in the area concerned manifested ambiguous and contradictory behaviour. In the work setting, individuals indentified themselves with union policy and in their areas of residence with the neighbourhood association.[21] It was pointed out by the researchers engaged in that particular study that in neither home nor work did the individual act out abstract generalised attitudes. The normative standards prevailing in any setting are also crucial. Thus underground workers may disregard racial distinctions while underground, but assiduously observe 'racial etiquette' when above ground.[22] Furthermore, the influence of friends and family extends to the types of racial contacts in which the individual is likely to engage.

One area in which beliefs and attitudes are widely considered to be related to behaviour is in the field of voting. A phenomenon which has puzzled a number of observers is that very often voters disagree with the policies of the parties which they support. The opinion poll undertaken for the Afrikaans Sunday newspaper *Rapport* during the course of the 1977 general election contained ten statements of opinion concerning Africans. Seven of the ten statements comprised an atitude scale according to the criteria of what is known as 'scale analysis'.[23] The seven statements reflect doctrinaire National Party policy concerning Africans. It was interesting to observe that there were a number of Nationalists who disagreed with every one of the seven National Party standpoints. There were also some Progressives who agreed with six of the seven National Party standpoints. It is also known that some Nationalists support the policy of a qualified franchise while some Progressives favour an independent parliament for Africans.[24] How then is one to understand the relationship between beliefs (attitudes) and behaviour (voting)?

Considerable progress has been made by social scientists in the past two decades in the development of 'causal analysis'. It should be acknowledged that causation can never be 'proved' in an absolute sense by these methods. What social scientists do is to construct some causal models in accordance with their theoretical orientations or expectations. Certain consequences flow from the models. It becomes possible, for example, to test whether any model is compatible with the data. If it is not, it is rejected. Thus progress is made by rejecting unsuitable models and confining oneself to the remaining models. Inferences of causal relations can then be made with a fair degree of confidence.

In South Africa (and elsewhere) there is a popular belief that the voter's views on issues predispose him to vote for a particular party. In technical terms, the political party is the 'dependent variable' and the opinions are the cause or 'independent variable'. Using the seven opinion statements of the 1977 *Rapport* opinion poll, it can be shown that the causal relations between the variables can be represented as:

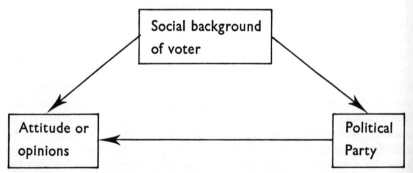

The arrows represent causal directions. The diagram shows that heretofore we have incorrectly identified the dependent variable. The political party which the voter supports is one of a number of influences that affect attitudes or beliefs. This conception does not mean that ideas have no reality or that they have no dynamic role to play in social life. However, in the context in which they occur, opinions are rationalisations (justifications) for political behaviour.

The logic underlying the derivation of the above diagram is fairly simple. However, the mathematical rationale on which the analysis is undertaken is more complex.[25]

Attitudes by themselves can never explain the social system prevailing in South Africa. Yet attitudes are never far away from such explanations. The division of the society on racial or ethnic lines is not due to an inherent characteristic of the peoples in a society. In Brazil there are blacks (of African origin), persons of 'mixed blood' (Coloureds), Indians (American) and whites. Yet race is not perceived as the major division in the society. Skin colour may differentiate various people, but skin colour is not always perceived as being of social importance. Attitudes therefore are important in telling us:

(a) what type of society we live in;
(b) what the major divisions of the society are;
(c) what the stratification system in the society is;
(d) the extent of inter-group tension;
(e) changes of inter-group tension;
(f) how to understand and interpret the behaviour of people in the society.

What we know about racial attitudes

Racial attitudes are influenced by a variety of factors. In a society which is stratified on racial and ethnic lines, as is South Africa, it is to be expected that the ethnic group to which the individual belongs exercises the most potent influence on the development and expression of attitudes. Social class and socio-economic status are, by comparison, of lesser importance. As MacCrone has pointed out: 'In a society organised upon the basis of two mutually exclusive white and black groups, it will be the individual's race membership which will be of far greater importance in determining his attitudes and behaviour than his membership of any particular class within his racial group.'[26] There are far greater differences in attitudes between members of different ethnic groups than there are differences between classes, and the former exercises a more potent influence than the latter.

The patterns of preference of some ethnic groups in South Africa are presented below.

Preferences of

Afrikaans Whites	English Whites	Jews	Coloureds
Afrikaans-speaking South Africans	English-speaking South Africans	Jews	Cape Coloureds
English-speaking South Africans	British	English-speaking South Africans	British
British	Afrikaans-speaking South Africans	British	English-speaking South Africans
Hollanders	Hollanders	Hollanders	Scotsmen
Germans	Jews	Afrikaans-speaking South Africans	Hollanders
Jews	Germans	Greeks	Portuguese
Italians	Italians	Italians	Indians
Greeks	Greeks	Portuguese	Afrik.-speaking South Africans
Portuguese	Portuguese	Japanese	Africans
Chinese	Chinese	Chinese	Jews
Coloureds	Japanese	Germans	Belgians
Japanese	Coloureds	Africans	Germans
Africans	Africans	Russians	
Indians	Russians	Coloureds	
Russians	Indians	Indians	

Indians	Zulus	Tswanas	S.Sothos
Indians	Zulus	Tswanas	S. Sothos
British	Swazis	S. Sothos	Tswanas
English-speaking South Africans	S. Sothos	Zulu	Zulu
Scotsmen	Tswanas	Pedis	Pedis
Cape Coloureds	Xhosas	Xhosas	Xhosas
Portuguese	Shangaans	Vendas	Swazis
Natives	Pedis	Shangaans	Shangaans
Germans	Vendas	Swazis	Vendas
Belgians	English-speaking South Africans	Coloureds	Coloureds
Hollanders	Coloureds	English-speaking South Africans	English-speaking South Africans
Jews	Indians	Indians	Indians
Afrikaans-speaking South Africans	Jews	Jews	Jews
	Afrikaners	Afrikaners	Afrikaners

Data in respect of the preferences of the English, Afrikaans and Jewish groups are taken from a study reported by the present author.[27] The preferences of Coloureds and Indians are taken from a study of Mac-Crone's[28] and the remaining groups from Edelstein's study of young Africans in Soweto.[29]

It will not come as a surprise to find that each group prefers the members of its own group. The groups which they feel closer towards come next and the groups to which the greatest 'social distance' is expressed are placed last. It is apparent that each group has its own distinctive pattern of ethnic preferences. The whites place Africans, Coloureds and Indians at a considerable social distance. Generally the Chinese and Japanese are placed above Africans, Coloureds and Indians. The attitudes of whites toward Russians are rather interesting. It is likely that this attitude is affected by political considerations rather than simply as an assessment in terms of ethnicity.

It will be seen that Afrikaans whites are not well liked by Coloureds, Indians or Africans. MacCrone has drawn attention to a 'Boer phobia'[30] in terms of which Afrikaners receive more than their fair share of blame and the English are treated more charitably than they deserve simply because the 'better of two evils' appears to be a common good. An interesting interpretation of the favourable attitude expressed by Africans towards the English is suggested by Brett and Morse. 'Since political power is controlled by the National Party', they say, 'the opposition parties which are more heavily English in composition, are able to oppose discriminating legislation without having to face the consequences involved in the modification of this legislation.'[31] It will also be seen that Jews are not particularly well liked by Coloureds, Indians and Africans. This attitude toward Jews may reflect economic disparities, personal ignorance of this numerically small group, or provide a substitute target for the hostilities felt towards whites in general.

It is evident from the preceding data that South Africa is not simply a society beset by white-black antagonisms. 'The best way of describing South African society', according to Feit, 'is to say that it consists of groups of peoples thrown together by history, all hating each other, but not enough to want to end their relationship. South Africa is, in other words, the same as everywhere else – only more so.'[32] In some respects, this view may be an over-statement. Yet it does make clear that South Africa is far from being a unified and harmonious society.

Social class, although not as potent an influence as ethnic group, does affect the way one perceives and reacts to the various groups which comprise the South African population. Generally, whites of lower status tend to regard the African as a threat, and consider him to be a poor worker who constantly needs to be supervised by a white and who is ungrateful for 'all' that he has received. The general pattern is also for whites of low status to enhance their ego through their attitudes towards Africans. Thus a white of low status and little accomplishment can always pride himself on being better than any African, no matter what the latter's accomplishments may be. Lower-class whites in South Africa are, therefore, likely to subscribe to the view that the African is childish and irresponsible, needs to be supervised in his work and behaves like an animal.[33] One of the accompaniments to wealth in contemporary society appears to be the acquisition of guilt feelings,[34] and South Africa is no exception in this respect. Thus the attitude of upper-class whites to Africans is characterised by guilt feelings. Statements such as: 'We should be ashamed at the low wages paid to Africans' are likely to be supported by members of the upper class. Upper-class whites are also less likely to perceive Africans as a threat and generally favour their educational, economic and political advancement. This tendency runs counter to the Marxist notion that the racial situation in South Africa is devised to enable the capitalists to exploit the masses or workers.

Education also has a bearing on ethnic attitudes. To a certain extent, education overlaps with social class. However, it can be shown that education has a distinct influence on ethnic attitudes apart from social class (viewed in terms of general life-style).[35] Generally, education tends to extend the intellectual horizons of people and to discourage biased and categorical views of people.

The relationship between a number of sociological variables affecting attitudes toward Africans can be represented in a type of 'path diagram'. The data are obtained from the seven opinion statements in the 1977 opinion poll undertaken for *Rapport*.

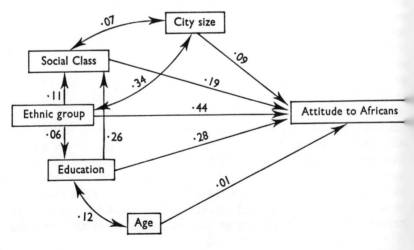

This is an over-simplified 'path diagram' since a great deal of relevant information has been excluded. The straight lines with arrow-heads represent the direction of causality. The bent lines with double-headed arrows represent correlation without an imputation of causation. The extent of causal influence is indicated by the values shown on each causal path. Each value represents the effect of each variable only, with the other variables 'controlled'. Thus ethnic-group membership is the most powerful influence and age the least powerful. The notion deriving from Marxist theory that attitudes simply reflect class background is thus over-simplified and inaccurate.

There are, of course, other influences on racial attitudes apart from the sociological ones. Certain types of personalities have been said to be prone to racial prejudices. Most research has been concentrated on the 'authoritarian personality' syndrome. The 'authoritarian personality' is rather complex and characterised, *inter alia*, by conventionality and submission to ingroup members, rigidity of outlook, anti-scientific attitudes, gullibility, compulsive religious beliefs, suspicion of others and admiration for the strong coupled with contempt for the weak. People with authoritarian characteristics are found in South Africa and are evident, for example, in those who admire *kragdadigheid*, that is, 'forcefulness'. Such personality characteristics are often correlated with hostile attitudes towards blacks. However, when the ethnic group of the respondent is 'controlled' in the analysis, the correlations are reduced to very small values. Thus Pettigrew claims that 'personality components do not in themselves account for heightened intolerance'.[36] Other personality characteristics have likewise been studied in relation to hostile attitudes. Amongst the most important of these are anomie (a sense of self-to-others belonging) and 'closed-mindedness' or dogmatism. Once again when ethnic group membership is 'controlled' the influence of these personality characteristics becomes negligible. According to Orpen: 'The consistent results indicate that personality factors should *not* be stressed in the explanation of prejudice in relatively "prejudicial" settings.'[37]

A third source of influence on racial attitudes is the historico-cultural one. The fairly stable patterns of ethnic attitudes which prevail in South Africa are the result of the transmission of norms of interracial conduct from generation to generation in the process of socialisation. Attitudes have thus become 'traditional'. As one authority has put it in discussing attitudes toward Negroes in America: 'Attitudes toward Negroes are now chiefly determined not by contacts with Negroes, but by contact with the prevalent attitude towards Negroes.'[38] Attitudes are acquired from one's peer groups, parents and teachers. The educational system in South Africa operates in several ways to perpetuate racial antagonism. Prejudice is found in the classroom in several forms. Many teachers impart prejudice, wittingly or unwittingly. History textbooks show a distinct bias in the selection and presentation of history.[39] Even grammar textbooks used in elementary schools reflect a prejudiced attitude toward blacks. MacCrone points out that one of the functions of the hostile attitude to Africans is that it facilitates the process of adjustment. According to MacCrone: 'There is no need for the individual to discover what adjustment he should make. . . . The place of the native is prescribed in the scheme of things.'[40]

Some attitudes of blacks

It was mentioned earlier that the study of the attitudes of blacks was less well developed than the study of the attitudes of whites. In part, this uneven development reflects the belief that it is the attitudes of whites which are responsible for the present pattern of race relations and for the preservation of political power in their hands. There are, of course, other reasons for the inadequate study of the attitudes of blacks. Whites, particularly university students, are more readily accessible as subjects for research. There is also the difficulty of securing adequately trained black interviewers who, until recent times, have been in short supply. There are also problems in the standardisation of attitude scales for members of different ethnic groups and other problems of instilling sufficient confidence in black interviewees to enable them to talk freely on matters of a political or near-political kind.

Although there is a voluminous literature on the attitudes of blacks, most research studies have been of an exploratory kind. It was only in the 1970s that any serious attempts at securing representative samples of blacks were made. At the time of writing, there has still not been a single study of the opinions of a nationally representative sample of blacks. However there have been a number of studies of important sections of the black community which yield reliable information on opinions and attitudes. There are, of course, numerous aspects of such attitudes to be considered. In the short space available here, it is necessary to be highly selective.[41]

An important area of interest is the perception by blacks of their major problems and grievances. Reliable information on the grievances of a cross-section of urban Africans comes from the *Quotso* survey of 197 based on a representative sample of 800 Africans in Soweto.[42] African were more than willing to talk about their problems. The research team

200

reported that a flow of words gushed forth when Africans were questioned on this topic. The most important problems of Africans, in order of importance, were found to be the following:

Insufficient money
Lower wages than whites
Poverty
The high cost of living
Pass laws and police raids
Influx control, not allowed to live and work where please
Oppression by whites
Job reservation
Housing
Crime and thugs
Bad treatment by whites
No unity of blacks
Lack of education

Some categories overlap to a certain extent with others. 'Insufficient money' was mentioned by 41 per cent of the respondents, 'lower wages than whites' by 22 per cent, 'poverty' by 19 per cent and 'high cost of living' by 15 per cent. The combination of these problems provide testimony of the very real economic deprivation experienced by Africans.

A similar type of question was asked by the Arnold-Bergstrasse Institute[43] in their study of urban Africans in Soweto, Durban and Pretoria in 1977. The improvements which Africans wanted to see most, in order of importance, were:

More work opportunities, better treatment and
    equal wages with whites
Improvement in housing conditions
The right to freehold property in the city
Abolition of the pass laws and influx control

Economic priorities were the most important for Africans in all three areas, but were highest in Pretoria.

Young Africans are apparently more politically conscious than their elders. Edelstein found the grievances of African matriculation students in Soweto to be, in order of importance, as follows:

Inadequate political rights
Influx control
Inadequate income
Inadequate educational facilities
Inadequate opportunities for employment

Inadequate accommodation

Restricted mobility within South Africa

The problems of Africans living in the homelands differ from those living in the towns, as was shown by the Markinor study undertaken of four homelands. The most important problems of Africans living in these areas were, respectively:

Insufficient money

Insufficient jobs

Poor transport

No water or unclean water

Land too small

No proper roads

The Theron Commission of Enquiry into matters affecting the Coloured population group followed the rather unusual but commendable procedure of commissioning a survey of the opinions of Coloureds. A representative sample of more than 2 000 Coloured persons in all regions of the country was obtained. Asked for their views on the most important problems, the following matters, in order of importance, were cited:

Housing

The financial position

Crime

Political rights

Educational facilities

Work conditions

Segregation and discrimination

No representative sample study of the opinions of Indians has been undertaken as yet. Indians are the most neglected group in the study of attitudes.

What type of political dispensation is desired by blacks? There is very little authoritative data on this matter. The indications are that urban Africans reject the notion of Bantustans in favour of the principle of a unified South Africa with equal opportunities for all races.[44] Support for the Bantustan idea is stronger amongst Africans who live in the homelands.[45] At one stage there was some support for a qualified franchise among educated Africans.[46] However, it is unlikely that this notion would enjoy much support to-day.

The survey undertaken for the Theron Commission did not examine the ideal model of South African society sought by Coloured persons. However, there was a tendency for Coloured persons to feel that their political future lay with the whites rather than with the Africans.

The converse of the grievances of blacks are their hopes and aspirations particularly as they apply to their children. One study of Africans sought to establish their life-goals.[47] The order of importance of their life-goals was as follows:

Education	Freedom
Security	Human rights
Material benefits	A home
Health and happiness	To help others
Comfort	A better government
Other personal needs	

It will be helpful to bear these aspirations in mind when considering attitudes towards change.

Attitudes and change

The changing character of racial attitudes during the fifty-year period under review is difficult to chronicle. There are no official statistics on attitudes which are comparable, say, to the gross domestic product, the number of registered voters, the international trade balance, or the size of the prison population. Attitudes are of principal concern to the social scientist and those reliant on them and are of less concern to governments except in so far as they relate to the government's mandate and ancillary matters.

There have been comparatively few studies in South Africa of changes in attitudes and opinions over periods of time. MacCrone has reported the changes in attitudes of university students during the period 1934 to 1944.[48] The American psychologist, Thomas Pettigrew, undertook a study of the attitudes of students at the University of Natal[49] which was replicated some years later.[50] The present writer has considered the changes in racial and ethnic attitudes characteristic of the white adult population of Johannesburg between 1964 and 1968.[51] The Arnold-Bergstrasse Institute in Freiburg has studied attitudes of the white electorate from 1974 to 1977.[52]

There are a number of difficulties in seeking to assess the extent and direction of changes in attitudes over the period of fifty years. The attitude studies are based on different types of subjects, different sampling plans, different measuring instruments and were undertaken in different parts of the country. One can never be sure, therefore, of the extent to which the differences in attitudes reflect differences at various points of time or any one or more of a number of confounding influences. An overall assessment of the differences in attitudes from the earliest to the most recent times and subject to the necessary qualifications attendant upon such comparison, suggests that there has been stability as well as change. It was seen earlier that many of the characteristic features of the racial attitudes which Mac-Crone described are recognisable to-day. Likewise the principal grievances of the African, Coloured and Indian communities of the 1920s have not been redressed to any remarkable degree. In some cases, particularly as regards Coloured persons, their grievances have been exacerbated. The patterns of ethnic preferences revealed in an early study by MacCrone[53] are essentially the patterns which prevail to-day. Those changes in attitudes and opinions which have occurred have been neither consistently favourable nor unfavourable to racial groups. Nor have they followed any cyclical or other discernible trend. Racial attitudes appear to have fluctuated from unfavourable to favourable over the years. In general, racial attitudes appear to have been modified as important events have occurred and general circumstances have changed. Thus the shootings at Sharpeville were accompanied by feelings of pessimism on the part of Africans as to the future.[54] Similarly, there was a sharp decline in the optimism of Africans following the disturbances of 1976 and 1977.[55] However, white university students appear to have become more sympathetic to Africans following these disturbances.[56]

Changes in economic conditions, international affairs and security problems have induced new attitudinal reactions. During the course of the Second World War, Malherbe found South African soldiers to be less desirous of according Africans improved employment opportunities than they were willing to accord them improved educational opportunities. 'This suggests', says Malherbe, 'that an important reason why many people oppose opportunities for Natives is the fear of economic competition. Education is a less direct threat than jobs or political power.'[57] The need for more skilled black labour and the consequent decline in the threat of competition[58] has been accompanied by the increased willingness on the part of whites to extend job and wage opportunities for blacks. The principle of 'equal wages for equal work' was supported by 62 per cent of a sample of the white electorate in 1974, 67 per cent in June 1976, 70 per cent in October 1976 (following the outbreak of violence in the townships) and 72 per cent in July 1977.[59]

There have also been changes in attitudes related to security matters. Thus in 1970 the majority of a sample of the white electorate (including one in every three Nationalists) declared itself opposed to the principle of detention without trial.[60] Yet when the Government ordered the detention without trial of a number of leading Africans on 19 October 1977 as well as ordering the closure of *The World* and imposed banning orders on a

204

number of individuals and organisations, nearly two-thirds of the electorate signified their approval (88 per cent of Nationalists, 56 per cent of South African Party supporters, 28 per cent of New Republic Party supporters and 11 per cent of Progressives).[61] It would appear that, in the abstract, there is opposition to infringements of the Rule of Law; but where such infringements seem calculated to put an end to continuing unrest they are regarded in a more favourable light.

There is a widely held belief that international reprobation of South Africa leads to a 'hardening' of attitudes on the part of whites. According to the eminent psychologist, Gordon Allport: 'Widespread disapproval throughout the world of the South African laws disenfranchising the Cape Coloured had the effect of strengthening the Nationalist Party of Malan and his supporters. Outside criticism is interpreted as an attack on the autonomy of the group. It usually results in greater cohesion. Hence the ethnocentrism that is under attack may become a necessary symbol of solidarity and flourish as never before.'[62] A similar view is expressed by Tiryakian.[63] It became possible to gauge the effect of the Security Council arms embargo on the views of the South African electorate by examining data from a panel study undertaken for the newspaper *Rapport* during the course of the South African general election of 1977. A panel study uses the same subjects, who are each interviewed on a number of occasions. A fairly precise estimate of effects can be obtained since information was obtained from the same people before as well as after the event. The effect of the Security Council resolution was only slight. In so far as changes of political allegiance occurred, such changes favoured the Progressive Federal Party.[64]

To a certain extent, changes in attitudes can be gauged from the very questions which are posed in opinion polls. That is, the questions may be as informative as the answers. The extent to which questions concerning change are posed is indicative of the fluidity of thinking, the perceived need for reform and of the changes which have already taken place in South African society. Thus in October 1977, two-thirds of a sample of the white electorate could say that there should be a new political dispensation for Africans living in the urban areas. (This view was shared by 57 per cent of Nationalists.)[65]

Following the disturbances which commenced in June 1976, increasing attention has been given to the need to bring about reforms. There have been some attempts to assess the extent to which the white electorate is willing to contemplate such changes. Valuable data have been obtained from an opinion poll undertaken for *Rapport* in 1976. The views of a sample of the electorate are presented in Table 1. The respondents were asked to indicate the changes which they would be willing to accept or which they would not accept.

Table 8.1

PERCENTAGE ACCEPTANCE OF CHANGES ACCORDING TO ETHNIC GROUP (*RAPPORT* POLL, 1976).

Change	Afrikaans	English	Total sample
1. *Repeal of the Immorality Act*			
Would accept	24,0	54,4	36,2
Would not accept	66,4	25,9	50,2
Uncertain	9,0	18,2	12,6
2. *Repeal of the Mixed Marriages Act*			
Would accept	17,9	49,4	30,5
Would not accept	73,0	33,1	57,1
Uncertain	8,4	16,5	11,7
3. *Universities which so choose, to be open to all races*			
Would accept	41,0	77,5	55,6
Would not accept	43,5	9,7	30,0
Uncertain	14,6	11,2	13,2
4. *Opening theatres to all races*			
Would accept	36,9	77,0	52,9
Would not accept	50,4	10,7	34,5
Uncertain	12,0	10,7	11,5
5. *Churches to be opened to all races*			
Would accept	31,4	90,0	54,8
Would not accept	54,9	4,5	34,7
Uncertain	13,2	3,8	9,5
6. *Abolition of job reservation*			
Would accept	41,7	81,5	57,6
Would not accept	33,8	6,3	22,8
Uncertain	22,6	10,2	17,7
7. *'Mixed Sport' up to club level*			
Would accept	50,4	88,3	65,6
Would not accept	34,4	5,5	22,8
Uncertain	14,3	4,9	10,5
8. *Freehold property rights for all races*			
Would accept	29,5	74,3	47,4

Change	Afrikaans	English	Total sample
Would not accept	47,8	10,2	32,8
Uncertain	20,8	13,9	18,0
9. Abolition of taxi apartheid			
Would accept	26,5	63,7	41,4
Would not accept	60,1	20,2	44,1
Uncertain	12,0	14,5	13,0
10. Abolition of ambulance apartheid			
Would accept	43,6	84,1	59,8
Would not accept	43,1	7,7	29,0
Uncertain	12,1	5,8	9,5
11. Abolition of passes, provided that everyone, White and Black, carries identity documents			
Would accept	68,9	83,9	74,9
Would not accept	17,2	7,0	13,1
Uncertain	13,2	7,8	11,0
12. Willing to work under a Black, if he is promoted on merit			
Would accept	34,5	72,4	49,7
Would not accept	43,4	10,1	30,1
Uncertain	21,2	16,2	19,2

It will be seen that there are considerable differences between English and Afrikaans voters in the changes that they would be willing to accept. The Mixed Marriages Act and the Immorality Act appear to be the most sacrosanct. There is apparently little objection to the abolition of passes, job reservation, ambulance apartheid, 'mixed universities', and to 'mixed sport' up to club level. There is greater resistance to taxi apartheid, working under a black, freehold rights for all races, and opening theatres and churches to members of all races.

In his monumental study of American society, the eminent Swedish social scientist, Gunnar Myrdal, pointed out that the fears of whites were inversely related to the aspirations of blacks.[66] A similar tendency is discernible in South Africa, although the rank orders do not follow the inverse form exactly. In the previous section it was seen that the desire for intermarriage or for interracial sex was of little or no relevance for Africans. Yet whites are more concerned with preserving the Mixed Marriages Act and Immorality Act than with the preservation of passes, job reservation, restricted universities or other forms of segregation. When marriages across the colour line were legal, there were comparatively few such marriages.[67] The prohibition of interracial marriages, therefore, was of greater symbolic significance than of practical importance. One cannot help but feel that the key to understanding the fears of whites was enunciated by MacCrone fifty years ago!

There are some authorities who believe that the views of whites on the changes which they are willing or unwilling to accept should form the basis for the formulation of a policy geared towards bringing a realistic modification of the society. This is reputedly the approach of the Arnold-Bergstrasse Institute at Freiburg. There is a three-fold fallacy underlying such a belief. In the first instance, it assumes that the crucial aspect of attitudes towards change is the opinion which the subjects express on the matter. But the salience of the opinion and the tenacity with which it is held are not taken into account. There is a tendency for social scientists to consider that the questions which they formulate are not only important for themselves, but also important for those to whom the questions are put. The questions, of course, may be of varying significance for different people. The salience of opinions and the tenacity of adherence to them are of paramount importance in considering the potentialities for attitude change.[68] Yet there have not been any studies in South Africa which have sought to assess these two particular characteristics and their consequences for significant change.

The faith in the value of data such as presented in Table 1 for forming a basis of a policy on change also ignores the role of political leaders in shaping attitudes and opinions. The data from opinion polls are not as clear as they could be on this influence, yet the indications are that when the government initiates change, such as in the sports policy, the opinions of the electorate generally follow behind them. It is likely that if the Prime Minister were to announce that the Immorality Act was itself immoral and should be repealed, the electorate would 'change their opinions' and support the repeal of the Act. This is in conformity with studies of voting which show that when there is a conflict between opinions and support for the party of one's choice, the conflict is usually resolved in favour of the party. The exact limits to which political leaders may succeed in carrying their supporters with them are not known. It is likely that the ability or inability correctly to perceive and react to the mood and needs of the times is one of the determining factors. Division within the party and the perceived self-interests of voters are also relevant.

Finally, the view that opinions on change should prescribe policies on change does not take account of the fact that opinions on the desirability of change are themselves subject to change. Thus an opinion poll undertaken

208

for *Rapport* in 1978 showed that there was less resistance to the repeal of the Immorality Act in 1978 than there was in 1976. Only 46,8 per cent of Afrikaans voters were unwilling to accept the repeal of the Act in 1978 compared with 66,4 per cent of such voters in 1976. The opposition of English voters remained at about the same level (26,6 per cent and 25,9 per cent respectively). There was very little change in the view that churches should be opened to members of all races. Thus 30,8 per cent of Afrikaans voters found this acceptable in 1978 compared with 31,4 per cent in 1976.[69] Attitudes towards racial segregation in churches would appear to be more tenacious than attitudes toward sex across the colour line. Church leaders, rather than political leaders, are best equipped to initiate changes in this regard.

A final matter which needs to be considered is the ability to change attitudes and opinions through deliberate efforts. It is reasoned that if members of the public can be persuaded to purchase brands of soap or cereals, it should be possible to market racial tolerance. Of course, predelictions for brands of soap or cereals do not have the same social significance or consequences as racial tolerance. While there is scope for changing racial attitudes, people are not as malleable as this naive marketing approach would suggest. Studies of the effect of the mass media on changing attitudes show that very often prejudiced people do not 'understand' the message of tolerance. Very often the message is distorted. Thus it is possible for a prejudiced person to believe that anti-prejudice material is actually designed to encourage people to express their prejudices openly.[70]

Education remains a powerful weapon in the war against racial intolerance. During the course of the Second World War, Malherbe found that courses designed to educate South African soldiers led to more favourable attitudes toward racial and ethnic groups. 'I have found', says Malherbe, 'that the careful and objective presentation of facts and allowing men to draw their own conclusions does bring them to revise their prejudices on the race question. At any rate, it makes them realise that they *are* prejudices.'[71] Yet Malherbe expressed regret at the fact that the progress which had been made through education in the army was lost when the men returned to civilian life. Malherbe was referring to a phenomenon which was later designated 'the re-entry effect'. For example, children's attitudes may be changed during the course of an interracial camp. These attitudes may be 'compartmentalised' in the sense that their changed attitudes and behaviour are confined to the camp environment. When they return to their communities or 're-enter' these communities they encounter standardised norms of behaviour which are regarded as appropriate for that particular setting. Thus there may be racial bias in one context and the lack of such bias in another. It is for this reason that a preference is expressed for attempting to change groups rather than individuals, or to attempt to change individual attitudes in group settings. The 'Springfield Plan', an educational programme designed in Springfield, U.S.A., accordingly attempted to educate the community at the same time as educating the school children. It was reasoned that it was futile and even harmful to attempt to change attitudes in one setting which would bring the child into conflict with attitudes in another setting. It needs to be recognised that attitudes never exist in isolation. The key to understanding attitudes and attitude change, therefore, consists in considering them in their social contexts. Any programme designed to change racial attitudes should also be co-ordinated with a programme designed to remove racial discrimination.

1. I. D. MacCrone, 'Psychological Factors Affecting the Attitude of White to Black in South Africa', *South African Journal of Science*, 27 (1930), 591–8.
2. *Ibid.*, p. 591.
3. L. Schlemmer, *Privilege, Prejudice and Parties* (Johannesburg, 1973).
4. H. Adam, 'The South African Power-Elite: A Survey of Ideological Commitment' in *South Africa: Sociological Perspectives*, ed. H. Adam (London, 1971), p. 80.
5. Mark en Meningopnames, *Meningspeiling vir Rapport* (Cape Town, 1974).
6. *Ibid.*, p. 596.
7. *Ibid.*, p. 598.
8. Personal communication from Professor MacCrone referring to the earliest version of his scale of attitudes towards the 'Native'.
9. Some of the more interesting exploratory studies of the attitudes of blacks will be found in *Contemporary South Africa*, ed. S. J. Morse and C. Orpen (Cape Town, 1975).
10. D. D. T. Jabavu, *The Black Problem* (Lovedale, 1920).
11. *Ibid.*, p. 2.
12. *Ibid.*, p. 6.
13. *Ibid.*, p. 9.
14. Quadrant, *Quotso 1973* (Johannesburg, 1973); Markinor, *Homelands Study* (Johannesburg, 1974); Markinor, *Quotso 1975* (Johannesburg, 1975).
15. M. L. Edelstein, *What Do Young Africans Think ?* (Johannesburg, 1972).
16. G. E. Simpson and J. M. Yinger, *Racial and Cultural Minorities*, 3rd ed. (New York, 1972), ch. 9.
17. R. T. LaPière, 'Attitudes vs Actions', *Social Forces*, 13 (1934) 230–7.
18. N. C. Weissberg, 'On De Fleur and Westie's "Attitude as a Scientific Concept" ', *Social Forces*, 43 (1965), 424.
19. M. Jahoda, 'Consistency and Inconsistency in Intergroup Behaviour', *Journal of Social Issues*, 5 (1949) 4–11.

20. M. L. Kohn and R. M. Williams, 'Situational Patterning in Intergroup Relations', *American Sociological Review*, 21 (1956) 164–74.
21. J. D. Lohman and D. C. Reitzes, 'Deliberately Organised Groups and Racial Behaviour', *American Sociological Review*, 19 (1954) 342–4.
22. R. D. Minard, 'Race Relations in the Pocahontas Coal Field', *Journal of Social Issues*, 8 (1952) 1.
23. L. Guttman, 'A Basis for Scaling Qualitative Data', *American Sociological Review*, 9 (1944) 139–50.
24. H. Lever, 'Public Opinion and Voting', in *The Government and Politics of South Africa*, ed. A. R. C. de Crespigny and R. Schrire (Cape Town, 1978), 146–7.
25. The rationale is set out in H. Lever, 'Inferring the Intervening and Dependent Variables', *British Journal of Sociology*, 30 (1979), 81–90. The detailed application of the method to the field of political sociology is set out in a forthcoming article, namely: 'The Issue in Issue Voting'.
26. I. D. MacCrone, 'Race Attitudes' in *Handbook on Race Relations in South Africa*, ed. E. Hellmann (Cape Town, 1949), 669–705.
27. H. Lever, 'Changes in Ethnic Attitudes in South Africa', *Sociology and Social Research*, 56 (1972), 202–10.
28. I. D. MacCrone, 'A Comparative Study of European and Non-European Differences in Race Preferences', *South African Journal of Science*, 35 (1938), 412–16.
29. *Ibid.*
30. I. D. MacCrone, 'Reaction to Domination in a Colour-Caste Society', *Journal of Social Psychology*, 26 (1947), 69–98.
31. E. A. Brett and S. J. Morse, 'A Study of the Attitudes of Some Middle Class Africans', in *Contemporary South Africa*, ed. S. J. Morse and C. Orpen (Cape Town, 1975) 163.
32. E. Feit, 'Community in a Quandary: The South African Jewish Community and "Apartheid" ', *Race*, 8 (1967), 403.
33. For a consideration of the differences in beliefs held by the various classes, see H. Lever, 'Social Class and Ethnic Attitudes in South Africa', *Social Science* (forthcoming).
34. E. Van den Haag, 'Economics is not Enough – Notes on the Anti-capitalist Spirit', *The Public Interest*, 45 (1976), 109–122.
35. See 'Social Class and Ethnic Attitudes', *art. cit.*
36. T. F. Pettigrew, 'Personality and Socio-cultural Factors in Intergroup Attitudes', *Journal of Conflict Resolution*, 2 (1958) 32.
37. C. Orpen, 'Authoritarianism Revisited: A Critical Examination of "Expressive" Theories of Prejudice', in Morse and Orpen, *op cit.*, p. 109.
38. E. L. Horowitz, 'Development of Attitude Toward Negroes', *Archives of Psychology*, 194 (1936), 34–5.
39. F. E. Auerbach, *The Power of Prejudice in South African Education* (Cape Town, 1965).
40. I. D. MacCrone, 'The Functional Analysis of a Group Attitude Towards the Native', *South African Journal of Science*, 30 (1933), 687–9.
41. For a more detailed treatment, see Morse and Orpen, *op. cit.*
42. Quadrant International S.A. (Pty) Ltd., *Quotso* (Johannesburg, 1973).

43. T. Hanf, H. Weiland and G. Vierdag, *Südafrika: Friedlicher Wandel?* (Munich, 1978).
44. P. Mayer, *Urban Africans and the Bantustans* (Johannesburg, 1972).
45. Markinor, *Homelands Study* (Johannesburg, 1974).
46. L. Kuper, *An African Bourgeoisie* (New Haven, 1965).
47. Brett and Morse, *op. cit.*
48. MacCrone, 'Race Attitudes,' *art. cit.*
49. T. F. Pettigrew, 'Social Distance Attitudes of South African Students', *Social Forces*, 38 (1960), 246–53.
50. R. H. Lent, W. Holtzman and E. C. Mosely, 'Sociocultural Factors and Personality in Intergroup Attitudes', paper read at April meeting of Eastern Sociological Society, 1967. Cited in J. W. Mann, 'Attitudes Toward Ethnic Groups' in Adam, *South Africa: Sociological Perspectives* (London, 1971), 50–72.
51. Lever, 'Changes in Ethnic Attitudes', *art. cit.*
52. Hanf *et al.*, *op. cit.*
53. MacCrone, 'A Comparative Study', *art. cit.*
54. P. L. Van den Berghe, 'Race Attitudes in Durban, South Africa', *Journal of Social Psychology*, 57 (1962), 55–72.
55. H. Lever, *South African Society* (Johannesburg, 1978) 204–5.
56. P. C. L. Heaven and H. J. Groenewald, 'New Social Distance Data of English-speaking South Africans', *Psychological Reports*, 40 (1977), 247–9.
57. E. G. Malherbe, *Race Attitudes and Education* (Johannesburg, 1946), 14.
58. See Sheila T. Van der Horst, 'The Changing Face of the Economy', chapter 5 of this volume.
59. Hanf *et al.*, *op. cit.*, 243.
60. H. Lever, 'Opinion Polling in South Africa', *Public Opinion Quarterly*, 38 (1974), 400–08.
61. H. Lever, 'The Effect of Restrictive Government Measures and the Security Council Resolution on the South African General Election of 1977' (forthcoming).
62. G. W. Allport, *The Nature of Prejudice* (New York, 1954) 230.
63. E. A. Tiryakian, 'Sociological Realism: Partition for South Africa', *Social Forces*, 46 (1967) 211.
64. Lever, 'The Effect of Restrictive Government Measures', *art. cit.*
65. Mark en Meningopnames, *Meningspeiling vir Rapport* (Cape Town, October 1977).
66. G. Myrdal, *An American Dilemma* (New York, 1944).
67. H. Sonnabend, 'Population' in *Handbook*, ed. Hellmann, *op. cit.*, 10–12.
68. C. W. Sherif, M. Sherif and R. E. Nebergall, *Attitude and Attitude Change* (Philadelphia, 1965).
69. Mark en Meningopnames, *Meningspeiling vir Rapport* (Cape Town, March 1978).
70. E. Cooper and M. Jahoda, 'The Evasion of Propaganda: How Prejudiced People Respond to Anti-Prejudice Propaganda', *Journal of Psychology*, 23 (1947) 15–25.
71. *Ibid.*, p. 7.

9 South Africa in a Changing World

JOHN BARRATT

The development of South Africa's external relations during the past five decades has involved an interaction between a rapidly changing world order (especially since the Second World War) and a changing South Africa. As with any other country, neither the world environment nor the South African situation can be viewed in static terms. However, as a small-to-medium power, South Africa's impact on the world generally has been minimal, although this has probably increased in recent times as the conflicts of southern Africa have moved nearer the centre of the world's stage. South African foreign policy in the past has thus been largely a matter or responding to stimuli from the external environment, and this essay will attempt to assess the nature of the responses over the years.

At the same time, there is another level of interaction, namely that between the government's foreign and domestic policies. No government can isolate its foreign policy from domestic considerations, but for many years the South African Government has tried to do just that, in spite of – or perhaps because of – the fact that its domestic policies have increasingly become the central issue in its external relations. A further related problem on this level is that domestic influence on South African foreign policy has been mainly confined within the limits of the white electorate. Thus, when one speaks of a South African response to an external stimulus, one is thinking in fact of the response of the Government and the whites who support it. The response of the majority of black South Africans, which would probably have been different in many cases, if clearly articulated, has not had a significant impact on South Africa's external relations in past years. However, black attitudes are now increasingly influencing the policies of other countries towards South Africa. The changing world order has forced Western governments, in their own interests, to try to ascertain and then take into account, more than in the past, the views of the black majority.

The two levels of interaction are, of course, linked, and they come together especially at those points where the changes in the world environment impinge directly on aspects of the domestic situation. Specifically, in South Africa's case, the growing and now universal condemnation of racism and the ending of colonialism are such changes.

Before 1945

Before and throughout the Second World War South Africa, although a small power, was a respected member of the Western-dominated world community. As a part of the Commonwealth, following Britain's lead, South Africa's foreign policy was less than independent, but the country was widely seen as playing a constructive international role, which was personified in the figure of General Smuts. Smuts was a principal architect of the League of Nations; he shared in the councils of world statesmen, especially during the war years; and he contributed to the evolution of the Commonwealth and to the founding of the United Nations. Though ties with Europe were the main consideration for South Africa, there were many contacts, economic and technical, in Africa, and South African leaders, not only General Smuts, had a vision of a growing South African role in Africa that extended even to the idea of federations in South, Central and Eastern Africa, in which South African influence would predominate.[1] But that was an Africa under colonial control, and the links and influence were through colonial governments. In the 1930s, and even during the War, few people in Europe, let alone South Africa, could have imagined that the colonial system would so soon be seriously and fatally challenged.

South Africa administered its own 'colony' of South West Africa under a mandate from the League of Nations. While there was some criticism within the League's Mandates Commission of the Government's administration of the Territory,[2] there were no problems which significantly affected South Africa's respected standing in the League or in the international community generally. Similarly, although racial problems within South Africa itself were growing, in the 1930s they were not an overriding issue in domestic politics, and they did not figure as an international issue. At the most, there was concerned interest in Western countries as to how these problems would be handled, but there was no articulated world opinion on them, let alone pressures to which South Africa had to respond.

South Africa's position internationally was nevertheless the subject of some controversy domestically, and this was focused on the constitutional question of the limits imposed on independence by membership of the

214

men and things. And to grow is to survive. Yet this also means change, adaptation, tolerance and a committed acceptance of the new, an employing of the new to one's own advantage.'[26]

Dr Verwoerd laid the basis for this new approach, for instance in his acceptance of the principle of independent black-ruled states living in harmony with a white-controlled Republic of South Africa. Initially this applied to the British High Commission Territories, with two of them due to become independent in 1966 (Botswana and Lesotho), although he saw this in the context of his policy which provided for future independent homelands. But Dr Verwoerd proved to be very cautious and slow-moving in giving practical effect to this principle, even as it applied to the political development of the homelands. The Transkei alone was placed firmly on the road to self-government by Dr Verwoerd. It was left to Mr John Vorster as Prime Minister, after Dr Verwoerd's assassination in September 1966, to develop what became known as the 'outward movement' or 'outward policy' on a more pragmatic basis. In May 1967 Mr Vorster said in a Republic Day address: 'It is not my intention to try to build Rome in one day, but slowly and systematically to establish relations to our benefit and the benefit of the neighbouring states in Southern Africa and further North where saner attitudes prevail.'[27] A year later, after there had been considerable debate about the phrase 'outward movement', Dr Hilgard Muller, who had succeeded Mr Eric Louw as Foreign Minister in 1963, stated: 'What is happening must be seen as a purposeful attempt to bring South Africa's international position back to normal. The principles and aims of our foreign policy remain unaltered, but the methods and the strategy depend on changed circumstances.'[28] The outward movement gathered strength after its first notable success in the establishment of diplomatic relations with Malawi and the appearance of black diplomats in Pretoria. The private sector also became involved, at a time of great economic confidence in South Africa, by reaching out for new economic links in Africa.

The relationship with the nearest newly independent states of Lesotho and Botswana (and later in 1968 also Swaziland) started well. These small states had little choice regarding their relations with South Africa when they became independent, given the existing factors of economic dependence, the Customs Union and the common currency system, and the employment of thousands of their nationals in the Republic. But the South African Government made clear its desire to assist with their development, and Lesotho, and later Swaziland, took advantage of some assistance, including the secondment of South African officials to their civil services.

231

Botswana took a more independent position, both in its political attitudes and in refusing official South African assistance, although it did not do anything to disturb the economic links and co-operation on the technical level in many fields.

One of the arguments of the Government in favour of the outward movement in Africa was that it was designed to counter the threat of communism by contributing to the stability, economic development and welfare of South Africa's neighbours, thereby contributing to South Africa's own security. The anti-communist motive had been a constant refrain in government statements for many years, but it now lent some strength to the criticism that the real aim of the outward movement was to create a buffer zone of friendly states around South Africa. Another criticism was that the main motive was economic,[29] and that South Africa was moving to exploit the developing countries in southern Africa and further afield for its own benefit, in the same way as blacks within South Africa were exploited to maintain the power and privileged position of the white minority. There are no doubt elements of truth in these criticisms, as the strategic and economic advantages to be gained from expanding co-operative relations in Africa are obvious. But the conscious and overriding motive seems to have been the general political one of breaking out of the threatening isolation in the world and of trying to obtain legitimation of the internal policy of separate development. In any case, strategic and economic objectives are not unusual in any country's foreign policy.

The outward movement did not apply only to Africa. Special efforts were directed at expanding trade and diplomatic contacts in Asia and also in Latin America, and more success was in fact achieved in these areas than in Africa. In Latin America, for instance, the number of South African diplomatic and consular missions increased from three in the mid-sixties to about ten in the early seventies, whereas there was no extension of diplomatic relations in Africa, apart from Malawi.

One proviso always mentioned in relation to the outward movement by government spokesmen was that the policy was being pursued on the basis of non-interference in internal affairs. This was a cardinal principle of South African foreign policy, as has been seen in relation to the United Nations, and the Government made it clear that any links established with African countries could not be used by them to try to effect changes within South Africa. This assurance was given more in order to satisfy doubts among the Government's own supporters than for external consumption. But, in spite of this assurance, there were aspects of the outward movement which caused serious problems for Mr Vorster within his party and con-

232

tributed to the small split in the party in 1969 and the establishment of the Herstigte Nasionale Party (H.N.P.) under Dr Albert Hertzog.

One particular aspect was the willingness of the Government to have black diplomats in South Africa and to accord them all the rights which other diplomats enjoyed. This was a change from the position of Dr Verwoerd who was not prepared to receive black diplomats in South Africa, where they would have to be treated differently from other blacks. The fears of the H.N.P., and the expectations of many others, that the presence of black diplomats would seriously disturb the system and force the Government to make further concessions internally, were not really fulfilled, mainly because the number of black diplomats remained very limited. But their presence has no doubt contributed in a small way to the gradual relaxation of some discriminatory measures in the social sphere.

Looked at against the background of South Africa's increasing isolation in the early 1960s, the increasingly hostile resolutions of the U.N. and O.A.U., and the support given by the O.A.U. to liberation movements seeking to change the situation in southern Africa by force, the achievements of the outward movement by the end of the decade were fairly significant, but in concrete terms they were decidedly limited. There were the diplomatic and growing economic links with Malawi, increasing contacts, official and unofficial, with Madagascar and Mauritius, and the tentative development of links, commercial and official, with other states, often not known publicly. The Foreign Minister stated several times, for instance in Parliament in May 1969, that South Africa was in direct contact with many more African states than he was able to mention.[30]

While the Government felt that it was making progress by 1969, most of Africa appeared to be maintaining a hostile front, with only a few signs that some African leaders were reconsidering their policy of confrontation with South Africa, which did not seem to be producing constructive results. One such sign, which was not taken seriously by the Government at the time, but which was later more widely recognised to have been very important, was the adoption by a meeting of the Central and East African states of the Lusaka Manifesto in April 1969. It was subsequently endorsed by the O.A.U. and the U.N. The Manifesto was strongly critical of the existing political system in South Africa, and of those in the Portuguese territories and Rhodesia, and it made clear the belief of the states which issued it that all men are equal and have equal rights to human dignity and respect, regardless of colour, race, religion or sex. We believe that all men have the right and the duty to participate as equal members of the society in their own government. We do not accept that any individual or group has any

233

right to govern any other groups of sane adults without their consent, and we affirm that only the people of a society, acting together as equals, can determine what is fair for them, a good society and a good social, economic or political organisation.' But, while the Manifesto reaffirmed that the objective of the African states was liberation in southern Africa, it stated: 'We always preferred, and we still prefer, to achieve it without physical violence. We would prefer to negotiate rather than destroy, to talk rather than kill . . .'

Furthermore, in calling for a commitment to change in the white-ruled states of southern Africa, the Manifesto maintained that if such a commitment existed, 'any disagreements we might have about the rate of implementation or about isolated acts of policy, would be matters affecting only our individual relationship with the states concerned. If these commitments existed, our states would not be justified in the expressed and active hostility towards the regimes of Southern Africa such as we have proclaimed and continue to propagate.' The Manifesto recognised, too, that there might have to be transitional arrangements while transformation from group inequalities to individual equality was being effected. The authors of the Manifesto acknowledged imperfections in their own states, with regard to their social, economic and political organisation, the standard of living, individual security and the administration of justice, and they admitted 'that within our own states the struggle towards human dignity is only beginning'.[31]

The South African Government's response to the Lusaka Manifesto was luke-warm at best. There was some acknowledgment by government spokesmen, including Dr Hilgard Muller, of the Manifesto's moderate terms, but there was a tendency to dismiss it as not very significant and as not providing a basis for negotiation, because of the criticisms it contained and its demands for change in the political system. However, in a real sense the Lusaka Manifesto could have been interpreted as a positive response to the South African outward movement, and even as a sign that by 1969 the outward movement was achieving some success in causing the African states to reconsider their approach towards southern African questions. Instead of responding in turn to this African overture, the Government claimed that its policies in Africa were bearing fruit and that there was no need to enter into negotiations which would involve South Africa's own internal policy. Here again emerges the basic problem, namely the effort to keep domestic policies completely distinct from foreign policy, and to try to make progress in external relations without realistically acknowledging that the internal policy creates the main barrier against such progress. Dr

Verwoerd sought to resolve this dilemma, even if the political path he chose did not prove acceptable internationally. But Mr Vorster's Government tried to keep the new initiatives in foreign policy in a separate compartment, without examining realistically their domestic base or trying to integrate foreign and domestic policies. The reluctance of the Government to assess effectively the implications of the outward movement for domestic as well as foreign policy, may well have been due to the dissension within the National Party towards the end of the 1960s. The Prime Minister's overriding concern appears to have been to maintain the unity of the Party, or at least to prevent the split from widening. Boldness in either domestic or foreign policy did not serve that purpose. It therefore became a question of marking time, while opportunities for the re-thinking and development of both domestic and foreign policies were lost – when political and economic conditions were more favourable for the Government than at any time since before 1960.

However, the Lusaka Manifesto was not the last word from Africa in response to the outward movement, and the beginning of the 1970s witnessed the emergence of new voices from further north. In November 1970 President Felix Houphouët Boigny of the Ivory Coast announced that he was planning to urge other African leaders to have direct talks with the South African Government, because he considered that force would not solve the problems of apartheid. His country, he said, supported negotiation and dialogue. 'We hope to succeed by dialogue. For seven years we have had nothing but grand and violent speeches, with tragic and sometimes ridiculous results. We cannot make threats without the means to apply them.'[32]

Support for President Houphouët Boigny's position came from the leaders of several other French-speaking African states, notably Gabon, Madagascar and the Central African Republic. President Banda of Malawi and Prime Minister Jonathan of Lesotho also welcomed the announcement, although their dependence on South Africa lessened the significance of their support. More important was a statement by Prime Minister Busia of Ghana who said, on a visit to Canada soon after President Houphouët Boigny's announcement, that neither trade embargoes nor guerrilla warfare was likely to break the rule of the white minority government in South Africa. Instead, he suggested, African states should negotiate with South Africa, while encouraging 'constitutional and moral change' from within the white-ruled country.[33] The following month, in a statement in Parliament in Accra, Dr Busia posed the question as to whether Africans were right 'in maintaining that the policies of violence and isolation are the only

235

ones on which we must rely' in dealing with the South African problem.[34] There was considerable opposition to Dr Busia's point of view within Ghana, but in March 1971 he was able to have a motion carried in the Ghanaian Parliament supporting his case for a dialogue which would be 'one of the weapons which could be used in the struggle to eliminate apartheid'.[35] (The divisions within the Ghanaian Government on this question were reflected in the fact that in June 1971 the Ghanaian delegation at the O.A.U. Conference did not support the dialogue proposals of the Ivory Coast, although Dr Busia himself stated later that he felt he had 'a moral obligation' to pursue his call for a dialogue between Black Africa and Pretoria.)[36]

Dialogue now became the new word in any discussion of South Africa's external relations, and there was a certain euphoria in the country about the possibilities which appeared to be opening up in Africa and the expectations that improved relations with African states would provide the road back to acceptance in the West (which still remained of prime concern in South African foreign policy). At the 8th Summit Conference of the O.A.U., which met in Addis Ababa in June 1971, a significant division appeared among the members on the question of how to approach the South African issue. In the past this issue had been a unifying factor, but now for the first time a few African states were willing openly to propose a new approach. These states were in a minority, and the decision to reject the dialogue proposals was adopted by twenty-eight votes to six against (Ivory Coast, Gabon, Lesotho, Madagascar, Malawi, Mauritius) with five abstentions (Dahomey, Niger, Togo, Swaziland, Upper Volta) and two states absent (Central African Republic and Uganda). However, this minority amounted to almost a third of the O.A.U. membership, and an observer at the Conference commented afterwards that 'it is doubtful that the dialogue issue will end there' and that the voting suggested 'considerable support for the dialogue concept', especially in view of the fact that in the O.A.U. forum strong pressure could be brought to bear on delegations to accede to majority opinions.[37] There thus seemed to be some momentum developing, and from a South African perspective the change in the African approach was impressive, seen against South Africa's earlier isolation in the continent.

It is not possible to analyse here the possible motives and aims of the African states who supported dialogue.[38] What is relevant is South Africa's response to this opportunity in Africa. From the statements of President Houphouët Boigny, Dr Busia and others on the subject of dialogue it is clear that none of them condoned apartheid or showed any signs of accepting the South African Government's policies of separate development as a possible solution to the problems of relations between black and white in southern Africa. What they were arguing for was a different way of attempting to bring about change, in place of the trend towards violence. President Houphouët Boigny argued that the threats encouraged South Africa to accumulate more arms and created a defensive reaction from which only African states north of South Africa would suffer. Dr Busia argued, for instance, that the support from African countries for 'freedom fighters' was 'woefully and hopelessly inadequate for them to wage a successful struggle'. He maintained: 'What we appear to be doing so far, is to send our African brothers to the slaughter.'[39] Prime Minister Jonathan of Lesotho stated that he was convinced that dialogue 'would provide a realistic and conclusive solution', and that if this was supported 'the situation in South Africa is bound to change'.[40] President Banda argued that there was no difference between him and his fellow African leaders as far as apartheid was concerned; but, he said, the difference was on the methods of fighting 'these evils'.[41]

There was a tendency in South Africa to ignore this aspect of the dialogue concept, reflected in the above statements, and to concentrate on other aspects, such as the expressed desire for peace of the African leaders concerned, their opposition to communism (with their fear that conflict would be exploited by the communist powers) and their desire that South Africa should be able to play a constructive role in African development. The emphasis, however, on the unacceptability of separate development as a political solution (which was also the factor preventing other African states from joining the dialogue campaign) provided a real dilemma for the South African Government, in view of its well-known and determined stand against interference in the country's domestic affairs. This prevented it from agreeing to any dialogue aimed at changing its internal policies, and from accepting the challenge implicit in the dialogue proposals (and explicit in the Lusaka Manifesto) of discussing frankly with the other African states the real issue dividing South Africa from the rest of Africa. This would have meant accepting the possibility of compromise in negotiations with other governments about South Africa's future political development, which was not a course the Government was ready to follow, given its own domestic political constraints.

In an effort to keep the dialogue moves alive, Mr Vorster did express a willingness to discuss *any* subject, including internal policies, with other African governments.[42] This was in the nature of a concession by Mr Vorster, although it is clear that by 'discussion' he was not thinking of any substantive policy concessions (which would not have been acceptable to his Party in any case), but rather perhaps of opportunities to *explain* South African policies. Within the Government there always had been, and still is, a strong feeling that the external problem lies in a misunderstanding of the aims of separate development, and that therefore the removal of such misunderstanding could lead to acceptance by other governments. At the same time, the attitude was growing within the Government that it was not the policy itself, but the way in which it was implemented, including especially the many discriminatory measures (known as 'petty apartheid') which could and should be eliminated, so that the positive aspects of the policy could emerge more clearly. However, even this trend towards the elimination of 'petty apartheid' had not met with unreserved support within the National Party and had therefore not moved as quickly as might have been expected when the outward movement and dialogue were creating a climate for change.

One of the strong criticisms of the dialogue move on the part of many African governments, and also of blacks within South Africa, was that the Government was not engaged in any effective dialogue with blacks inside South Africa, and it was argued that this should begin first, before external dialogue could take place.

In spite of the rejection of dialogue by the O.A.U. in June 1971 and the condemnation of South Africa's outward policy as being 'deceitful propaganda and manoeuvres', some initiatives by pro-dialogue states continued, including a state visit by Dr Hastings Banda to South Africa in August 1971. President Houphouët Boigny also continued to maintain contact with South Africa and to advocate the dialogue approach. But, when the East and Central African States (who had adopted the Lusaka Manifesto in 1969) met in Mogadishu in October 1971, they condemned the initiatives of Malawi and the Ivory Coast, and they adopted a Declaration strongly rejecting dialogue and arguing that any dialogue had to be between the peoples within the countries of Southern Africa themselves. A further set-back to dialogue was the military coup in Madagascar in May 1972, and the replacement of the pro-dialogue government by one strongly opposed to the links which had been growing with South Africa.

When the O.A.U. Summit Conference met again in mid-1972 the question of dialogue with South Africa was not even raised publicly, indicating that, although a few countries (notably Malawi and the Ivory Coast) continued to maintain their contacts with South Africa, the movement had run out of steam. Even the countries nearest South Africa, the small B.L.S. states, were showing no inclination to follow the dialogue path, in spite of their great dependence on South Africa. Lesotho was the only country which had taken a public stand in favour of the initiatives of President Houphouët Boigny, but now Chief Leabua Jonathan began to take a much more critical public position. Swaziland had maintained a low profile and has continued to do so, while Botswana had opposed the concept of dialogue from the start. For instance, in March 1971, speaking in Lagos, President Sir Seretse Khama said: 'The outward looking policy is for export only – it has nothing to do with internal liberation.' He also maintained that the condition imposed for dialogue was 'the acceptance of the *status quo*', and that South Africa's rulers had 'made it quite clear that the dialogue with Black Africa can be about many things, but it cannot at this stage be about political change or self-determination.'[43] Thus, as already indicated, more was required from the South African Government as a response to Africa than it was willing or able to give.

The period between the mid-1960s and 1972 was a buoyant one for the South African Government, with considerable economic strength being evidenced by the Republic, the internal situation seemingly under control (although without any dramatic forward movement politically, even with the homelands concept) and with the opportunities for initiatives in external relations. In fact, the willingness of some African states to advocate dialogue may well have been due to the perceived growing strength of South Africa and the ineffectiveness of measures proposed in the U.N., the O.A.U. and elsewhere, against the Government. Outside observers, too, writing in this period, were impressed by the evidence of South Africa's strength and its ability shown to survive the crisis of the early 1960s.

However, certain dramatic developments were about to take place on the world scene and within southern Africa itself, which would fundamentally change South Africa's position. The first of these was the Arab-Israeli war of October 1973, which was to lead to the oil crisis and the profound effects which the increases in the price of oil had on the world economy. In common with other countries, South Africa was to suffer the effects of the world recession, combined with inflation and, as its economic strength declined severely, so did the confidence which had marked the previous period. All this would have created problems for South Africa anyway, but more serious were the political effects of the changes let loose in southern Africa by the military coup in Lisbon in April 1974.

Turmoil in Southern Africa

For South Africa the revolutionary changes in Mozambique and later in

Angola, which resulted from the Portuguese coup, removed what had been both physical and psychological buffers against the threat of militant black nationalism. What had been perceived as the protection of South Africa's flanks by Portugal was replaced by the uncertainty of a situation where revolutionary movements were coming to power. Moreover, Rhodesia which, like South Africa, had gone through a buoyant economic period, and which had successfully resisted the pressures following U.D.I. in 1965, seemed especially threatened. Following the change in Mozambique, where power was fairly rapidly transferred to Frelimo, the Rhodesian issue was seen as the one which could lead to wider confrontation, given the direct interests of Rhodesia's neighbouring countries of Zambia, Mozambique and South Africa.

However, the immediate effect of the change in Mozambique was a drawing back from confrontation by all the countries directly concerned. Diplomatic negotiations began and they emerged into the open towards the end of 1974, when agreement was reached to begin discussions on a Rhodesian settlement. The aim was to find ways of achieving a peaceful resolution of differences through meaningful accommodations, and the South African Prime Minister stated in December 1974 that the consequences of failure in these efforts would be 'too ghastly to contemplate'.[44] The relaxation of tension and the negotiations which followed in the so-called détente period, were based mainly on a degree of coincidence of interests between South Africa and Zambia, concerning the need for a Rhodesian settlement and for the avoidance of disintegration in Mozambique. The basis of Prime Minister Vorster's policy in this regard was indicated in a speech on 23 October 1974 in which he said that southern Africa had come to a crossroads, where it had to make a choice between peace and the escalation of strife. Zambia's response came in a speech by President Kenneth Kaunda a few days later, in which he referred to Mr Vorster's 'crossroads' speech as 'the voice of reason' which Africa had been waiting a long time to hear.[45]

The South African and Zambian Governments were both responding to the dramatically changed and critical situation which had arisen in southern Africa, and it was significant that this was the first time that a serious effort was made to settle differences within and between the countries of the subcontinent through direct negotiation, without the involvement of outside powers. This effort to resolve the conflict situation, at least as far as Rhodesia was concerned, on a regional basis, had also the positive effect of drawing attention to the factors which linked the countries of southern Africa together and to the opportunities for co-operation which existed within the region, if only the political divisions could be overcome. The negotiations were, however, limited to the Rhodesian issue as a matter of urgency, and therefore the basic problem which had prevented the dialogue initiative from progressing, namely South Africa's internal policies, did not initially affect these negotiations. But success in the regional initiative over Rhodesia could well have led to further realistic discussions on other issues standing in the way of South Africa's acceptance in southern Africa and Africa generally. It is relevant to note in this regard that, at about the same time as Mr Vorster's 'crossroads' speech, Ambassador Pik Botha made the statement in the U.N. Security Council, which referred to the Government's commitment to move away from racial discrimination.[46] This statement raised considerable expectations in South Africa and externally at the time.

Although the year following Mr Vorster's 'crossroads' speech did not see the beginning of meaningful negotiations within Rhodesia itself, the wider negotiations continued within the regional context, and in August 1975 a dramatic South African/Zambian summit meeting was held on the Victoria Falls bridge (between Rhodesia and Zambia) in a major initiative aimed at bringing together Mr Smith and the black nationalist leaders of Rhodesia. This initiative did not fully succeed, although within a few months Mr Smith did enter into negotiations with one of the main leaders, Mr Joshua Nkomo (who, together with the Rev. Ndabaningi Sithole and other nationalists, had been released from detention in Rhodesia at the end of 1974 as a result of the influence of Mr Vorster on Mr Smith's Government). Before the summit meeting of August 1975 the South African Government had withdrawn from Rhodesia its police units which were assisting the Rhodesian security forces, as an indication of its willingness to make concessions to the African demands, in order that a political settlement could be reached within Rhodesia.

While attention was focused on Mozambique and Rhodesia, however, a critical situation was developing in Angola, which was to lead to the South African intervention in that country in the months immediately following the Victoria Falls bridge meeting. The war in Angola, which preceded and followed Angola's formal independence on 11 November 1975, and in which the Soviet Union and Cuba were also involved, effectively marked the end of the brief détente period.[47] Since then, there has been increasing involvement by outside powers, including the two super-powers, in the disputes of southern Africa and the opportunity to resolve them on a regional basis was lost.

It was not simply South Africa's Angolan intervention which brought to an end the détente period. It was as much the intractable nature of the Rhodesian conflict which had remained the most critical one, threatening peace generally in southern Africa, as it did even before the Angolan war. But with the new dimensions introduced into the southern African situation by that war, including super-power rivalry, it was no longer possible to look simply for regional solutions, and this meant that the circumstances in which South Africa's foreign policy had to operate had decidedly changed. In particular, the Western powers, led by the United States, became directly involved in trying to resolve the southern African conflicts, whereas previously they had been reluctant to do much to effect changes, in spite of their influence in all the countries concerned. As indicated above, the United States had been preoccupied with its own external and internal problems, and its attitude towards southern Africa in the early part of the 1970s had been based on the assumption that the *status quo* would generally be maintained for the foreseeable future, and that the changes needed and advocated by the United States and other Western countries would come about only through the action of the white governments concerned. The collapse of the Portuguese and what followed in Mozambique and Angola, together with the greater involvement of the Soviet Union on the side of the 'liberation' forces, destroyed that assumption and forced the United States to change its policy.

This change and the beginning of active diplomatic invlovement on the part of the United States was heralded by the policy statement of the U.S. Secretary of State, Dr Henry Kissinger, in Lusaka in April 1976. There then followed a period of 'shuttle diplomacy' on the part of Dr Kissinger, which culminated in a meeting in Pretoria in September 1976, at which Prime Minister Ian Smith finally agreed to accept the principle of black majority rule for Rhodesia. This achievement was the product of a joint effort by Dr Kissinger and Mr Vorster, which had involved hard bargaining between them and between Mr Smith and Mr Vorster, whose task it was in these negotiations to convince Mr Smith to agree to a plan for settlement which he (Mr Smith) clearly indicated subsequently he would have preferred not to have to accept.[48] That the settlement plan did not succeed was due to the fact that Dr Kissinger had not also been able to obtain the full agreement of the African front-line states (Zambia, Tanzania, Mozambique, Botswana and Angola) who were now working together on the Rhodesian issue, and of the main Rhodesian black nationalist leaders. While Dr Kissinger continued his efforts for a time, they were affected by the American presidential campaign and President Ford's defeat by Mr Jimmy Carter in the November elections. This meant that further meaningful American initiatives had to await the inauguration of the new President in January 1977, and the various changes involved in installing a new administration in Washington.

Mr Vorster's willingness to co-operate with Dr Kissinger (in spite of the strong South African feeling earlier in 1976 that the Government had been 'let down', if not betrayed, by the United States over the Angola incident) was no doubt due both to a real desire to resolve the Rhodesian conflict in the interest of South Africa's own security, and to a desire to use this opportunity of drawing closer to the West. But this was also made easier for Mr Vorster's Government by the apparent understanding reached with Dr Kissinger that the question of South Africa's internal problems would be put on the 'back burner', as it were, and that Dr Kissinger would even be supportive in this regard, at least in giving South Africa more time to work out its internal policies. The indications that this was the approach of Dr Kissinger gained some credence from the United States decision to abstain on the U.N. General Assembly's resolution in October 1976, rejecting the independence of the Transkei (Resolution 31/6A).

After the advent of the Carter administration, this position changed, because it was soon made clear that the United States would no longer treat the three issues of southern Africa (Rhodesia, Namibia and South Africa itself) in an order of priority, and a new, more critical, tone emerged in official American statements about South Africa. Mr Vorster still hoped to contribute to a resolution of the Rhodesian conflict through co-operation with the West, but the rapport established with Dr Kissinger was now missing, and this was dramatically illustrated by the outcome of the meeting between Mr Vorster and Vice-President Mondale in Vienna in May 1977. The strains between the United States and South Africa became more acute after that meeting and were aggravated during the South African election campaign in the second half of the year, when government spokesmen responded to the critical attitude of the Carter administration by launching emotional attacks on American policies and political personalities.

The much greater attention now being paid to South African internal questions, not only by the American administration, but also by other Western governments and by world opinion generally was, of course, not due simply to a decision in Washington to change the order of priorities of the previous administration, but rather to the fact that very serious unrest and violence had erupted within South Africa, beginning with the Soweto disturbances of June 1976. This had focused world attention on South Africa more strongly than at any time since Sharpeville in 1960 and, for

South Africa, it was a much more critical situation than Sharpeville had been, because it occurred under radically changed circumstances in southern Africa. In 1960 the liberation movements had not yet started their wars in Angola and Mozambique. None of the black countries of the region was yet independent, and Rhodesia had not yet become an international issue. By 1976 South Africa was almost surrounded by independent black states in southern Africa, plus a situation in Rhodesia where the white government was fast losing control, and a situation in South West Africa/Namibia where international pressure was increasing, and where the threat of insurgency in the north, supported from across the border in Angola, was growing. Not only was the Government under much greater pressure from all these external factors than ever before, but the dramatic changes in the region had affected the attitude of blacks within South Africa, creating more militancy, especially among younger people, and greater expectations in respect of political emancipation.

While the unrest in the country continued sporadically after June 1976, the Government attempted to contain it by use of its extensive security legislation and by some concessions designed to reduce racial discrimination in the social and economic fields. But the wide-spread bannings and detentions which occurred on 19 October 1977 demonstrated that the Government's main efforts were directed at maintaining internal security, and there were no signs of political accommodations to meet the demands being made by black leaders, particularly in the urban areas. Instead, the Government moved even more vigorously in the implementation of separate development. Bophuthatswana became independent in December 1977, and Mr Vorster spoke of the likelihood of several more independent homelands within the coming few years. The implications for those Africans who did not identify with the homelands became more serious, as their citizenship of South Africa was now brought into question.

The events of October 1977, together with the death of Steve Biko a month earlier, and the subsequent inconclusive results of the inquest into the circumstances of his death, had a profoundly negative impact internationally, especially in the United States and other Western countries. An immediate result of 19 October was a resolution adopted unanimously by the U.N. Security Council imposing a mandatory arms embargo on South Africa (Resolution 418 of 4 November 1977). For the first time the Western countries in the Council (United States, United Kingdom and France) agreed to support a resolution on South Africa under Chapter VII of the United Nations Charter. Even France, which had continued to supply military equipment to South Africa in spite of many U.N. resolu-

244

tions and criticism from African states, now decided fully to observe the embargo. Following this action by the Security Council, the threat of further action under Chapter VII, possibly in the economic field, is ever-present and is likely to become a real one should there be a repetition of events in South Africa, such as Sharpeville, Soweto, Biko's death and October 1977.

Outside the U.N. pressures have also mounted in the economic field, particularly on international companies which have interests in South Africa. These pressures by relatively small groups, which have been building up for many years, are now having more effect than ever before in influencing the decisions of organisations on their investment in South Africa, because they contribute to the uncertainty which many abroad feel, in any case, about the future stability of the southern African region. Although Western governments have shown themselves very reluctant to adopt any economic measures against South Africa, the domestic and international pressures on them to move in that direction are increasing.

The one area in which there has been considerable movement, involving political change and accommodation, has been South West Africa/ Namibia. In spite of the U.N. General Assembly's decision (first taken in 1966, endorsed by an advisory opinion of the International Court in 1971 and by the Security Council, and supported by the Western states) that South Africa's presence in the Territory was illegal, the Government continued for several years simply to resist U.N. and African demands for South African withdrawal and for independence of the Territory as one integral unit. Instead, plans went ahead for the implementation of the policy of separate political development of each of the eleven ethnic groups (i.e., the South African policy exported to the Territory). However, a new sign of flexibility emerged in the Government's approach during discussions with the U.N. Secretary-General and his special representative, Dr Escher, in 1972/73, when the Government indicated it would respect the wishes of the whole population on the future constitutional organisation of the Territory and would not impose any system. It explicitly accepted the principles of self-determination and eventual independence, and did not rule out the possibility of the Territory becoming independent as one integral whole, if the various groups accepted that.[49]

Then in September 1975, during the southern African détente period, the Turnhalle Constitutional Conference was launched for the purpose of preparing the Territory for independence. Although this Conference was composed of ethnic group representatives, and although it evolved a constitutional system which included the separation of groups at the

245

second level of government, the preservation of the territorial integrity of Namibia was fully accepted. But internationally the Turnhalle concept was not acceptable, and so the South African Government, with the agreement of the Turnhalle delegates, decided to suspend that process and enter into negotiations with the five Western members of the Security Council, who were acting in terms of a Security Council resolution (No. 385 of 30 January 1976). The negotiations began in April 1977 and a year later the Western group's proposals for a U.N.-supervised process leading to independence were accepted by South Africa. After several months' delay the African front-line states also agreed and, with the somewhat ambivalent acquiescence of Swapo, the Security Council set the process in motion in July 1978 and adopted a detailed plan in September (Resolution 435).

The difficulties of implementing the Western-sponsored U.N. plan, given the deep distrust on all sides, may not be surmounted. But the fact that the negotiations reached such an advanced stage was nevertheless a considerable achievement. South African acceptance of a plan involving elections on a 'one-man, one-vote' basis, supervision of the elections by the U.N., a ceasefire monitored by a U.N. force, participation in the process by Swapo (which has been engaged in an armed struggle against South African forces) and the removal of all discrimination, demonstrated how far the South African Government was willing and able to move from its position of only a few years previously, in order to resolve this dispute. These 'concessions' by the Government resulted in part from the sustained determination of the five Western states, whose Foreign Ministers even visited Pretoria as a group in October 1978 in order to prevent the plan from collapsing. But, coupled with this Western pressure, was a recognition by the Government that a positive response to facilitate decolonisation of this remnant of the colonial era was in South Africa's own interests, if the further spread of violent conflict in the region was to be avoided.

Even if the new problems which arose in early 1979 prevent the implementation of this U.N. plan, further negotiations should still be possible on the basis of what has already been achieved without having to start again at the beginning – *provided that* there is the political will on all sides to reach a negotiated agreement and thus avoid escalating war. If the Government's willingness to negotiate a transfer of power in Namibia is maintained, and if it can renew its considerable efforts of recent years to achieve a settlement in Rhodesia/Zimbabwe, then there will be stronger grounds for hoping that the Government will also respond realistically to the need for new initiatives to resolve through negotiations the much more

246

difficult political issues in South Africa itself. The advent of a new Prime Minister, P. W. Botha, in September 1978, has produced signs at least of greater flexibility in the approach to domestic questions, although it is too early to predict whether this new approach will be an adequate response to the growing political expectations of black South Africans and to the pressures of the changing world. Meanwhile, the 'Information affair' has hopefully taught South Africa a hard lesson, that futile attempts to manipulate world opinion do not provide a realistic alternative to the accommodations required within the country.

1. Amry Vandenbosch, *South Africa and the World* (Lexington: Univ. Pr. of Kentucky, 1970), pp. 66–8 and 156. *See also:* J. Spence, 'South Africa and the Modern World' in the *Oxford History of South Africa*, ed. Monica Wilson and Leonard Thompson (Clarendon Pr., 1971) vol. 2, p. 492.
2. J. Dugard, ed. *The South West Africa/Namibia Dispute* (Berkeley: Univ. of Calif. Pr., 1973), pp. 82–8.
3. J. C. Smuts, *Selections from the Smuts Papers*, ed. Jean van der Poel, (Cambridge Univ. Pr., 1973), vol. 7, p. 48.
4. *Ibid.*, p. 129.
5. J. Spence, 'South Africa and the Modern World' in the *Oxford History of South Africa* (Clarendon Pr., 1971), vol. 2, p. 525.
6. J. C. Smuts, in his 'explosive' speech made in London on 25 November 1943. *Selections from the Smuts Papers* (Cambridge Univ. Pr., 1973), vol. 6, p. 464.
7. G. C. Olivier, *Suid-Afrika se Buitelandse Beleid* (Pretoria: Academica, 1977), pp. 126–128.
8. J. E. Spence, *Republic Under Pressure* (Oxford Univ. Pr., 1965), pp. 69–70.
9. Quoted in J. Spence, *ibid.*, p. 70.
10. Speech by Mr Eric Louw at the University of Pretoria on 30 March 1957. *Southern Africa Record*, no. 5, July 1976 (Johannesburg: South African Institute of International Affairs), p. 44.
11. Quoted in J. Spence, *op. cit.*, p. 69.
12. Quoted in J. Spence, *op. cit.*, p. 16.
13. South Africa, *House of Assembly Debates*, vol. 99, 1959, col. 63.
14. *Ibid.*, cols. 64–5.
15. South Africa, *House of Assembly Debates*, vol. 100, 1959, col. 6221.
16. South Africa, *House of Assembly Debates*, vol. 107, 1961, col. 4191.
17. South Africa, *House of Assembly Debates*, vol. 101, 1959, cols. 5254–5.
18. See ex-Prime Minister Vorster's references to the meeting between Dr H F. Verwoerd and Chief Jonathan, in South Africa (Republic), *House of Assembly Debates*, vol. 17, 1966, cols. 2554–7.
19. Mr Harold Macmillan's 'winds of change' speech in Cape Town on 3 February 1960, and the reply by Dr H. F. Verwoerd, in *Southern Africa Record*, no. 3, October 1975 (Johannesburg: South African Institute of International Affairs), pp. 20 and 29.
20. South Africa, *House of Assembly Debates*, vol. 75, 1951, col. 6948.

21. Gerrit Olivier, 'South African Foreign Policy' in *South Africa: Government and Politics*, ed. Denis Worrall, 2nd ed. (Van Schaik, 1975), p. 292.
22. *Ibid.*, p. 293.
23. See: B. M. Schoeman, *Van Malan tot Verwoerd* (Cape Town: Human and Rousseau, 1973), pp. 234–44.
24. U.N. Document S/5723 and Corr. 1.
25. *The Kissinger Study of Southern Africa* (Nottingham: Spokesman, 1975).
26. *News/Check* (Johannesburg) 24 September 1965.
27. Quoted in John Barratt, 'The Outward Movement in South Africa's Foreign Relations', *Newsletter*, no. 3, 1969 (Johannesburg: South African Institute of International Affairs), p. 15.
28. *Ibid.*
29. S. Nolutshungu, *South Africa in Africa* (Manchester Univ. Pr., 1975), pp. 122–124.
30. South Africa (Republic), *House of Assembly Debates*, no. 13, 1969, col. 5450.
31. Quotations from the text of the Lusaka Manifesto, as reproduced in *Southern African Record*, no. 2, June 1975 (Johannesburg: South African Institute of International Affairs), pp. 1–7.
32. *Malawi News*, 17 November 1970.
33. *The Times* (London), 11 November 1970.
34. Quoted in *The Star* (Johannesburg), 23 March 1971.
35. *Ibid.*
36. *The Star* (Johannesburg), 12 July 1971.
37. Frederick Hunter, in *The Christian Science Monitor*, 28 June 1971.
38. See, for instance, the author's article, 'Dialogue in Africa: a new approach', in *South Africa International*, vol. 2, no. 2., October 1971.
39. *The Star* (Johannesburg), 23 March 1971.
40. *Koena News* (Maseru), 18 January 1971.
41. *Daily Digest*, Malawi: Department of Information, 21 January 1971.
42. For example, at a Press Conference in March 1971. *The Star* (Johannesburg) 30 March 1971.
43. *Africa and America in the 70s*. Address by the President of the Republic of Botswana, Sir Seretse Khama, to the Third Annual Conference of the African-American Dialogues, Lagos, March 1971, p. 8.
44. *Southern Arican Record*, no. 4, February 1976 (Johannesburg: South African Institute of International Affairs), pp. 2–3.
45. See *Southern Africa Record*, nos. 1 and 2, 1975, pp. 1–8 and 14–21, respectively, for the texts of these speeches. Also: the author's article in *Foreign Affairs*, vol. 55 no. 1, October 1976, for more extensive comments on the developments in the détente period.
46. See *Southern Africa Record*, no. 1, March 1975 (Johannesburg: South African Institute of International Affairs), p. 21.
47. See the author's article in *Foreign Affairs*, vol. 55, no. 1, October 1976, for a view on the implications of the Angolan War and the reason for South African involvement.
48. See *Southern Africa Record*, no. 7, December 1976 (Johannesburg: South African Institute of International Affairs), p. 39.
49. See, for instance, U.N. document S/10921 of 30 April 1973.

10 In the Crucible: A Situation of Change for South African Literature*

ADAM SMALL

Heraclitus tells us that everything is always changing, that the world is continually in flux. Says Bertrand Russell: 'The metaphysics of Heraclitus are sufficiently dynamic to satisfy the most hustling of moderns.' In a Heraclitic world 'perpetual change was to be expected'.[1]

I believe that we do in fact live in a Heraclitic world. If Heraclitus over-stated his case, that does not lessen its truth. (There are times when over-statements of this kind are very necessary.)

The changes that have come over literature in South Africa during the past four or five decades are part of the broader metaphysical picture of change in the country and, of course, of the total picture of change in the world.

Social change has occurred in South Africa during this time, and even political change. Things may only have been changing like the pyramids, but the Heraclitic law could not be broken. It holds for the universe, it holds for South Africa, and it holds for South Africa's political regime. Verwoerd could still speak of his wild dreams for the country in terms of *graniet* (granite) which, apparently, he believed to be a material of no change. However, even at the time of his death (it will be recalled that he was murdered in the white Parliament in 1966), 'things were changing'. One of the very last press pictures taken of Verwoerd before his death was of this white Prime Minister of South Africa actually shaking the hand of a black man. Before this, the idea of the white ruling clique was that when they had to meet blacks, blacks were kept at a distance – there was no physical contact between white person and black person. The greeting exchanged was simply 'Molo!' – at that distance.

---

*I have tried to reflect in this chapter only my own intuition about change in our literary situation. I did not intend to write an academic piece.

However, even Verwoerd proved to be no exception in respect of Heraclitic metaphysics.

Then Vorster took over as Prime Minister and, despite the image that he had acquired as Verwoerd's minister of police and justice, he became white South Africa's symbol, *par excellence*, of pragmatism. What this meant was that the Calvinistic façade of no change was kept up – 'We are still, and always will be, exactly the same chosen race of God in Africa'; kept up in respect of the white masses 'out there', while in fact, under John Vorster's guidance, things were changing all the time – like the pyramids.

The schizophrenia of this pragmatism took its toll. It appears to me that on the one hand Vorster was a really convinced, no-change Afrikaner Calvinist, and a dyed-in-the-wool *bittereinder*, who would and could never live down his internment by the government of the day at a time when he, too, was an 'agitator'. On the other hand, he was reasonably conscious of the fact that the world, also the political world, was round, that times pass and that, indeed, things must change.

In the end he left the political scene as a man thoroughly defeated by this split in his own person. According to the Erasmus Commission of Enquiry into the so-called Information Department scandal, even his old buddy from Koffiefontein days, the general (Van den Bergh), had misused his solid – or, to other minds, perverted – no-change Calvinism, though not in terms of itself, but in terms of the other side of him, his 'pragmatism'. Exit John Vorster. And so the world changes.

It is quite a thought, if one thinks of 'change' in this country, that the once strictly puritanical (or at least strictly puritanical-looking) people who, on behalf of all of us in South Africa, were never going to put a moral foot wrong, have now reached the point where (at the time of my writing this) they have a son of theirs *op vlug*, fleeing through Europe, and, indeed, as rumour has it, through the world. A fugitive hunted by former buddies. Something like that, a symbol – I should think, and this is meaningful – that these white chosen ones of God in South Africa are 'just people', quite ordinary people in this country and in the world. If this is the meaning of Eschel Rhoodie, then certainly he has 'served a purpose'. Perhaps, now, some real change becomes possible in South Africa.

So far I have been speaking mainly of Afrikaans white South Africa. What of English white South Africa? Not very much, except the fact – which of course is important – that time on the sub-continent and life on the same soil as the destiny-obsessed Afrikaner, have landed these people in the middle of an identity crisis. It is not exactly the eye of a storm, but serious enough: in South Africa, these people just 'don't know what to do'.

Another large minority group are the 'Coloureds'. To which the writer of this is supposed to 'belong'. Then, of course, there are 'the blacks', the majority of the people of the sub-continent. Perhaps there was a time of docility of black people in respect of white oppression, but change is indicated by the place-names – rather, concepts – of Sharpeville and Soweto; and the change is confirmed by the fact that the white regime, in whose clumsy hands 'Bantu' had become a term of denigration (in spite of its meaning, 'being human'), have started talking about 'blacks' instead. 'Bantu Affairs' has been changed to 'Plural Relations' and, silly though it sounds, this sensitivity to nomenclature is also – slight though it is – a sensitivity to the situation. And, as I write this, I hear that 'Plural Relations' is to be changed, perhaps to something less ridiculous? The sensitivity prevails.

This is no longer Verwoerd's granite white South Africa. Heraclitus must have been right. The scene does change.

There was a time when J. C. Smuts – world statesman, holistic philosopher, mountain climber and racist – could describe South Africa as an *uithoek* (far-away corner) of the world. The great Afrikaans poet, N. P. van Wyk Louw, was right to reject this view – but this was a matter of philosophical insight deeper than that of Smuts. For the 'ordinary man in the street', South Africa at Smuts's time was indeed a 'far-away corner' in relation to Europe; it was so in every way. But this has changed. Today South Africa is an established part of world news. The apartheid policy of its regime is even called a threat to world peace. When the Secretary-General of the U.N., or some such personage, speaks about this part of the world, one's impression is: The world (whatever that might mean) is watching us closely; we are important in 'the world'.

I say again that Van Wyk Louw was right to reject Smuts's idea of the country as an *uithoek* in the world.[2] Now, when we speak of a 'far-off corner of the world', writes Van Wyk Louw, 'we presume a capital or main area, as a centre . . . that the world has a fulcrum, somewhere. Such views often also express a value judgement: the centre is the heart or brain, the outlying areas are subject to it; the centre is of primary importance, the outlying areas only of secondary consequence; the centre is spontaneous and the seat of initiative, the outlying areas derivative. . . . This is cultural colonialism.'[3] Of course it is.

And where in the world was the 'centre'? Unconsciously/subconsciously – and even very consciously – for someone like Smuts it was London, Cambridge, Oxford ('surely', writes Louw, 'the idea was never that it was Bombay or Peking or Buenos Aires'). .

Of course, Van Wyk Louw still had his own Afrikaner axe to grind with Jannie Smuts; quite apart from that, however, it was correct for him to believe that no culture could be considered to be a spiritual fulcrum for the world. Certainly for every culture – as for every developing culture – there are 'influences', yet every culture stands 'immediately before God'.

Louw concludes that 'there is *no centre*, and *no far-off corners*'. There is what we might call world culture, in which we may share, the only condition being 'a wide knowledge of other philosophies, an open attitude in respect of our own problems. . . . A people (*volk*) that manages to free itself from a colonial consciousness – what mouldy little world does it escape from.'

English literature in South Africa has never really escaped from this 'mouldy little world'. Afrikaans literature, on the other hand, has never really had the problem. Paradox is part and parcel of the meaning of life in the sub-continent (as, for that matter, anywhere else) and the problem for Afrikaans literature – young as it is – has become the one about which Alexander Solzhenitsyn warns: power – political power. This has happened precisely to the extent that the Afrikaner has wanted to free himself from English colonialism. He has indeed crushed the English in South Africa – at least politically. To use – or misuse – Mao Tse-Tung's phrase, the power that resides in the barrel of the gun has become his.

But soon – all too soon – he has felt himself threatened by all the world. The reason, of course, being apartheid. So he asserts himself, with this power, also in respect of his own youthful literature.

Solzhenitsyn writes: 'Woe to that nation whose literature is disturbed by the intervention of power. Because that is not just a violation of "freedom of the press", it is the closing down of the heart of the nation, a slashing to pieces of its memory. The nation ceases to be mindful of itself, it is deprived of its spiritual unity, and despite a supposedly common language, compatriots suddenly cease to understand one another.'[4]

Fortunately, in this sub-continent we are still working on the construction of a memory. Power is always dangerous, but much more dangerous in old environments of the world than in new ones. What 'heart of the nation' can be closed down here? What 'memory' slashed to pieces? We are still constructing a heart, building a memory. Literature in South Africa is still young. We, writers, are still discovering the sub-continent. Nothing is settled for us – nothing ought yet to be settled.

And yet it is good – a sound principle – even now to be warned of the danger of power.

Therefore when I say that 'things are changing', I intend more than merely that the country is changing like the pyramids – the sort of change which means movement from a position decades ago, under, say, J. C. Smuts, where a Mahatma Ghandi could not travel first class on a main-line train, to a position under Vorster's regime where it has become possible for even lesser black souls than the Mahatma to stay overnight in five-star hotels designated 'international'. I also have in mind that most important kind of change which means to be *in the crucible.*

It is only now that a culturally Africa-centred consciousness is emerging among our writers. This, of course, is happening at the same time that (for instance) any rubbish of the theatre that comes from the 'West End' is still patronised overwhelmingly in preference to culturally indigenous work.

But what does 'African writing' mean? Nadine Gordimer tries to answer the question: 'What is African writing? Must one be black or brown in order to write it, or may one be any old colour? Must the work deal with situations that couldn't come about in quite the same way anywhere else in the world? Or can it deal with matters that preoccupy people everywhere? May it be written in one of the world languages which came to Africa in colonial times, or must it be written in African languages?

'My own definition is that African writing is writing done in any language *by Africans themselves and by others of whatever skin colour* who share with Africans the experience of having been shaped, mentally and spiritually, by Africa rather than anywhere else in the world. One must look at the world *from Africa,* to be an African writer, not look *upon Africa* from the world. Given this Africa-centred consciousness, the African writer can write about what he pleases, and even about other countries, and still his work will belong to African literature.'[5]

I can fault this definition only in respect of the phrases that I have italicised. Under the impact of 'Western standards' – the better and the worse – there is no longer any guarantee for any black man that, because of his blackness, he is spontaneously African – which this definition appears to imply.

There are people of other-than-black pigmentation who do not only 'share with Africans' the experience of having been formed here and now, but who are African, as spontaneously as any black person.

I believe that it is part of the change that has already come over some of us, that we are careful not to equate the concepts of 'African' and 'black', for such an equation is still tinged with colonial sentiment – that colonial sentiment in terms of which, long ago, the word 'native' started to be used here, not so much to indicate indigenousness, but rather blackness:

253

as we know, this is the word that later became 'Bantu' – and today, even in the law-book, it is 'black'.

Changes in this kind of terminology – the vicissitudes of such terms – are of course informative. Here I should also mention that the first use of 'black' to include all people who, in South Africa, are not white, even though their skin colour may be all but visually black – the first use of 'black' in this manner was by blacks themselves, in the black consciousness movement initiated by young men such as Steve Biko and Barney Pityana. If I have understood them correctly, then what they achieved was to realise that being African was a more complex matter than being black, so that they did not make the simple equation of black = African.

To my mind, these first initiators of 'blackness' or 'black consciousness' had a strong sense of cultural discipline. In any case, when I first met Biko and Pityana – it was in 1970 – there was no cheap or easy talk: a fiercely proud blackness, yes, but no sentimental 'mother Africa' attitudes.

These were the first years of the South African Students' Organisation (SASO), which is now banned. I was associated with the movement at the University of the Western Cape (UWC), so that I speak here with a measure of knowledge. In fact, as head of the Department of Philosophy at UWC at the time, I was the first person to introduce concepts of this new black awakening at the University and in the Western Cape. I recall that, at the time, I required my students also to pay attention to Senghor's ideas on negritude and African socialism. For young people in the Western Cape this was a novel experience – something quite new.

I dwell on this matter too long. However, its importance for our changing literary situation must be understood, or at least sensed, very clearly.

In South Africa the literary languages are English and Afrikaans. Much has been done in other languages – think of Mofolo, think of A. C. Jordan. Still it simply is a fact, as Claude Wauthier has remarked, that 'even taking South Africa's contribution into account, African literature in the vernacular falls far short of the literary output in French and English'.[6] In our sub-continent the language is English – and, of course, Afrikaans.

The new black consciousness has come to terms with the fact that it cannot throw off or escape the language of the English colonialist. After all, it is necessary for purposes of communication in the world. And then, beyond this pragmatic level, the colonialistically outraged people can never again rid themselves of the language of the former overlords – for that language is a great language, one which had what Solzhenitsyn calls a 'heart' and a 'memory' so long ago that even the new people who start sharing in that heritage – though they might have been outraged by the colonialists – start caring for it in its new habitat.

But as people of the continent, as Africans, as people 'shaped, mentally and spiritually, by Africa rather than anywhere else in the world', our use of English will be different from the use of English in London, or Oxford, and so on. In fact we do not, and cannot, know yet what our English will look like; what we know, already, is that it does not look like English from the 'United Kingdom'.

What the new black writer insists on is that English as he uses it here and now should be accepted for the reason that it is English moulded – 'shaped, mentally and spiritually' – by Africa, here and now! English has come to Africa, also to South Africa, but now, as used by Africans it looks 'at the world from Africa'. And far too many literary critics and academics who teach English in our schools and universities, still, even now, 'look upon Africa from the world'. These people have not yet changed; so many of them, despite their learning, do not understand – and have not sensed the changes in the air. They remain colonialists, 'mentally and spiritually' – even though many of them, already, have been born here, on African soil. Apparently they still suffer from the feeling that was also that of Smuts, that somehow it is better to be associated with 'the centre' of the culture than with the culture itself. Unfortunately for them, as Van Wyk Louw points out, 'the centre' does not exist, and their cultural – or, shall one say, cultured – lives, are illusory.

If anything, then this – so far – is the literary achievement of the new black writers: that their work draws attention to the literary meaning or meanings of looking at the world from Africa (Gordimer's phrase), through the medium of the English language as the positive colonial input into our sub-continent. Culturally, I suggest, we have just started. Culturally we are in the crucible.

Is the work of poets such as Mtshali, Serote, Sepamla, Gwala, being fairly heard by the literary critics? What are their criteria for such work? It is not an easy question, and the matter is not simple. One colonialistic way out, of course, is to be snobbish about these writings, as if they were merely 'attempting to write English'; another colonialistic way out is the well-known pat on the back for anything that looks like achievement by blacks.

Sydney Sipho Sepamla probably expresses the literary problem of black writers working in English as much as any other problem of being black here and now, in the following lines ('Remake the World').

255

For years I've known the native problem
It worried me
It worried me
Another man to lose sleep
Another man to lose appetite
Because I was a problem
Even as I ate into myself
Even as it ravaged my soul
I couldn't face the night without fear
I couldn't walk the day without fear
I've come to live with myself
Having learnt to read problems from faces
And my worry is the greater
I want to remake the world
For everything about me is white
The lush green grass is white
The pitch-black night is white
The dream I scream is white
The cry I shout is white
God! where can the end lie
If not in me
I want You to trample the world once more
And I shall make it in Your image.[7]

I mention the following as an example of the literary, shall I call it snobbery, that I have in mind in respect of our struggle with ourselves as African. Dr Richard Rive in a review of the 1978 production of *The Orange Earth*, my first drama in the medium of English (a review which I considered to lack understanding of an indigenous human situation), remarks on the manner of speech of the actor Bill Curry that 'one ought not to be too fastidious about his very cultured accent. After all, some of them do speak like that.'[8]

It is the phrase 'some of them' that worries me. Here is an attitude of cultural superiority (snobbery?) that – at least on this evidence – does not identify with people in the cultural crucible.

In fairness to Dr Rive, however, it is necessary to say *also* that as a teacher of English in South Africa, he has been pleading for the 'right to teach students indigenous literature' in our schools and universities; he does this insofar as he believes (correctly, of course) that the 'future of the country is tied up with its literary development and vice versa'. He points out that the attitude of academics opposed to the teaching of indigenous literature is that they want to teach their students 'to recognise true works of literature' and that, according to them, indigenous work does not make the teaching of this recognition possible. Dr Rive considers the attitude to be – well, wrong *and* right. Still he insists that 'it is right for students to take an interest in all aspects of life on the continent on which they live. . . . They have a right to such a right,' he says, 'a right to study their own literature in addition to the best that can be provided for them in the English language.'⁹

Of course, this rightful concern about students studying 'their own literature' does not really touch my problem yet – which is about the making of culture in the sub-continent, about the meaning of 'being in the crucible' here.

In any event, it is almost unbelievable that in the world of English literature in South Africa, Dr Rive and others should, in the seventies, have to find it necessary to state that 'in order to teach African and South African poetry, one must first acknowledge its right to be taught'.

For this, the seventies is rather late in the day. Which simply means that colonialism in the English literary world in South Africa has been persistent – and still is.

But even here we are progressing. The literary journal *Speak* reports that 'The Association of English Teachers of South Africa have at last recognised the right of African literature to be studied'.¹⁰ (Period. But an exclamation mark would have been more to the point here.)

There was a time Afrikaans had this kind of problem in respect of Dutch. Just as South African English may be considered to be not fit for teaching in the university, Afrikaans was considered to be not fit to use anywhere in public – not fit in the schools, naturally, and, above all, not fit to be used in church. Dutch was the language.

But the indigenous language won, culture took its course. And entangled with power though Afrikaans is, the language has settled down to Africa.

Consider Afrikaans as used by N. P. van Wyk Louw, D. J. Opperman, Breyten Breytenbach, Elsa Joubert. This is a language of this place, this time. It is African. The image of Afrikaans only as the 'language of the oppressor' is superficial – after all, the regime, or the majority of its people, must use *some* language. And in any case, in Africa English too holds a high place as a 'language of the oppressor'.

But to return to Afrikaans. In respect of this language, too, Solzhenitsyn's warning about power is to the point. Power endangers its own culture. And here, where everything is still taking shape, the tremendous power of the regime, which is so overwhelmingly Afrikaans, is a stumbling block which at times appears insurmountable to the Afrikaans writer.

As long ago as 1960 (it is long ago in terms of the flight of time today), the Afrikaans poet, D. J. Opperman, warned that Afrikaans power, if it continued on the way it appeared to be going at the time, was taking us all to (what he then called) 'cold spiritual hell'.[11]

N. P. van Wyk Louw has warned the regime about the dangers of power, to the point where Verwoerd heaped scorn on this poet. At the very moment that I am writing, in 1979, the Administrator of the Cape Province is trying to bludgeon a section of theatre in the Cape into accepting that the only plays to be put on stage are ones that will put 'steel in the bones'[12] of white South Africa with a view to the future defence of itself to the bitter end. Heroic work. Years ago, in 1966, Verwoerd blacklisted Van Wyk Louw in similar terms, when Louw wrote a play in which for the Afrikaner (and the country) the question was raised: What is a nation?

In Afrikaans:

> Wat is 'n volk?
> Uit stof en stof-in-tyd is ons gemaak:
> Boere en knegte, trein-masjiniste,
> passers, laboratorium-assistente,
> motoriste, meisies in swemklere,
> bestuurders, direkteure en rekenmeesters,
> meisies op voorblaaie en agter
> op motorfietse; anoniem: 'n massa,
> maar elkeen met sy naam en eie aard,
> elkeen met sy kiesheid, wat 'n kuisheid kan word.
>
> En stof-in-oordeel? Goeies, slegtes, dapperes –
> dapperes en banges – niemand
> heilig voor God nie, maar
> almal sondaars:
> Van die slegtes soms verloste sondaars;
> van die goeies soms hovaardig op hul goed-
> heid en hul strewe;
> geen dappere altyd dapper,
> en banges soms tog bang om bang te wees.

In English:

> What is a people?
> Derived from dust we are, we're dust-in-time:
> farmers and foremen, fitters and
> turners, engine-drivers, lab. assistants,
> motorists, bikini-girls, bank managers,
> directors of companies, accountants, chartered,
> cover-girls and girls on pillions
> of motorbikes – a mass anonymous, yet
> each with his own name and nature
> and peculiarity which might become his holiness.
>
> Will dust in judgment sit? The good, bad, brave
> the scared-to-death, none holy
> before God
> all sinners:
> The bad ones sometimes are salvation's children,
> the good ones haughty in their goodness
> and ambitious
> the brave ones not so brave, and
> those afraid sometimes afraid to be afraid.[13]

What sort of spineless questioning is this, Verwoerd had wanted to know. What is a people? Have Afrikaners to ask such questions? Don't Afrikaners know, then, what a nation is? No, said Verwoerd, this type of art is not for Afrikaners. Afrikaners need writers who can, and who are willing, to say: *This* (emphatically) is the nation. The Afrikaner needs portrayals of the heroic deeds of the *volk*, not questioning such as that of Van Wyk Louw.[14]

Naturally, Verwoerd also mentioned 'patriotism', insinuating that Van Wyk Louw was not patriotic, or not patriotic enough. To climax it all, this hard-headed politician, in schoolmasterish fashion, pontificated and read Louw a lesson in 'spirituality'. Apparently Verwoerd's arrogance was something to reckon with! Perhaps he was aware of another poem of Louw's, written as far back as the fifties, in which Louw, without mentioning names, pictures Afrikaner leaders – *Afrikaners in aansienlike posisies* (Afrikaners in important places) – who, despite all their hardness, would not survive – *En hulle gaan nie bly nie*. He was bitter about these people. They were destined for the dung-heap, he said – *hulle gaan mis-*

hoop word; however, they might take all of us with them – *en ons almal saamsleep na die mishoop.*[15]

No wonder that Verwoerd did not like this man. I may be wrong, but Vorster, in his political career, never referred to Louw. Certain lesser Afrikaners *in aansienlike posisies* do refer to and quote Louw – mostly, however, in the way in which many – in fact, most – Christians refer to and quote Jesus. Without understanding, without any understanding at all.

This great poet was, in his youth, a leading figure in the Afrikaans literary movement of the thirties – a leading (*the* leading) *dertiger*. D. J. Opperman, another great poet of Afrikaans, calls Louw the *hooffiguur* (main figure) in the development of literature at the time.[16] This was a movement of poets in the first place (not novelists, not dramatists). Theirs was a reaction – not necessarily conscious – to writing in the service of a 'struggle', in the service of 'politics'. As far back as the thirties, these writers felt that the Anglo-Boer War was over and that humiliation at the hands of 'the English' was not the only thing in the world to inspire poetry. The very young Van Wyk Louw could, of course, still write in the idiom of the 'struggle' for, and of, Afrikaans:

> With ever harder discipline
> We'll bind our strengths and our desires
> Until everything soft in us will die . . .
>
> Life that surges without form
> in circles, wide and undefined,
> We'll seize upon and narrow down
> to a few things that are hard and clear.
>
> (Ons sal met altyd strenger tug
> ons wense en kragte samegord
> tot al wat sag is in ons sterf . . .
>
> Die lewe wat gestalteloos dein
> deur ewig wyer, yler kringe,
> die sal ons saamgryp en vereng
> tot enkele harde en helder dinge)[17]

Like all good Afrikaners, Louw at the time was impressed with this idea of hardness and clarity in the cause of *Afrikanerskap* (Afrikanership).

He had read Nietzsche. But then, he was also reading Dostoevsky and my hunch is that he came to understand many things – also Nietzsche's writing – more and more in terms of Dostoevsky. He is impressed by the 'mighty winds' and 'great force' of Nietzschean philosophy, but he calls Dostoevsky 'deep' and admires this great writer's 'patience and humility' (*geduld-in-lydsaamheid*).[18]

Ultimately, it is not the 'will to power' aspects of Nietzsche that impress Louw, but the culturally critical aspects of Nietzschean philosophy. As early as the thirties, Louw already resisted negative nationalism, that frivolous brand of nationalism which, culturally, exists on the level of petty, that is bourgeois, 'Streben' and, politically, involves power merely for the purpose of brute existence. But Louw's resistance remained 'loyal' (*lojale verset*). He believed that truly great cultural criticism could exist only when 'the critic does not place himself outside, but in the very midst of those that he criticises, and knows that he is inviolably bound, in love and destiny and guilt, to the people (*volk*) that he dares to reprove; when he does not say "they" but "we". Then it is not attack any longer – except in the sense in which one's conscience attacks you inside your own breast. Criticism is a nation's conscience.' (*Kritiek is 'n nasie se gewete.*)[19]

Louw thought of himself as a 'nationalist' throughout his life, but as far back as the thirties he had overcome the kind of nationalism (rife in Africa and rife in the world) with no holds barred, and for which no rules apply. Louw was dreaming of a nationalism that would be beautiful, or 'liberal' – a *liberale nasionalisme*. (In the world of Afrikaans these phrases – *lojale verset* and *liberale nasionalisme* – are synonymous with the name of Van Wyk Louw. Perhaps in the end both phrases are contradictions in terms.)

In terms of these concepts, Louw's view of the Afrikaans language as an African language, whose home is this soil, but one that must open itself to the total reality of being human, explains itself. So does Louw's critique of censorship.

Towards the end of his life (he died in 1970) Louw, clearly, was doubting the possibility of the beauty he had in mind for Afrikaans nationalism. Sheer power had taken over the house, and was corrupting it. 'The pathos of our human endeavour', he wrote some forty years ago, 'is that, time and time again, we seek to realise justice, but then our own system brings injustice . . .; we seek freedom, and then again our own system enslaves people.'[20]

Towards the end of his life, then, Louw was questioning – all over again: What is a nation? This irked Verwoerd. And is it bitterness or Dostoyevskian 'patience and humility' that we hear in lines such as these from

Tristia? He says 'She' as if he is talking about a bride that was expected, for a long time, and then did not come:

> Sy sal nooit kom nie. Moenie luister.
> Moenie wag. Moet niks verwag nie.
> Leer die verwagting af. Leer die wag af.
> Leer af om te luister. Leer af.

> (She will never come. Do not listen.
> Do not wait. Do not expect anything.
> Unlearn expectation. Unlearn to wait.
> Unlearn to listen. Unlearn.)[21]

Perhaps the miserableness of the position in which the Afrikaner power élite now finds itself will cause Afrikaners to look at the work of Van Wyk Louw – either again, or for the first time. And perhaps they will discover there, again, or for the first time, the great philosophical input of Louw into literature in South Africa, which they can transform into a constructive input into their life in South Africa. (When will Afrikaner children be taught some of the real meaning of Van Wyk Louw at school? What happens at the moment is that some of his poems are 'studied' for purposes of the end-of-year departmental examinations. So many of these scholars, so many of them, achieve 'A' symbols in the examination and go on to become teachers, at school and at university, themselves!)

And English-speakers are as isolated in their world as Afrikaans-speakers are in theirs: many English-speakers, for example, have never even heard of the poet – a great poet of their own country – called Van Wyk Louw.

I have dwelt somewhat lengthily on Van Wyk Louw for the simple reason that he, more than any other writer, had prepared the way for 'changes' in literature in South Africa – especially in so far as changes in South African literature during the past decades are changes in Afrikaans much more than in English literature. And during forty and more years, until his death, Louw was himself part of the change. Technically, too, he was renewing his work all the time.

However, important as are the technical changes, it is the large human changes in our literature that interest me.

What has happened, then, is that Van Wyk Louw and other so-called *dertigers* (Uys Krige, for example) had already at that time laid the foundations for poetry that was indigenous, but no longer merely self-indulgent (in terms of oppression by the 'English', and the idea that Afrikaners were

God's people and would, despite everything, come out on top). The new poetry had to speak about the entire, complex situation of being human. Which it did.

The change from pre-1930 until now is quite remarkable and has happened in the face of and, indeed, in opposition to Afrikaner nationalist politics. It is symbolised most strongly in the Van Wyk Louw/Verwoerd incident of the sixties. And then, of course, there is the well-known episode of the seventies: *the State* v. *Breyten Breytenbach*. The fact that this famous Afrikaans poet was pathetic in his efforts to work against the regime is irrelevant; what is important is the fact that here is an Afrikaans poet incarcerated. It is a symbol illustrating the fact that the literature of Afrikaans finds itself beyond the point of being the handmaiden of Afrikaner politicians.

English literature in South Africa has, of course, never historically found itself in a position where this kind of breaking away from politics was a real issue. But, then, English literature here – or rather literature in English – has a far less complicated history and position than Afrikaans literature. Books in English have been banned by the regime – Nadine Gordimer, Jack Cope, even Stuart Cloete. Then, of course, there are the banned black writers in English, whether in exile or in the country: Ezekiel Mphahlele, Alex la Guma, Lewis Nkosi, James Matthews, the writers of *Staffrider* (now banned), also of the banned Azanian Poets and Writers' Organisation, later called Medupe, and so on. They have suffered banning of their works for many years, whereas, I think I am right, the first Afrikaans work to be banned outright was André P. Brink's novel, *Kennis van die Aand* (*Looking on Darkness*),[22] which took place as recently as 1974. But a fight against censorship is a far lesser burden than the total cultural fight that the Afrikaans writer has to carry on against the regime. The language – the cultural mould – of the regime is overwhelmingly Afrikaans. I have said 'the Afrikaans writer works in the language of the oppressor'; it is his language too. And the achievement of Afrikaans literature at this moment is that it has in fact, over a period of the last fifty years, changed so much that the literature can be seen by everybody not to be continuous with the regime. At the same time, the change that has occurred again raises the paradox of culture that Van Wyk Louw had expressed in the concept of *lojale verset*. The evil in the culture is also 'yours', if it is your culture. And the relationship at any point in time with a culture which, at that moment, exhibits the evil in it obtrusively, can be an experience of frustrating hell on earth. Consider, therefore, the impact of apartheid on the Afrikaans writer.

The (white) Afrikaans writers of today – the novelists, Jan Rabie, André P. Brink, Etienne Leroux, Elsa Joubert; Breyten Breytenbach and all the other poets; all the writers have to live with this cultural feeling of guilt, that the language in which they write is not 'innocent of the horrors' of apartheid – roughly just as, in George Steiner's words, 'the German language was not innocent of the horrors of Nazism'.[23]

Steiner asserts that 'Brecht, Kafka and Thomas Mann did not succeed in mastering their own culture, in imposing on it the humane sobriety of their talent. They found themselves first the eccentrics, then the hunted. New linguists were at hand to make of the German language a political weapon ... and to degrade the dignity of human speech ...' Nothing quite as vicious, yet certainly something similar, has happened to Afrikaans writers and to the Afrikaans language. The difference is only that for the Afrikaans writer, the problem is not a mastering of his culture, for, as I have said, the culture is still in the making. The problem for the writer is, rather, the fear that Afrikaans may not survive the crucible as an acceptable vehicle of humane communication between man and man in the sub-continent. The Afrikaans writer is working against time. If the cut-off point was not Sharpeville, was it Soweto? Perhaps there is a turning-point – the 'Information scandal'? (Or could it be true in this case, that whom the gods want to destroy, they first make mad?)

We cannot say, and so we keep on working. Or perhaps we *can* say that a language that can express the ongoing events in this land as vitally as Afrikaans does, will not die here. And it may be, also, that Afrikaans has already infiltrated – as culture does – the communications process of black people, the very people who, naturally, believe the language to be (only) that of the oppressor. Is Elsa Joubert only whistling while walking in the terrifying dark, when she suggests that this may be the case? Miss Joubert has explored this development, tentatively. First let us say that Miss Joubert underscores the fact that we find ourselves in the crucible. We live, she says, at a time 'when something that is not yet defined, must acquire form. Something is taking shape.' She thinks of Afrikaans as an African language and says that the language has already taken root and put out feelers in Africa to a far greater extent than we might, superficially, surmise. It has entered the life-system of other languages. (*In baie groter mate as wat ons besef, het Afrikaans hom reeds ingewortel, is Afrikaans vasgeslik in, het hy sy voelers uitgesteek, amper soos 'n rankplant, en begin vasklou in ander tale van Afrika.*) And, says Miss Joubert, it may be that Afrikaans will survive here even if every person who now speaks it as a mother tongue were to disappear from this sub-continent.[24]

Afrikaans may not remain as a language that is 'pure, stylish, and accepted by the Akademie', but it will remain as something vital, with staying power, just as (what is now) Afrikaans itself remained and grew in Africa as a language distinct from Dutch. It may become something different from what it is now, but it will stay.

Miss Joubert suggests that already Afrikaans has reached out into black experience in a process of cultural spreading and integration. This has happened despite the politics of the country, despite the regime, despite the 'system of things', and I speak not only of the *platteland*, but indeed also of Soweto. This Afrikaans is not the Afrikaans spoken in an Afrikaner environment – it is mixed with English, and both languages in turn are mixed with the black languages. The fact is that Afrikaans is holding out. Surviving. And Africa has accommodated the language without any regard to official sanction, without permission, without permit. (*Die land het die taal in hom opgeneem, buite amptelike beslissing om, sonder verlof of permit.*)

In terms of the cultural snobbery that I have mentioned, of course there are those Afrikaans critics, too, who would consider this growth of Afrikaans to be an unfortunate, 'bastard' phenomenon to be discouraged. The fact, however, is that it has happened and is happening, and whatever the feelings of the literary purist (whoever that might mean), the world, also this world of language, is moving around him and there is nothing he can do to stop it. He can only, shortsightedly, lament it. Historically it is always the case that culture develops without any regard to 'special' people, or, as it is said in Afrikaans, '*sonder aansien des persoons*'. And so, as Miss Joubert says, perhaps already Afrikaans 'has many tongues' (*het baie tonge*) – for instance,

> Hela baby!
> Zwakala daarso
> Of hoe sê ek?
>
> Jy moet my notch
> Kyk my mooi sweetie
> Ek is nie een van hulle
> Jy ken mos
> Die Hillbrow type.
>
> Hela Sisi!
> Look sharp
> Otherwise jy val
> Met my 'M'
> Jy val soos 'n sak kool.

Ek wil jou weedie
Of praat jy net met situations
Die manne met 'n ntanjana
Die Stetson oukies
Die Mpala-mpala outies
Wat jou rwa
Met Manyeledi
And Mgababa
Of hoe sê ek?

Baby jy's 'n washout
Hulle vang jou
Sluit jou toe
For Immorality
'Strue met my 'P'
Jy's 'n has-been.

Kyk, ek mca jou baby
Ek is serious
My hart maak shandies
Jy ken mos
Die downtown beat
Van Jimmy Smith se mojo.

Ek praat die real ding
Moenie dink
Ek wala-wala net stof
Ek wil jou cover
Ek wil jou smekana
Jy ken mos
Die movie-star ding.

Jy's my number one mbuzana
Die neneweet
Jy's my eie ding
Met my ma!

Baby come duze!
Come duze baby![25]

Then there is my own work. Perhaps I should not be speaking about it myself, but in this place I simply have to say something about the position of those South African writers who, politically, are 'black' (that is, who politically, are not 'white') but, as far as literal skin colour is concerned, are neither 'black' nor 'white'. It is a complex thing to describe, but there is such a position in the country, there are such writers. I am one of them.

In the ethnic jargon of the country, they call us 'Coloured'. (Sarah Gertrude Millin used to call us 'God's stepchildren'!) One resents the tag. You resent it, you are bitter about it. It is a stamp that brands you, marks you for life, and that brands your children. You are disgusted, then, by a regime that legislates 'race classification'; you detest it, hate it. You have hated it for so long now that your hatred – and bitterness – have grown sublime. But this is part of the general experience of being black in South Africa.

The special problem for a writer who is burdened by this particular position in terms of the colour categories of the country, arises when he writes in Afrikaans – which, in my case, is the mother tongue of the majority of the people labelled in this manner. For the writer who has grown from such roots, but who works in the medium of English, the response to the world and to his own bitterness, is less difficult; in fact, his position is reasonably straightforward. English does not bind him to a cultural situation which he necessarily shares with people and things that abhor him. English, after all, is a 'world language'. When he 'tells freedom' in it (I am using Peter Abrahams' phrase), the telling of freedom involves no special cultural problem for him. (Or perhaps it does; but the problem of the Afrikaans writer is far more serious.) In this sense, the position of all the black writers who work in the English medium is relatively uncomplicated.

For the politically black writer whose cultural shade is 'Coloured' and whose medium is Afrikaans, there exists the frustration of working in a language which is straightforwardly associated with the regime: Afrikaans, it is said, is 'the language of the oppressor'. At the very same time, of course, it is the language that my mother taught me first, it is my mother tongue, the language in which I express myself best. And through the language which I share with 'them' and 'they' with me, I am, culturally, intimately related to 'those people'. In a deep cultural sense, the oppressors are 'family of mine', and there is nothing I can do about it. Culture is simply like that. No one can change the fact.

The following lines (overleaf) by S. V. Petersen are, at least partly, to the point (of course, the problem reaches even deeper than this).

Weet dit:
Vir my bly jy 'n vreemdeling,
niks meer:
Jou vader was a slaaf,
en myne was 'n heer!

As dit,
as dit by vader kom, is ons
verwant!
En vreemde broer, durf jy
ontken die broederband?

(Know this:
To me, you are a stranger,
nothing more:
Your father was a slave,
mine the master!

When we . . .
When we speak of fathers,
we are one!
Strange brother, dare you
deny our brotherhood?)[26]

Also, insofar as one writes in Afrikaans, you cannot just leave this place as, for instance, Peter Abrahams did years ago, to 'tell freedom' from outside. Writing about his decision to leave South Africa, Abrahams explained that he had 'submitted' to the system of things for so long. 'But submission can be a subtle thing. A man can submit today in order to resist tomorrow. My submission had been such. And because I had not been free to show my real feeling, to voice my true thoughts, my submission had bred bitterness and anger. And there were nearly ten million others who had submitted with equal anger and bitterness. One day, the whites would have to reckon with these people. One day their sons and daughters would have to face the wrath of these embittered people. The two million whites cannot for ever be overlords of the ten million non-whites. One day they may have to submit to the same judgement of force they have invoked in their dealings with us. . . .' Then he says: 'For me, personally, life in South Africa had come to an end. I had been lucky in some of the whites I had met. Meeting them had made a straight "all-blacks-are-good-all-whites-are-bad"

268

attitude impossible. But I had reached a point where the gestures of even my friends among the whites were suspect, so I had to go or be for ever lost. I needed, not friends, not gestures, but my manhood. And the need was desperate.

'Perhaps life had a meaning that transcended race and colour. If it had, I could not find it in South Africa. Also, there was the need to write, to tell freedom, and for this I needed to be personally free . . .'[27]

I agree with Abrahams on this theme of 'submission'. It is as valid now as it was when he wrote these lines (only we don't say 'non-whites' any more, we say 'blacks'. Things have changed, have they not?) And I, too, do not need 'white' gestures. However, in life, even in life in South Africa, I do need friends – and they may be 'white'. (My blackness is not sacrosanct, as little as other people's whiteness.) Then, I do not understand Abrahams' point about 'manhood'. And does the 'need to write' not mean precisely that you are rooted here, and that, really, you can't ever leave? You may go – you may have to go (fleeing, on a one-way travel permit, that sort of thing); but the 'need to write' prescribes that somehow, somehow you have to be here – have to be 'in touch' – all the time. Once, Alex la Guma admitted to me that he had reached a stage where meaningful writing had become impossible for him. He had been away, an exile, for so long – yet *this* was what he had to write about: but, after all these long years, how does one write about this place, and about its time? For another kind of exile, the news that reaches him in the media is sufficient: he can act on it. For the writer, the position is different. He cannot act merely on information from the media. The only channel that can inform him 'to fulfil the need to write', is his own existential experience. *Personal* experience.

So, I have to stay. Or, should I leave, I shall have to return. If I cannot return, then I shall have to accept the bitter fact that my writing will dry up. Sooner or later it will. Too soon, it will.

And so, if you are black, and your medium is Afrikaans – well, there is a problem for you: a problem of real dimension, real complexity.

When literary criticism in South Africa comes to grasp this kind of problem fully, that will be the time when it achieves real insight into the cultural situation here. Literary criticism here is in a bad state. It is still very much a 'white' monopoly, practised by those isolated in the universities, who are much more concerned about their status as professors, or if they are not yet professors, about rising in the hierarchy, than about *trying to understand – really understand – the realities of South Africa.* In this respect, too, the change – measurable change – that has occurred during the past years, has taken place in Afrikaans. (Consider the advent of a literary critic such as André P. Brink, or the young University of the Western Cape critic, G. J. Gerwel, who adds, or may add, a new dimension to literary criticism here, insofar as he is black ('Coloured') *and* Afrikaans, and the first critic of this 'kind' in our literature.)

From what I have written, it appears, almost, that, except for the appearance of the new black writers, change during the past ten to twenty years has been in respect of Afrikaans only; and as if the hard judgment of an English-language poet on English literature in South Africa is true: the poet is Christopher Hope, and the reference to his view of 'the English South African' which I quote is from James Polley's introduction to *Poetry South Africa*. 'I suspect', writes Polley, 'there is much truth in Christopher Hope's assertion that the English South African is a "displaced" person – "flotsam left high and dry after the tide" of colonialism had passed. The emphatic way in which many of us pledge allegiance to Africa – in a windy monument in Grahamstown, or in poems about an "Africa within" – betrays insecurity. The traditional answer, of course, is to return to the homeland, England, if one is white – as Hope himself has done. This after all was the route of the premier ancestors of our modern poetry, Roy Campbell and William Plomer. Plomer begins his autobiography by stating (a) that he was born in Pietersburg and (b) that he is an Englishman. He became one of the great literary Englishmen of his generation.'[28]

For the Afrikaans writer, the white one too, there is no 'home' elsewhere in terms of which to think. He is naturally an African, and consciously co-responsible for the sub-continent.

On the whole, my judgment of 'the English South African', also in literature, agrees with that of Christopher Hope, or of James Polley; or of the philosopher Martin Versfeld, who, writing about education in Africa, remarks: 'My conviction is that the fact that one is working in Africa is a powerful reason for discarding nineteenth-century attitudes and bringing to bear on the situation what is most modern in philosophy, theology, and educational theory. The teacher who tries to re-create a pale reflection of his home or cultural past is missing his vocation. The Englishman finds it particularly difficult to avoid this failure to the extent that he has failed to create something new for himself in Africa, and is still parasitic upon an overseas culture.'[29]

There is some light. If a writer such as Plomer 'became one of the great literary Englishmen of his generation', there is the phenomenon of Athol Fugard to compensate (shall I use this bold expression?) for the lack of ability of 'the English South African' to take root. Fugard, today, is the outstanding symbol of change as far as South African literature in the medium of English is concerned – no doubt about that; the outstanding writer in the English medium to have broken through the defences of the English-speakers' cultural colonialism. Certainly, it is still the case that Fugard's plays are enthusiastically put on in South African theatres, not so much because of their indigenous meaning for the arts in this country, but rather because Fugard has had successes in London. (An excellent re-commendation.) But this is not Fugard's fault. *He* certainly rejects the old idea of Jannie Smuts, that we are a 'far-off corner' of the world. His work is completely contemporary, and a meeting place for English and Afri-kaans – a place of meeting *in Africa*, and consciously so.

But Fugard merits an essay to himself alone. I wish only to leave his name standing at the conclusion of these notes. Also because I feel myself related to his work; for I recognise in him something that I, myself, have been working towards from my side of the spectrum: a drawing together of the different worlds of this country, even if it is only in literature.

This is so important. After all, literature has implications for real life. And this meeting together of the different worlds is the only direction that change should take (I say *should* take) in 'this wide and sad land' that may yet be happy – South Africa.

1. Bertrand Russell, *History of Western Philosophy* (Allen & Unwin, London, 1971), pp. 61–2.
2. From Smuts's introduction to Monsignor F.C. Kolbe, *A Catholic View of Holism*, which was Kolbe's response to Smuts's work *Holism and Evolution*.
3. This quote and those that follow are from N. P. van Wyk Louw, *Liberale Nasionalisme* (Nasionale Boekhandel Bpk., Cape Town, 1958), p. 9 *et seq.*
4. *Solzhenitsyn*, ed. Leopold Labedz (Penguin, London, 1974), p. 314.
5. Nadine Gordimer, *The Black Interpreters* (Sprocas/Ravan, Johannesburg, 1973), p. 5.
6. Claude Wauthier, *The Literature and Thought of Modern Africa* (Pall Mall Press, London, 1966), p. 32.
7. Sydney Sipho Sepamla, *Hurry up to it* (Ad. Donker, Johannesburg, 1975), p. 25.
8. In *Speak: Critical Arts Journal*, October/November 1978, pp. 54–5.
9. This and the following quotes from *Speak*, March/April 1978, pp. 37–9, 63.
10. *Ibid.*, p. 63.
11. From a supplement to *Die Burger* at the time of the Union Festival, 1960.
12. This statement emerged from a controversy quoted in the press at the beginning of 1979.

13. From Adam Small, *Oh Wide and Sad Land* (Maskew Miller, Cape Town, 1975), pp. 126–31.
14. Quoted in *Die Burger*, 4 June 1966.
15. From N. P. van Wyk Louw, *Tristia* (Human & Rousseau, Cape Town, 1962), pp. 114–17.
16. D. J. Opperman, *Digters van Dertig* (Nasionale Boekhandel Bpk., Cape Town, 1953), p. 163.
17. N. P. van Wyk Louw, *Die Halwe Kring* (Nasionale Boekhandel Bpk., Cape Town, 1967), p. 40. English translation by Adam Small.
18. N. P. van Wyk Louw, *ibid.*, pp. 14, 32.
19. N. P. van Wyk Louw, *Lojale Verset* (Nasionale Boekhandel Bpk., Cape Town, 1939), p. 169.
20. *Ibid.*, p. 174.
21. N. P. van Wyk Louw, *Tristia*, p. 99. English translation by Adam Small.
22. Published by Buren Uitgewers (Edms) Bpk., Cape Town, 1973.
23. George Steiner, *Language and Silence* (Penguin, London, 1969), p. 140.
24. These quotes are all taken from two articles published in *Rapport*, 17 September 1978 and 1 October 1978.
25. From Sydney Sipho Sepamla, *op. cit.*, p. 21.
26. S. V. Petersen, *Die Enkeling* (Maskew Miller, Cape Town, 1944), p. 13. English translation by Adam Small.
27. Peter Abrahams, *Tell Freedom* (Faber and Faber, London, 1954), pp. 310–11.
28. Peter Wilhelm and James Polley, *Poetry South Africa* (Ad. Donker, Johannesburg, 1976), p. 10.
29. Martin Versfeld in *Education for Reality in Africa* (Mambo Press, Gwelo, 1963), p. 15.

INDEX OF PERSONS

GENERAL INDEX

Dominion Party 32
Dutch Reformed Churches 22, 135

Economic and Wage Commission 124
Education 157 *et seq.;* ethnic 178 *et seq.;*
    expenditure on 171; language medium
    174; racial segregation 80, 86; statistics
    160 *et seq.;* teachers 172 *et seq.;*
    technical 172; *see also* Universities
Electricity Supply Commission (Escom)
    109
English as an African language 179, 255
English-speakers 31–2, 133–4, 250
Erasmus Commission of Enquiry 250
Ethiopia 227–8
Extension of University Education Act,
    1959 86, 181

Fagan Commission 11, 20, 116, 138–9
Federal Party 45
Ford Foundation 9, 25
France, arms embargo 227, 244
Franchise: Cape 33; Coloured 36, 43
    et seq.; qualified 29; Indian 36;
    Progressive Party 37
Freedom Charter 48
Freedom of assembly 81, 90–1
Frelimo 62, 63, 290
Front-line States 242
Fusion Government 30, 32, 34

Gabon 235
General elections 34–6
Ghana 225, 235–6
Group Areas Act, 1950 17, 36, 45, 49, 85,
    86, 143, 148–9

Habeas corpus 92
Herstigte Nasionale Party 53, 86, 233
Hertzog Bills 10, 33
High Commission Territories 221, 231
Hoernlé Memorial Lecture 14, 19, 67, 70
Homelands: agriculture 122; as buffer
    states 77; economic development 121
    et seq.; independence 39, 68–9, 71, 244;
    leadership 42, 56, 66 *et seq.;* mining 123;
    political developments 66 *et seq.* 75;
    'Umtata summit' 56 68, 70; *see also*
    Markinor homelands survey
Housing 150 *et seq.*
Human Awareness Programme 21
Human rights 82–3, 93, 215 *et seq.*

Immigration 118
Immorality Act 79, 84, 207–9
India 47, 216
Indian Affairs, Department of 48
Indian National Congress 48
Indian Representation Act 46, 47
Indians 46 *et seq.*, 58; education 157
    et seq.; employment 99 *et seq.;* and

Group Areas 149; land ownership
    restrictions 80; racial attitudes 196–7;
    segregation 148; urbanisation 148;
    wages 125
Industrial and Commercial Workers'
    Union 2
Industrial Conciliation Act 99–100, 117
Industrial Legislation Commission 100
Industrial Development Corporation 110
Influx control 85, 103, 127, 139 *et seq.*
'Information affair' 247, 250, 264
Inter-Cabinet Council 46, 49
Internal Security Act 17, 90, 92
International Court of Justice 227–8
Inkatha 66, 70, 73, 74
Investment: domestic 110, 113 *et seq.;*
    foreign 113–14 *et seq.*, 127
Iron and Steel Industrial Corporation
    (Iscor) 110
Ivory Coast 235, 238

Jews, attitudes towards 192, 196–7
Job reservation 53, 85–6, 100, 117, 119
Joint Councils 5, 21

Kliptown Charter 57

Labour, legislation 101; *see also* Job
    reservation; South Africa; economy;
    Trade unions; Works committees
Labour Party 45, 75
Latin America 232
League of Nations 214
Lesotho 231, 239
Liberal Party 38
Liberal tradition 3, 29
Liberation movements 233
Liberia 227–8
Local government 132–3
Lusaka Manifesto 233–4, 237–8

Madagascar 233, 235, 238
Malawi 231–2, 238
Markinor homelands survey 191, 202
Marxism and racial attitudes 191–2, 198–9
Mauritius 233
Medupe Writers' Association 263
Migrant labour 141
Mines and Works Act, 1911 2; Amend-
    ment Act, 1926 99
Mining *see* South Africa: economy
Minister of Posts and Telegraphs vs *Rasool*
    84
Mission education 157, 179
Mixed Marriages Act 207
Moller vs *Keimoes School Committee* 80
Mozambique 31, 76, 239

Namibia *see* South West Africa/Namibia
Natal: devolution idea 29
Natal Indian Congress 47, 49, 58

276